Producers' Choice: Six Plays for Young Performers

Promise, Oedipus/Antigone, Tory Boyz, The Butterfly Club, Alice's Adventures in Wonderland, Punk Rock

Promise: as the media descends on a small community haunted by loss, one journalist is determined to report a story of sensational tragedy. But when instead a teen romance blossoms, will she still get her scoop? This uplifting drama wonderfully captures the soul of a community and the difficulty of expressing what we really think. It offers a real treat for performers and audiences alike.
Age range: 11–25; **cast**: m9, f9, m/f1; **running time**: 40–60 minutes

Oedipus/Antigone: a thrilling adaptation of one of the greatest family dramas of world literature, the play skilfully dramatises Sophocles' tragic tale of the Theban king's relentless quest for truth and his daughter's fatal defiance of her uncle. This is a fast-moving piece for large ensemble casts.
Age range: 11–25; **cast**: m8, f3, m/f1 & chorus; **running time**: 60 minutes

Tory Boyz: set in Westminster, in the offices of parliamentary researchers, *Tory Boyz* is a political comedy about ambition and prejudice among young Tories. Moving between the past and the present, the play asks if Ted Heath had to suppress his sexual instincts to rise in the Tory party and whether a person's sexuality remains a barrier to political success today.
Age range: 16–25; **cast**: m14, f7, m/f1; **running time**: 60 minutes

The Butterfly Club: written in response to the wave of teen suicides in and around Bridgend, South Wales, Sarah May's play captures with black humour the fractured lives and vulnerability of young people living in the shadows of tragedy and the emotional failure of adults.
Age range: 14–25; **cast**: m6, f8; **running time**: 60–70 minutes

Alice's Adventures in Wonderland: when Alice is confronted by a white rabbit and follows it down a rabbit-hole, she is toppled into a fantasy world that has delighted generations of readers. This dramatic retelling of Lewis Carroll's classic fantasy offers a spellbinding array of pleasures and challenges for actors, directors and designers.
Age range: 11–25; **cast**: 20+, open to interpretation; **running time**: 60 minutes

Punk Rock: young, bright and privileged, the characters of Simon Stephens's gripping grammar-school drama have the world at their feet. But in this pressurised world where awkward affection and simmering violence dispel myths of 'the best days of your life', things are about to explode.
Age range: 16–25; **cast**: m5, f4; **running time**: 100 minutes

Producers' Choice: Six Plays for Young Performers

Promise
Megan Barker

Oedipus/Antigone
D. J. Britton

Tory Boyz
James Graham

The Butterfly Club
Sarah May

Alice's Adventures in Wonderland
Simon Reade

Punk Rock
Simon Stephens

introduced by

Paul Roseby

Methuen Drama

1 3 5 7 9 10 8 6 4 2

This collection first published in Great Britain in 2010 by Methuen Drama

Methuen Drama
A & C Black Publishers Limited
36 Soho Square
London W1D 3QY
www.methuendrama.com

Promise copyright © Megan Barker 2010
Oedipus/Antigone copyright © D. J. Britton 2010
Tory Boyz copyright © James Graham 2010
The Butterfly Club copyright © Sarah May 2010
Alice's Adventures in Wonderland copyright © Simon Reade 2010
Punk Rock first published by Methuen Drama in 2009.
Copyright © Simon Stephens 2009

Introduction copyright © Paul Roseby 2010

ISBN 978 1 408 12885 5

Typeset by MPS Limited, a Macmillan Company
Printed and bound in Great Britain by CPI Cox and Wyman, Reading, Berkshire

329582

Contents

Introduction

I write this introduction at a time of economic uncertainty. If it weren't so serious, I'd be tempted to make light of the phrase 'double dip recession' as some kind of new joy ride at Alton Towers, but that would not be taking my role as a producer and director seriously. However, we artists are brilliantly resilient to economic change owing to the sheer nature of what we do: it is our job to create 'more' for 'less', which allows the words 'show' and 'business' to work so well together. Despite these turbulent times, theatre has been enjoying something of a renaissance – be it above pubs, in unusual spaces, on London's West End or touring venues across the UK – theatre audiences are bucking the doomsday trend. You could argue, and you might well be right, that recent successes have largely been down to the popular Saturday night TV shows as the nation votes for their favourite 'Nancy' or 'Dorothy' and that the popularisation of a genre can only increase the curiosity of new audiences wanting to experience an entertaining night out at the theatre. Of course, the reality TV shows only focus on musicals and this collection of plays has no room for any Nancys or Dorothys, although there is at least one Alice and an Antigone. Another recent TV phenomenon that also has theatrical roots at its heart is *Glee* – the US all-singing, all-dancing sensation that we watch with part ironic dismissal and part karaoke joy. Although you could still argue that this feeds more interest in theatre, could these accessible musical shows spell trouble specifically for plays for young people? Well, to quote a line from a young troubled soul in Shakespeare's *Hamlet*, 'The Play's the thing / Wherein I'll catch the conscience of the King', and those familiar with the plot know that is exactly what happened. Interesting that I choose to use a line from Shakespeare to illustrate a current point, but the play is *still* the thing that can catch the consciences not just of kings but of entire audiences of all backgrounds and ages, and this new anthology of work proves exactly that.

These six plays, selected by a panel of producers from the industry, showcase some of the best work produced for young actors by companies from around the UK. All the plays have already been staged successfully and you will note that the range, diversity and status of the companies serve as an early indicator of the high quality and unique subject matter of these plays. You'll find too that each of them is packed with engaging new characters for young actors to cut their teeth on.

The title *Producers' Choice* also gives the anthology the 'top billing' it deserves. In the theatrical food chain producers get to eat everything, although with the weight of responsibility often comes ulcers and chronic indigestion. A producer finds the cash, and sometimes *is* the cash, but ultimately, be it a producing house or an individual, the financial risk is all theirs. Timing is everything, not just on stage but also off. The subject matter of the play has to engage the target demographic the producer believes the play will appeal to. The recent West End example of the Olivier Award-winning *Enron*, written by Lucy Prebble and directed by Rupert Goold, is a beautifully crafted piece of theatre that sold out in London. Given that it is about the collapse of the American-based company a natural assumption was to take it to Broadway, but after just fifteen performances and twenty-two previews *Enron* the production went the same way as Enron the company, proving that some subjects can be just too relevant for an audience to endure. For the producers that must have been a hard pill to swallow, but even the most experienced producers and theatre companies can get it wrong. As a renowned producer once said, 'a sure way to make a million in theatre is to start with ten'.

You will be relieved to know that such figures will not be needed in producing any of these chosen plays and their appeal is about how to stage them with a small budget to maximum theatrical effect. As a young theatre-maker you are part of the next generation of producers, directors, actors, technicians and indeed audiences, so do not forget what you would like to see as a member of that audience.

Because some of the subject matter dealt with in this collection goes beyond the average experience of a young person it is important to do your research, to seek out the subtext and to go beyond the story as much as possible. Each play has a cast of at least six and room for large ensemble theatrical moments that cannot fail to entertain and inspire. Each will provoke a very different type of 'glee', thereby keeping the experience of live theatre very much alive.

The first play in the volume, *Promise*, was written in response to the spate of suicides in Bridgend, Wales, but chooses to focus on something positive amid the tragedy. All writers and audience are looking for good stories, and *Promise* is about exactly that: a good news story overshadowed by the mass-media frenzy for a darker tale in and around Bridgend. Written by Megan Barker and performed at Sherman Cymru as a result of collaboration with homeless charity The Yellow Project, it has at its heart a beautiful poetic story that would never get the attention of the press, but will certainly hold the attention of the audience lucky enough to see this little gem. The play offers up a challenge to a company because the central character is played not by one but by three members of the cast, which is a perfect opportunity to share and explore myriad teenage emotions without the heavy burden of playing them alone.

The dialogue and setting of *Promise* is in stark contrast to classic Greek tragedy but the Sherman Cymru also became the perfect place to reinvent the site-specific nature of this well-trodden genre with D. J. Britton's pacey script *Oedipus/Antigone*. The director Phil Mackenzie likes to break the rules when staging a production and often regards theatre spaces as unnatural locations. He likes to animate spaces that normally do not see the light of day or indeed the light of a follow spot. Staging Greek tragedy almost demands an unusual setting in my mind, because the Chorus lends itself to leading an unwitting audience around the twists and turns of a building which can echo the cries and despair of the bloodied heroes and spurned counterparts. Be it your choice to promenade in and around the dressing rooms and corridors of the theatre as Mackenzie did, or to stage the performance in more traditional settings, this play is Greek tragedy at its best – not least because you get two for the price of one! The stories of Oedipus and his daughter Antigone are commonly told as separate tragedies, but here the efficiency and speed of the script will allow a large cast to tell the stories in an appealing easy-on-the-ear way without missing any of the fatalistic cruelty that rips this family apart.

The next exciting new drama, entitled *Tory Boyz* and written by the award-winning James Graham, deals with class and re-engages us with the political argument of what's 'right' and what's 'left'. But most poignantly it grabs a well-known rumour about the sexuality of an ex-Prime Minister, Ted Heath, and brings it bang up to date by paralleling his struggle with that of a young Tory suffering bullying and suppression of his own sexuality in a draconian atmosphere among the corridors of power. The National Youth Theatre produced the play and it was an instant hit, proving that a fascinating subject with a topical sting can put those bums on seats. James Graham is masterful at political playwriting and one of the few young British writers daring enough to tackle the genre. The *Tory Boyz* appeal went beyond the loyal NYT audience because the play, maybe not surprisingly, attracted many MPs and junior researchers who all nodded in a knowing way. However, it did receive the odd complaint, particularly in the shape of one Tory blogger, Ian Dale, who said that the talent on stage wasn't attractive enough. But the fact that this play reached 'blog appeal' is a producer's dream, even if the actors weren't dreamy enough for Mr Dale.

The Butterfly Club, written by Sarah May, explores the consequences of history and inheritance on a group of young people. Like *Promise*, the play was written in response to the teen suicides in Bridgend and it is this hard-hitting reality that makes it so devastating to read and watch. The statistics are there for all to see, and it is a sad fact that the majority of suicide victims are under the age of twenty-five. The renowned playwright Sarah Kane wrote of the haunting suicidal tendencies that became clearly and tragically autobiographical. It is not an easy subject to write about and a brave choice for any producer too because you can't exactly market it as a 'fun night out'. What is so welcoming to see is Sarah May's use of much needed dark humour. As a performer it's important to remember that what I call the 'slash your wrist style of acting' is not necessarily the way to go! I see many auditions – up to 1,000 in any one year – and my heart sinks when a young actor does a speech from a Sarah Kane play and gushes with OTT emotion that ends up as being about as truthful as an MP's expenses claim. Do not try too hard: there are very few young actors who can pull on such raw emotion from genuine experience, and so the old adage 'less is more' is key to acting such sensitive subject matter.

There's a different, more wholesome, kind of fantasy altogether with Simon Reade's *Alice's Adventures in Wonderland* which enjoyed its premiere at the Bristol Old Vic for the theatre's 2004–05 Christmas season. It is important to appeal to adults and children alike because this festive season is a traditional time to give the family a theatrical treat. It is rare for all ages to genuinely enjoy the habitual outing but mercifully here's a treat that puts the cliché firmly back into the genie's lamp and instead allows for a fantastical adaptation of this classic logic-bending tale. Carroll's work often remains challenging to adapt and there have been some cracking flops, such as *The Hunting of the Snark* in the early 1990s where the line 'Don't let the memory die, children of the sky' haunted an empty auditorium soon after opening night.

Thankfully, Reade's adaptation of Carroll's most famous and hallucinogenic work will keep the memory and fantasy alive, but unlike the other plays in this collection there is an added challenge here for any producer and director of such a well-known story. Whether the audience have read *Alice in Wonderland* or not, they will nonetheless recognise and love the characters and so there is a greater expectation from those watching. Therefore, your designer is key here and I suggest a very collaborative process at the earliest stage to allow the vision and ambition of the play to be fully realised. Be playful, subvert the ordinary and break all the conventional rules of perspective for a timeless classic.

You could be forgiven for thinking that the title of the final play, *Punk Rock*, is about the music scene of the late 1970s. Think again. Staged at the Lyric Hammersmith and the Royal Exchange, Manchester, in 2009 and dubbed one of the best plays of the year by several critics it cleverly dissects the issue of class in a classroom. Simon Stephens has combined his skill as a teacher and a dramatist to thrilling effect and written a compelling new play set in an old, safe, traditional library of a fee-paying grammar school. There is nothing safe about the story, however, or the outcome. It's a portrait of dangerously edgy, middle-class adolescents with dark humour and a mounting sense of doom, and it proves that writing about turbulent teens with all their agonies and ecstasies makes great theatre. Stephens's experience in the classroom can clearly teach us all a lesson in brave story-telling.

So there you have it: from gay politicians to grieving mothers and from murderous pupils to struggling journos you are spoilt for choice in characters, plots and inspirational opportunities, be they as producer, actor or even both. Britton's Greek Chorus declares, 'Hope lifts our feet from the mud', and if we can lift the audiences' feet from the proverbial stuff then as theatre makers we have done our job, and the renaissance in live performance continues – definitely something to be gleeful about!

Paul Roseby
Artistic Director, National Youth Theatre
June 2010

Promise

Megan Barker

About the Author

Megan Barker's writing has been performed since 2000. As well as *Promise/Adewidd* (Sherman Cymru, 2008), her most recent work includes *The Gingerbread House* (The Courtyard, Hereford, 2009); *Anaphylactic* (Soho Theatre, London, 2009); *Monaciello* (Tron Theatre Company at Naples International Theatre Festival, 2009); *Cria* and *Tongue Lie Tight/The Bad Drive Well* (The Arches, Glasgow, 2008); and *Pit* (Traverse Theatre, Edinburgh, 2007). She often writes pieces to be performed in non-theatre spaces (such as a cloakroom, a public-toilet cubicle, an underground labyrinth, a farmyard or a multi-storey car park) and regularly designs her own work.

About the Play

During February of 2008 Sherman Cymru's youth group Acting Out Cardiff collaborated on the development stage of a performance with The Yellow Project, a charity for homeless young people based in Bridgend. During this time Bridgend was featuring heavily in the news as the location for a spate of teenaged suicides. In discussion participants passionately opposed the sensational media portrayal of these events. We decided I would make a piece that responded to this situation. In contrast to the press, we would not purport to explain why the suicides were taking place – it was too raw and current for that. Instead we would offer some positivity to an otherwise bleak period. The group felt that better communication between adults and young people and across social divides needed to take place to learn from the situation and the way it was being represented. This discussion fed straight into the story I eventually decided to tell. I also wanted to explore the ideas in form as well as content. My decision to divide Jay's character into three performers is intended to give a sense of the subjective experience I remember about being a teenager myself. I remember feeling that I was playing many roles at once, like Jay, but I also remember a persistent sense of being outside myself, watching myself, trying to monitor and edit my own social performances and frequently surprising myself, as though I was watching action I could not entirely control. For me, the Jays watching the scenes unfold are just as important as the Jay narrating. All the characters are heightened and the direct-address narration is poetic rather than naturalistic. I wanted to create a world that is obviously fictionalised – by the press and by Jay. The characters are all squashed flat by social, economic, cultural, even literary conventions and restrictions. However, if given the chance to escape the little boxes they are put into by society, the press, even the playwright, they are more surprising, more promising, than they might at first appear.

Producing the Play

Two plays – Dylan Thomas's *Under Milk Wood* and Samuel Beckett's *Waiting for Godot* – hung around in the back of my head while I was writing this piece, and the idea was that these two references would meet in the stage design. The lights inside the little houses were very important to me: as well as being an actualisation of Jay's point of view from the tree they also conjured the feeling of melancholy curiosity you get when you are in the street on a cold evening looking in on lots of private but seemingly connected worlds. Although the original production's design stayed fairly true to the text, the budget wouldn't stretch to the little houses being internally lit and in the event it didn't matter at all. Their tree was a mock-up made stable enough to climb, which they had dressed with newspaper (a nice touch I wish I had thought of myself). However, if the budget is tight, any structure that allows the performers to gain height will be adequate, because the tree is vividly described and is as much symbolic as anything. The candles at the end could also cause problems. You could always turn the relevant stage direction into a line of narration and just let the audience imagine what it looks like for themselves.

Characters

The young characters (all aged fourteen to fifteen, approximately):

Jay 1
Jay 2
Jay 3
Pritti Patel
Bryn
Tania
Elen
Bethan
Tommi Tomos
Newspaper Boy/Girl
Morris Muggins, *any age*

The adult characters:

Pauline, *Jay's auntie, Danny's mum*
Terry, *Jay's uncle, Danny's dad*
Tony, *Jay's dad*
Annie, *Jay's mum*
Pamela, *Pritti's mum*
Miss Owen, *the head teacher at the school*
Jenny, *a journalist*

Chorus: Kids, Crowd, Media

(It is assumed that young people play the adult characters. For smaller casts there are various possibilities for doubling-up.)

Staging

Centre stage there is a large tree which has been struck by lightning. It is bare limbed and the wood has been scorched white. Downstage is a miniature street of houses, the school, possibly the church – all simple, uniform, small-town. The buildings are simply represented in plain white with windows cut out of them. When a domestic scene is played out, the corresponding house lights up from within. The central playing space is a fluid area – becoming a living room/school classroom, etc. through use of simple walk-on props/pieces of set.

Scene One: Mornin! Media Madness

Upstage, a tree. Bare limbed. White. In front of the tree, far downstage, a street of miniature terraced houses, stretching in both directions. It is quiet. Peaceful. Early morning.

A **Newspaper Boy/Girl** *rides across the stage on a bike. Stops centre.*

Newspaper Boy/Girl   Mornin. The town asleep. Tucked up tight between two valleys. Peaceful. Quiet. Dawn. Not a whisper. Just a yawn and a stretch and a – (S/*he yawns and stretches.*)

Until the world arrives.

Crowd. Half of them are townspeople, opening and reading newspapers, the papers held up in front of their faces. Half of them are voices from the media, crowding in to everybody's day.

Media 1   Extra! Extra! –

Media 2   And the headlines today –

Media 3   More news, coming up!

One journalist – **Jenny** *– stands aside from the others. She is speaking to the crew and to her editor, who is directing proceedings through an earpiece she is wearing.*

Jenny (*to crew*)   Is this the place, then? Right. Is this good? I'll stand more like this so you can get that creepy tree up there in behind me. Yup. OK? OK. Yup. Go.

She speaks to audience – as though to camera.

Good evening. I'm standing in the centre of a town which, later this week, will be marking the ten-year anniversary of a suicide cluster that shook the –

(*to her editor*) Sorry? What? Oh. Right. OK, yup –

(*to camera*) – the ten-year anniversary of a . . . a suicide terror cult. How has the community moved on from –?

Erm . . .

(*to editor*) Er sorry? Er yes, that's it. What do you mean where's the story? Sam, it's a *Real People* piece.

Well there isn't a high-impact current event –

No. It's a reflective . . .

Right. What? Well what do you want me to do about it? – We're in the arse end of nowhere here.

Oh. Has there? Right. Yes, I suppose it could work . . . Well . . . Who? A girl? Well how old? OK. Erm . . .

(*to camera*) I've come here today because . . . just hours ago, a young woman was found – apparently dead – apparently a suicide . . . has been found . . . somewhere . . . just thirty miles from . . . (*she listens to her earpiece . . .*)

(*to camera*) Only thirty miles from this town, where just ten years ago, the err . . . suicide terror cult . . . struck.

I . . . I'm here to investigate whether or not there is a link – (*puts her hand up to earpiece – she is being shouted at, coughs, corrects herself*) I'm here to investigate the *certain* link between this latest loss and the events of all those years ago. Stay tuned for more on this exclusive breaking news.

(*to Sam, her editor, but on camera still*) Thirty miles away? That's not a link is it? Surely . . . ? Sam? Sam? Surely we're stretching this a little too far – Sam are you there? – I said surely we're – Alright! Don't bite my head off.

(*coughs, regaining authority*) And now for the weather.

She pulls out the earpiece in pain because the editor is shouting in her ear so loudly.

Ow! OK, OK, we need a story. (*Shouts into earpiece.*) I get you boss. Loud and bloody clear.

We hear a crash of thunder and lightning, rain . . . Lights up on the tree. **Jay 1** *has appeared in the crown of the tree.* **Jays 2** *and* **3** *are just visible elsewhere on stage, watching.*

Scene Two: My Tree

Jay 1 *zips up his coat and pulls hat down tight over ears. We hear the thunder rolling around.*

Jay 1   There's a tree on the hill behind our house. They say it was struck by lightning. In 1982. The year my cousin Danny was born. They say it's dead now, like him. It's not though. I know it's not cuz I come up here. I'm always up here, me. Love it, I do.

Flashback to earlier that evening in the Joneses' home. A light comes on in one of the miniature houses in the terrace, downstage. Elsewhere on stage we see **Tony** *and* **Annie** *sitting in the front room, while* **Jay** *is on his way out, in the hallway.*

Tony   Jay, where you off? Not up by that damn tree again I hope.

Jay 2   No Dad.

Jay 1 *(directly to audience, from tree)*   That's me in the cap. Well, supposed to be me. Tell the truth, don't know *what's* the real me, really, see?

Jays 1 and 2   There's the me that's me when I'm at home

Jays 1 and 3   and the me that's me when I'm at school

Jay 1   and the me that's me when I'm up here. On my own. Just hangin about.

Jays 1, 2 and 3   Know what I mean?

Annie   Leave him, Tony. He's not doing any harm, are you son?

Tony   It's weird. Hangin around that place. Spooky.

Annie   Eat your puddin Tony. *(Beat.)* Blancmange, it is.

Tony *(calling out)*   Not still thinking about that bloody loony cousin of yours?

Annie   – Tony – Don't speak like that about Danny, Tony. Especially not now.

Tony   Son –

Annie   Jay? Jay, love? Jay?

Pause – we hear **Jay** *slam the door as he exits.*

Annie (*calling after him, defeated*)   Be careful love.

Tony   There's something not right with that boy. I'm telling you – he's a loner.

Annie   He's probably just a bit upset. Bound to be. Anniversaries do mean something you know.

Tony   The past's the past, Annie –

Annie   Well it's not helpful you saying those things about poor young Danny. You dare let my sister hear you speak like that, and –

Tony   Pauline knows perfectly well I'd do anyth– that I'd . . . that I care for her.

Silence.

Annie   Don't you like blancmange? I thought you did. You always liked blancmange, Tony.

Tony   Bloody anniversary.

Annie   Ten years. So long . . .

Tony   Raking it all up. It'll be a bloody circus here again. Especially with that girl over in – Did you hear? On the news?

Annie   That poor girl.

Tony   Bloody circus.

Annie   They've got a point though, Tone. I mean this girl. She was only young. A kid. Just like before. Like Danny.

Silence . . . **Tony** *pokes at his pudding with his spoon.*

Annie   It *could* happen again, Tony. Things do happen again.

Tony   Oh for God's sake. The girl in the news is thirty miles away!

Annie   Thirty miles is nothing for an idea. The internet makes it all so quick, see? That's what it's all about on the news. We have to protect our young people.

Tony   Sensationalist crap.

Annie   Try not to get worked up love.

Tony   It's not me who –

Annie   I'm just saying.

Tony   You women. You'll believe anything. Can't you think for yourselves?

Annie   Your programme's on at six: *Crime Unlimited – Who's Watching Your Home?* Then it's *When Pets Kill.* You like that one. Why don't you sit down and watch your programmes?

She turns the TV on.

And eat your pudding, hm? (*Beat.*) It's blancmange, Tony. You *do* like blancmange, it's your favourite.

Tony *takes TV remote and changes channel.*

TV: 'And the headlines today: Young local woman is found dead at her home just ten years since the suicide spate that shocked the world. Could this be the start of –'

Tony *smashes his bowl of blancmange down and switches off the TV. Lights fade on the Joneses' home.*

Jay 1   I can see them from up here. Well, the lights at least. Can hear stuff too. If you get in just the right spot. Can hear so clear it's like I'm right up close. Whole street. Whole town. Everything. Reception's brilliant, it is. Like the tree is a sort of conductor. Not just for lightning. For all the airwaves. Like the air up here's full of ears. Listen.

*A light comes on in another of the miniature houses downstage, and elsewhere on stage we see **Pauline** and **Terry** in their home. **Pauline** is in bed and **Terry** is on the landing **Jay 2** is nearby, watching.*

Jay 2   There's my Auntie Pauline and Uncle Terry's house.
It's the quietest house of all. My uncle's down the pub most
nights and when he comes in –

Terry   Pauly? Pauly?

Pauline   I'm in bed, love.

Terry   Which bed, love?

Pauline   I'm in Danny's bed, love.

Terry   Won't you come to our bed, love?

Pauline   Not tonight, love. Tomorrow. Tomorrow
maybe I will.

Terry   Love?

Pauline   Hm?

Pause.

Terry   Night love.

Jay 2   And then sometimes, if you listen really closely, you
can hear her saying her prayers into her pillow, my Uncle
Terry standing in the doorway, watching.

Pauline   Gras ein Harglwydd Iesu Grist a chariad Duw – . . .

Terry   Pauly? Pauly is that you talking?

Pauline   Yes love.

Terry   What you saying?

Pauline   I'm praying.

Terry   Praying? What for?

Pauline   Don't know.

Terry   Oh.

Pauline   If you don't mind, love – Cadw ni'n ddiogel drwy'r
nos dywyll –

Terry   What sort of language's that you're speaking?

Pauline   Welsh, of course. What d'you think?

Terry   But you don't speak Welsh, love.

Pauline   So?

Terry   So how do you know what you're saying?

Pauline   I don't.

Terry   But –

Pauline   I learnt it at school.

Terry   You could be saying anything though!

Pauline   Terry. I don't care. I don't care if I'm talking absolute squit. I don't care what the words mean. I'm just saying them.

Terry   Oh. But why love?

Pauline   In case *somebody's* listening.

Terry   But –

Pauline   Just shut up, Terry.

Terry   But I'd listen, Pauline. Can't *we*? Can't *we* talk?

Pauline   Tomorrow, Terry, tomorrow OK?

Terry   But – why not now, love? I'm listening.

Pauline   Because I don't know what to say, you idiot. I don't know what to say. That's why I'm quite happy, talking rubbish, to someone who probably doesn't exist, in a language I don't even know. At least it's talking – letting the sounds out – without having to make sense. Of everything. Of anything. So. So if you don't mind –

Terry   Right.

Pauline   Right.

Terry   Tomorrow then, maybe.

Pauline   Maybe.

Terry   Right. (*Pause.*) Love?

Pauline   What?

Terry   Night love.

Lights fade on **Terry** *and* **Pauline**.

Jay 2   And on a really quiet night, if you listen closer still, you can hear Uncle Terry chewing the pillow and through the wall in the room next door, Auntie Pauline's shrivelly old heart, gurgling and drowning like a battered rat in a puddle of tears.

Jay 1   She don't lie in Danny's bed on nights when Terry's away driving his truck. Or on nights when my dad goes round. She goes in her own bed then alright. Or else they go on the sofa.

Lights up on group of kids, another part of the stage. They are huddled in a group, playing spin the bottle below the clock tower in the middle of town. The **Jays** *are still watching . . .*

All kids are chanting, except **Bethan** *and* **Tomos**, *who are snogging in the middle of the group, obscured from view.*

Kids   Ten, Eleven, Twelve, Thirteen, etc. . . .

Elen   Eurgh!

Marie   I can see your tongue!

Elen   Gross.

Tania   How's he score Bethan?

Bethan (*coming up for air*)   I'd say . . . a three!

Bryn   A three! Hear that Tommi boy?!

Tom   So? She's rough anyway. Minger. She got smelly breath.

Bethan   Have not.

Bryn   Ew! Tangy.

Bethan   It's not true, is it Tania?

Tom   Eurgh stop speaking, you're killing me.

Bethan   I wasn't talking to you.

Tom   You're doing it again. Every time you open your mouth to talk. All this. Hot. Stinky. Air . . . Ahhhhcccchhhh (*chokes himself*).

Bethan   Up yours.

Tom   And yours.

Tania   And yours.

They all sit in silence, staring ahead. They all get out mobile phones and start texting other people. They put their phones away, stare into the distance. Fiddling with lighters/thumbs/shoes/whatever . . . silent, bored looking . . .

Bryn   Well?

Tom   Drink up?

Tania   Cider?

Bethan (*looking away and trying to surreptitiously cover her mouth with her hand*)   You get it, Tan.

Tania   Eh?

Bethan (*trying to speak with her mouth closed*)   The booze. You gerrit.

Bryn   Speak up!

Bethan (*with hand over her mouth*)   Cider! You get it, *God*!

Tania   Why me?

Tom   Why d'you think? (*Does a big tits gesture.*)

Bethan (*forgets her mouth*)   Whatever. Nobody's listening to you, Tom.

Tom *gasps dramatically, choking.*

Bethan   What?

Tom   Done it again. I'm choking. I'm – that mouth. The stench –

Tania   Piss off. Come on Bethan.

Tom   Laters.

Bethan   Loser.

Jay 3   Those two like each other really. Just don't know how to say it. Sweet really. Romantic. Or something.

Jay 3 *moves over to another part of the stage, where* **Morris Muggins** *is sitting.*

And then there's Screwball Morris Muggins up in his attic. Playing with devices he's ordered off of the internet.

Morris *has a cardboard box of parts in front of him which include a bike helmet, copper sheeting, some crystals, tubes . . .*

Morris *(to himself)*   If I just fit this copper plate in there, and connect it with wires, here . . . These tubes are for the crystals there . . . And . . . There.

(reading the manual) Having trouble communicating? Having trouble being understood? This Copper-Plated Thought-Amplifier will increase the scale of your thoughts tenfold! Just assemble, apply, turn the dial and . . . *(he turns the dial)* one, two, three, four, think. Go on. Reach out.

He scrunches his eyes tight, thinks for a few seconds. Opens his eyes. Speaks directly to the audience.

Hello? Think it worked? Hello? I Am Reaching Out. Anybody? Hello? Anybody hear me?

Jay 3   Yeah. I hear you mate, and I think you're bloody bananas! Gotter respect you for trying though, eh?
At least you're trying to make a connection. Trying to be heard.

Lights start to fade and beautiful flute music is heard wafting across the town.

Scene Three: Pretty Petals

Lights do not fade after all.

Jay 1   Wait though. I haven't said yet about Pritti. Finally of course, there's still Pritti Patel. Hear that?

The flute music gets louder.

That's Pritti. She's practising. Not that she needs to.

Jay 3   She's new in our school and I remember the first day of term she had to stand up in front of the whole assembly.

A light goes on in the miniature school building upstage. We see the **Kids** *in assembly,* **Jay 3** *amongst them.* **Miss Owen** *addresses them.*

Miss Owen   Good morning everybody. I'd like you to meet our new friend and pupil, Miss ermm . . . (*looking searchingly at her register*) Ermm would you like to stand up and tell the rest of the class your name, Miss –?

Pritti *stands up but doesn't say anything . . .*

Miss Owen   Well dear?

Silence, some kids start to giggle . . .

You do speak English, don't you dear? Well? Introduce yourself.

Jay 1 (*to audience*)   The silence went on for ever but it was obvious Miss Owen had forgotten the new girl's name, or didn't want to say it wrong or something. Anyway there was no way she was gunner give in so she just stood there with her mouth all screwed up and thin. And she stared and waited and we all did and everyone was holding their breath just trying not to bust out and crack up.

Jay 3 (*to audience*)   Except me.

Jay 1   I was just letting my whole body slip into the sight of the pink in the new girl's cheeks creeping up the sandy brown beach of her skin towards her ears. Like watching a warm tide lap up her face it was and lap me up and wash over me like waves of I don't know what.

Jay 3 (*to audience*)   Something pink. Blancmange maybe.

Pritti   Pritti Patel.

Jay 3   She said. In the end. And everyone practically fell on the floor laughing, except me. To me it was like music.

Kids (*each taking a line*)

– Pretty? You? Having a laff was they, your parents?

– Blind are they?

– Praps she was born in the dark?! Don't they have lights where you comes from?

– They were hopeful at least!

– Yeah, or in denial.

Pritti (*straight to the audience*)   I stand here, and I know I'm going red. I know I am and I'm going redder because I'm so mad angry I'm boiling over, but you know when the kettle's filled too full and it's boiling and boiling and it doesn't spill it just sort of judders on its little stand? Well that's me now. I'm juddering like a kettle and what I want to do is burst off my lid. And by the way, I'm not not speaking because I'm shy, and I'm not not speaking because I don't speak English (duuh). I'm not speaking because I don't see why I should speak to anyone in this armpit of the world place with its armpit of the world people in their armpit of the world school. And I'm not speaking to my Mum for bringing me here and I'm not speaking to my Nan for dying and leaving us her rotten little bungalow to live in and I'm not speaking to my Dad for being too far away to speak to and I'm not speaking because I can't believe I'm here with all these small-town inbred freaks goggling at me. And by the way I'm not even really speaking now, I'm just standing here with my mouth shut. This is just a cheat to let you know that I'm not the bloody idiot I look like just standing here like a bloody idiot in front of a load of bloody idiots being so mad angry

I can't speak. Like this. (*Taut silence.*) And anyway then some cleverdick says:

Tom   Pretty Petal? Porky Poppadom more like!

Jay 3 *lunges at Tommi.*

Jay 3   And I'm over the aisle and down on the floor with him underneath and then it's –

Miss Owen   James Jones! Tommi Tomos! Detention! Both of you! 1000 lines. 'I will not express my anger through violence in class.'

Jay 1   And I'm there four nights later my arm crooked with cramp and the veins in my wrist thick and bulging not with what Miss Owen said but with two words.

Jay 3   Pritti Patel Pritti Patel Pritti Patel! In my very best joined up.

Jay 2   Pritti Patel Pritti Patel Pritti Patel . . .

Beat.

Jay 1   That is her real name. Honest. It's Indian or something I suppose but to me it sounds like a flower, right? And pretty. And she is and all. No matter what the others say. She is. In her own particular way. And it's a way I like alright. She don't speak, mind. Must be a quiet sort of a type. She's been at our school nearly a year now and they's still the only two words I ever heard her say.

Pritti (*still frozen to her spot*)   Pritti Patel.

Jay 1   Until tonight, that is.

We hear the flute music swell as we shift forward in time.

Scene Four: Crushed

Later the same evening. The group of kids at the clock tower are now a bit pissed. **Jays 2** *and* **3** *are each somewhere nearby, observing from different places. We see* **Pritti** *pass them with her flute case.*

Tania   Eh, Pritti, come and have a drink with us. Hey! I'm talking to you!

Elen   Leave her alone, Tan. She's shy.

Tania   So?

Bethan   Only being friendly. (*To* **Pritti**.) Want a fag?

Elen   She don't smoke, stupid.

Bethan   How do you know?

Elen   Can't you tell? And anyway, because of her flute.

Bryn   She's gotter be able to blow.

Tom   She can come and blow on me if she likes! Eh! Poppadom! I'll be your flute tonight!

Bethan   Shut up Tom. Idiot.

Tania (*to* **Pritti**)   Don't listen to him. He's a tit. Come over and chat with us girls.

Pritti *looks awkward,* **Tania** *goes to her, puts an arm around her, friendly, sits her down amongst them.*

Tom   You're good on that thing, I heard.

Pritti *shrugs.*

Tom   Real chatter box you, ent you?

Pritti *looks embarrassed.*

Elen   Why can't you leave her alone Tommi?

Tania   Fancies her, that's why. It's obvious.

Tom   Get real.

Bethan *giggles – hoping it's not true.*

Tania (*ignoring* **Tom**)   You know you'd look better with your hair down. Why don't you ever wear your hair down Pritt?

She pulls the clips out of **Pritti**'s *hair so it falls down to her shoulders.*

See? Much less. Harsh. What d'you think Beth?

Bethan *looks the other way, pretending not to have heard.*

Elen   Yeah. Nice. Better anyway.

Bryn   Yawn.

Tania   Beth? – *Beth*?!

Bethan (*looks at last*)   S'alright. Tom, get us some chips, Tom would you? And sauce.

Tom (*to* **Pritti**)   You must be able to say *something* though.

Pritti *shrugs, squirms again.*

Bethan   *Tom!* Sauce an all, I said.

Tom *lunges for the flute case and grabs it, takes instrument out of its case, roughly assembles it.*

Tom   Let's have a look then.

Bethan   God's sake.

Pritti *has jumped to her feet and is hovering, wanting to take the flute from* **Tom.**

Elen   Leave her alone.

Tom   Not til I hear her say something.

Bryn   What for?

Tom   Say something or play something. Come on.

Elen   Leave her.

Bethan   Yeah Tom. (*She tries to wrestle the flute from* **Tom***'s grip.*)

Tom (*holding on to it tight, trying not to let* **Bethan** *get it*)   No way, not unless she gives us a tune.

Bethan   Give it.

Tom   No way.

Tom *holds it behind his back, teasing* **Bethan.** *This has become a flirtatious game between* **Tom** *and* **Bethan** *now. She tries to grab it again, giggling. The others all shout at once:*

Elen   Watch it! –

Tania   Hold it! –

Bryn   You'll break –

Tom *falls backwards.* **Bethan** *falls on top of him. The flute is crushed underneath them. None of them notice* **Pritti** *gasp, and walk backwards, away from the group, with her hand over her mouth in despair, before turning and running off as fast as she can.*

Bryn   – it.

Bethan   Oops. (*She giggles.*)

Tom (*to Bethan*)   Look what you done now.

Bethan   Shutup!

Elen   You idiots.

Tania   You can fix it though, right Pritt? Right?

Elen   Pritt?

Jay 3   But Pritti's gone. As far and as fast as her mighty lungs will carry her she's just running all her breath crushed out of her til she stops and comes up for air, finally, and leans against my tree.

Bryn (*shrugs*)   Oh well. Who's for chips?

The group exit. **Pritti** *appears from behind the tree, leaning against it, out of breath. Tears in her eyes. Music.*

Scene Five: Me and Pritti – Up a Tree

Jay 1   So there she is at the bottom of my tree. Just a few feet away. And now I'm the one that's blushing.

He jumps down out of tree, startling **Pritti**.

Eh, it's alright. Din't mean to make you jump.

She starts to move away.

No wait. Pritti. Wait. It's only me. Jay. From school? –

She hesitates.

Get your breath back.

He offers her a swig of coke from a bottle in his pocket. She takes it.

OK?

She nods. She looks at her watch.

Late home is it? Don't worry. I'll give you a backy on the bike.

She shakes her head.

Don't like bikes?

She shrugs.

Don't like backies?

Shrugs.

Walk you home, then.

She shakes her head, distressed.

You don't want to go home?

She looks at the floor, distressed.

I'll . . . I'll make things right for you Pritti.

She thinks he's weird.

Honest. I mean . . . That Tommi's a prize asshole. You gunner be in trouble about your flute?

She nods. Still confused that he seems to know what's happened.

That why you don't want to go home?

She just looks at him . . . puzzling.

I know, I know. You're thinking what's he on about? He wasn't even there just now! You think I'm nuts. Or you are. You wanner know how I knows? Come on. I'll show you something.

He starts to climb the tree.

It's quite a trick to get up here because the branches are hollow, some of them, and you have to know where to put your hands. Where's safe. Just copy me, see?

She is not following him.

It's good.

Honest.

People say it's bad this tree. And well. It is lanky alright, and . . . and it's got a posture like a pudding – Dad would say, but –

He sees she's still not following him.

Oh I get it. Scared of heights isit?

She shrugs, embarrassed.

Scared of bikes, scared of heights . . . you're a scared sort of a person aren't you, Pritti Patel?

She shrugs, embarrassed.

Alright. I'll just tell you all about it instead. Only. It's a secret, right? All what I tell you. About this tree. It's a secret and I don't really know why but you're the only person I have ever wanted to tell. So. Well. There we are. OK?

She nods, sits at the base of the tree.

Jays 2 *and* **3** *are watching. They speak directly to audience.*

Jay 2   And I did. About the tree and how it picks up all the noises, all the voices in the town and how that's how I knew – about Tommi Tomos and what he done –

Jay 1   – and about how I love sitting up here and listening even though sometimes I hear things I don't want to hear, like the sound of my Auntie Pauline whimpering into my Dad's shoulder with the bedsprings going underneath and the sound of my Mum's back creaking as she buries her head even deeper in the shag pile carpet with a can of Shake and Vac in her hand.

Jay 3   I told her about Morris Muggins and his helmet and the knob saying one to ten and she laughed. (Ha!) She laughed! I couldn't believe it!

Jay 2   The moon grows big and shrinks small and sails off behind us and I reckon she's nearly nodded off when – shit –

He drops the knife in front of **Pritti** *and it makes her jump up, shocked and frightened.*

I drop the knife.

Jay 1 (*to* **Pritti**)   Oh my God. Sorry.

He jumps out of the tree and grabs his knife. She is scared.

Look. I'll put it away. See? (*He puts it in his pocket, shows her his empty hands.*)

I'd never hurt you, Pritti.

Nor no one come to that.

Honest.

Jay 3 (*to audience*)   And then I tell her about what I been doing. Every night. Just me and the knife. All night. Up a tree.

Jay 1 (*to* **Pritti**)   People say it's hollow because it's dead, see? People say it should be chopped down, that tree. After all what happened. But I say it weren't the tree's fault. The tree was just minding its own, whistling a tune to itself. It never asked for any of it. Never wanted the attention. Was just standing there, being a tree.

Jay 2 (*to audience*)   And I tell her how the tree's beautiful. No matter what the others say. In its own special way. And it's a way I like.

Jay 3 (*to audience*)   And then I tell her about Danny and the others and all what happened back then ten years ago.

Jay 1 (*to* **Pritti**)   Dad says I've gone weird for coming up here. He thinks I'm stuck on Danny and how he's dead. S'not like that. I remember Danny. Alive, I remember thinking he was pretty smart. But I was only six, so that's it.

Jay 2 (*to audience*)   And then I tell her the rest.

Jay 1   Dead, I remember Danny dead alright because it was me what found him. Really I only remember his shoes. Really that were all I could see of him. Just above my head.

Jay 3   And the rest.

Jay 1   And the knife. This knife. It was on the floor. About where you are now. His penknife see? I picked it up and I pocketed it and I never told no one. Goes everywhere with me this knife. Not because it was Danny's and he was my cousin and he was pretty smart and now he's dead. Just because it's a knife what I found and nobody knew I got it and I was only six and well, that's all isn't it? My knife now. To do what I like with.

Jay 2   And then I offer again. To show her. Up the tree. All what I've been doing up there. With the knife.

Jay 3   The only thing I don't tell her is what I'm gunner do next. The bit what's the bignuts, the slambam the grandfinale? That bit's a secret. For now. Even from her.

Jay 2   But she still won't come.

Jay 3   She's still scared of heights.

Jay 1   But I reckon she's not scared of me no more.

Jay 2   And that feels pretty good.

Jay 3   So I sit down the bottom of the tree with her. And I'm sitting close enough that I can feel she's shivering under her clothes.

Jay 2   So I –

Jay 1 *takes his jacket off and puts it over both their legs. He then takes off his cap and puts it on her head. As he does this,* **Jays 2** *and* **3** *take their hats off simultaneously. They sit down too, in their respective positions on stage. Relax.*

Jay *and* **Pritti** *sit leaning against the tree, looking out at the town. She puts her head on his shoulder. He is pleased. Eyes closed now, they sit in silence for a while.*

Pritti Jay?

He opens his eyes but doesn't say anything, not quite sure whether to believe she has spoken.

Pritti Thanks Jay.

Music, the sun rises.

Scene Six: Say Cheese!

The media crowd all rush and jostle and push each other again, speaking over one another. A hullabaloo. Each take individual lines.

– And the headlines today:

– I am standing just *thirty miles* away from . . .

– Ten years on, can this possibly be called coincidence?

– Could this be the start of a new spate of suicides?

– Valley echoes yet again with the sound of grief.

– The world will be waiting now to see, will there be another?

– (*all shouting*) And another!/And another?!/And another?!

– And now for the weather.

*We hear heavy rain beginning to fall. This wakes **Jay** and **Pritti** up with a start. They both leap up and pull themselves together, and **Pritti** speaks directly to the audience.*

Pritti I can't believe it when I wake up and it's morning and I've not been home. My mum'll kill me twice over! Once for not going home and once for the flute. I just cross my fingers and run down the hill. Course I say bye to Jay first though, and he says –

Jay 1 See ya. (*He shimmies up the tree.*)

Pritti And he's all a colour red and grinning at me and it's a colour of a grin I like.

Jay 1   Pritti wait! Hang on a sec. My hat. Sorry. It's just. It was my cousin's, see? I never go without my hat. And – sorry.

She shrugs and gives him back the hat.

Pritti   And I run down the hill down home and my stomach's churning up happy even though I know it's gunner be bad.

Jay 1   And it's mad what I can see. It's like there's been an invasion. Talk about a frenzy! The media's everywhere like piranhas biting people's heads off on their way to the shops – gnashing for that all important story.

Media (*each take individual lines*)

– Any comment – (*Snap.*)

– A word – Mr – (*Snap, snap.*)

– Just stand there and – (*Snap, snap, snap.*)

– Can you tell the world – (*Snap.*)

– You grew up *here*? (*Snap, snap.*)

– So you think it's not surprising? (*Snap, snap, snap.*)

– So the question is –

– Well, wouldn't you?

All Media   (*Snap, snap, snap, snap.*)

Jay 2   And there's poor Pritti arriving home and getting the biggest bollocking off her Mum you ever heard.

A light comes on in one of the miniature houses downstage. We see **Pritti** *at home with her mum,* **Pamela**.

Pamela   Have you no idea how worried I have been? I thought you'd killed yourself what with all this in the news. Have you no idea what you put me through Pritti Patel? There's nothing for it. You will have to go and live with your father in India.

Pritti (*to audience*)   Which is what she always says when she's cross as if going to live in India would be something terrible when really, I'd love to go there and see what it's like. But that was before and this is now and now I don't want to go to *anywhere at all*. All I want more than anything – except maybe to get my flute back, and maybe more than that – is to stay right here. Near. Jay. So please, please Mum, don't make me go.

Pamela   And you're grounded and while you are up there in your room you can think about how on earth you're going to get your scholarship to music school without a flute to play at your concert next week and you will have to cancel and no one will hear how good you are and you may just as well have killed yourself Pritti Patel and me and all, because what sort of a future is there for us now that you have thrown it all away? You've left me no choice. I'm calling your father.

Lights down on **Pritti** *and* **Pamela**.

Jay 3   And I'm up the tree, ragin at how Pritti's gunner get taken away from me and sent off to India all because of that prize asshole Tommi Tomos and how I'm gunner sort it for her and I'll make sure she still gets to go to music college.

Jay 2   As long as it's not too far.

Jay 1   From me.

Jay 1 *turns his back to us in the tree. He is busy at something. A flurry of sawdust comes from the tree and falls like snowflakes to the ground below.*

Jay 3   And I'm just working at things when –

Jay 2   Snap!

Jay 3   Flash!

Jay 1   Blinded, I am.

Jay 3   And then –

Jenny   Newsflash! Erm. Disaffected youth up death curse tree. Is this the beginning of the second suicide spate we have all been dreading? (*Calling out – down the hill.*) Someone call an ambulance! (*To* **Jay**.) Excuse me? You there. Just. Steady. On. Keep it. Calm, now. Now, can you give us a few words about – about how you feel? About why you feel drawn to this – the tree that stands for so much horror, heartache and – Young man?

Jay 1   Bog off would you?

Jenny   I can see you're angry. Of course you are. How else do you feel? I want to see things from your perspective. I'm doing a 'Real People' piece. If I can get it past my editor . . . If I could just come up there with you and – Yes! That's it! A report from up the tree itself! I'll do a piece that's quite literally from *your* point of view. She's bound to go for that. People like you need a voice and I won't let my editor or anybody else stand in the way of that.

She is attempting to climb the tree.

Jay 1   Get away from me, you nutter! Get away!

He swipes his knife in the air, in her direction, trying to scare her off the tree.

Jenny (*scared*)   Jesus Christ.

Jay 1   Get down!

Jenny   Alright, alright. Don't do anything stupid. With that. Not. Until. I've called. Your parents.

Jay 1   No way!

Jenny   Or the police, or –

Jay 1   What?!

Jenny   Do you understand me? You're going to be OK. (*Calls down.*) For God's sake, somebody call the police! Get that thing off him!

Jay 1   No! You can't. This knife. This knife is . . . It were my cousin's. I'm not doing bad. I'm just – It's just for – nothing bad.

Jenny (*trying to put on a calming voice*)   It's OK. I believe you. Why don't you show me. The knife? Just give it over – so I can have a look at it. That's all.

Jay 1   What, you think I'm stupid?

Jenny   If you would just. Let me –

Jay 1   But –

Jenny   I'm not a monster. I've got a degree. I want to help you people. I want to help you find a way out –

Jay 1   But I'm not doing nothing. Just sitting here. Up a tree. Minding my own. Taking in the view.

Jenny   Yes! And it's your view I'm interested in. You deserve to be represented.

Jay 1   You what?

Jenny   The world out there needs to know what it's like for people like you. All this.

Jay 1   I don't want nothing to do with you. Get. Off. My Tree!

Jenny   Look. Unless you can *prove* to me that you're not harming yourself, I will have to have that knife confiscated. Do you understand? (*Calls down again.*) Somebody?! Over here!

Jay 2 (*to audience*)   And she's got me, the cow. Got me by the short and curlies.

Jay 3 (*to audience*)   I mean what choice have I got? What choice –

Jay 2 (*to audience*)   Except to say –

Jay 1 (*to* **Jenny**)   OK. OK, but you promise you'll leave me alone then?

Jenny   I promise.

Jay 1   Say it.

Jenny   I promise to leave you alone.

Jay 1   OK . . . So. You put your feet on where the notches are. See?

She climbs up a bit and sees part of his creation.

Jenny   Good God, but that's incredible – amazing! What . . . what is it – some sort of sculpture . . . ?

Jay 1   Right that's enough. You seen. Now bugger off. You said you'd leave me alone. So. Go on.

He stands high in the tree, barring her vision.

Jenny   OK, OK. I'm going, I'm going.

Jay 1   And remember what you promised.

Jenny   I do. I will.

Jay 2 (*to audience*)   And does she?

A single bright camera flash.

Does she hell!

Jay 1 *jumps down from the tree . . .*

Jay 1   Next thing I know my ugly mug's plastered all over everywhere!

Jay 3   That's me! Stuck half way up a bloody tree!

Jay 2   And God knows where she got my name from!

Jay 1   Although, to be fair –

Jay 2   Not that I wanner be

Jay 3   And not that she deserves it

Jay 1   – to be fair she don't mention what she seen. It just says:

Jenny (*reading the headline in confusion and then horror*)   'Local lad takes to tree of terror. James Jones, the face of teenage death tree cult. The curse lives. Ten years on' . . . Oh no! NO! Sam?! Sam?! What the –? Where's my report . . . ? These aren't my words . . . ! Who is responsible for these words? Sam? Sam?! – Yes of course I understand that headlines sell. I just wanted to take a more positive angle . . . But you can't do that, I've put years of sweat into this company – I'm not a bleeding heart, I'm a –. Right. I hear you. One more chance. But it's got to be *my* words. Is that a promise? Right. A positive spin that sells or . . . Right. Yup. Or that's it.

Jay 1   But it's too late by now. And all the other vultures have pecked it up and cottoned on. Screaming out they are, saying:

Media, *each taking a line*

– And now the question leaving the world baffled is –

– Why has this tree been allowed to remain standing?

– Casting its shadow of death over this grim and gloomy town?

Jay 2   And the thing what gets me, really gets me, is how they're all sucked in. Mum, Dad, Auntie Pauline . . . the lot of em.

Scene Seven: A Right Regular Swampy

Jays 1, **2** *and* **3** *are all watching from their respective positions. Light up in miniature house and we see* **Pauline** *and* **Terry** *in their home.*

Pauline   I've been thinking, love.

Terry   Hm?

Pauline   How we never had that tree chopped down . . . Perhaps we should've. It might help.

Terry   Help with what love?

Pauline   Help us put it all behind us.

Terry   I thought we had. I thought we were . . . What'd be the point now, hm? Ten years ago now Pauline. It's such a long time.

Pauline   Maybe to you, Terry. Maybe to you.

Terry   It's just – Love, are you sure you're not just feeling like that because of all this fuss on the telly?

Pauline   But maybe they're right. Maybe we should have done it before. Maybe it makes us look like we don't care. Didn't care.

Terry   Rubbish.

Pauline   There you go! You see?!

Terry   What love?

Pauline   This is what happens when I try and talk to you –!

Terry   What love? What?

Pauline   You just dismiss everything I –

Terry   I don't!

Pauline   You do.

Terry   Do not.

Pauline   You just said I was talking rubbish. I wasn't.

Terry (*simply*)   OK.

Pauline   What, that's it?

Terry   Yes. That's it. We'll see about getting the tree chopped down, if –.

Pauline   If what?

Terry   If it makes you feel better.

Pauline   Right. Good. It will.

Terry   Good.

Pauline   Right.

Pause. They seem to get a tiny bit cosier together . . .

Love?

Terry Hm?

Pauline You will sort it *before* the anniversary service tomorrow, won't you love?

Terry *Before?* But that's no time!

Pauline Please, Terry. I just don't think I could stand to come out of the church and see the tree looming up there and have everyone thinking we didn't – when we should have –. It's like some sort of . . . a curse, Terry. It wouldn't be right.

Terry But love. It's been there every other year. After every other service.

Pauline Oh fine. Whatever. You just go on. I'll just sort it myself.

Terry But –

Pauline I'll phone Tony. He'll know what to do. He's the sort of bloke that gets things done when it matters.

Pauline *exits, huffy.*

Terry Love –?

She's gone and doesn't answer him.

– But – *Tony?*

(*Defeated.*) Right, love. (*Sighs.*) Bye love.

Assembly. We see **Miss Owen** *addressing the kids,* **Jay 3** *amongst them.*

Miss Owen Class, I want you all to pay attention. As you all know, tomorrow night is the annual memorial service. I want to remind you that there is an excellent school counselling service in place. That is, if any of you should wish to discuss your feelings about what happened, the school nurse or I myself are available during the morning break and, if absolutely necessary, during the first half of the lunch hour, to hear your concerns. I'm sure we are both, as the expression goes, all ears.

Jay 3   Well that's all well and good but then check this bit −

Miss Owen   Furthermore, I want to make it absolutely clear that any pupil seen spending time up at the waste ground or within a hundred-metre radius of the lightning tree during school hours or whilst wearing school uniform will be suspended immediately. The tree represents a real danger, children. I myself will be signing the petition to have the tree removed and I strongly urge that you do the same.

Kids (*each taking different lines*)

− Yeah, it's well creepy anyway.

− Did you know three people hanged themselves there?

− I heard it was four.

− Gross.

− No stupid, it was only one. The first one. The others did it other places.

− Still gross.

− They reckon it's cursed.

− Well I think it's spooky having it there as a reminder all the time.

− Me too.

− Me too.

All Kids   Chop it down! Chop it down! Chop it down!

Jay 3   Can't you see? It's them lot out there what's raking it all up! All this! It's just what they want! Stories for papers. You've *all* let those greedy piranhas eat your brains out!

Except Good Old Morris Muggins who's just minding his own with a new contraption.

We see **Morris Muggins**, *who has wires coming off his fingers which connect straight into the inner workings of an old record player.*

And then get this, that night, when the vultures have all disappeared to their trucks and I go home, it's –

Light up in miniature house downstage. We see **Tony**, **Annie** *and* **Jay 2** *in their home.*

Tony Jay, you are to stay away from that tree and there is an end to it.

Jay 2 But –

Tony No buts.

Annie Listen to your father, Jay.

Jay 2 But surely you don't buy into all that rubbish they're spouting out there –

Tony Don't you tell me what to buy into.

Jay 2 But it's tabloid crap, Dad. Sensationalism?! The circus – remember?

Annie Don't swear, Jay.

Jay 2 But – for God's sake! 'The past's the past', remember Dad?

Annie *Jay.*

Tony Do as your mother says, Jay. And stand up straight. Posture like a puddin.

Jay 2 But I'm not doing nothing.

Tony Precisely, son. Perhaps you should stop doing nothing and start doing something. It's wasters like you end up with a bloody screw loose and wind up hanging from that cursed bloody tree.

Annie Tony! Mind what you're saying to Jay.

Tony I will say what I goddam well like, Annie. This is my house and it's time for a bit of straight talking.

Annie Yes well let's all just calm down and have a cup of tea and a biscuit shall we?

Jay 2   Straight talking? Is that a joke? *You* want straight talking do you Dad?

Tony   Don't you answer back to me son.

Annie   Now, now Jay don't be cheeky to your father. So. Bourbon or a Nice?

Tony   He's not to go hanging about that tree. He's to stay in with us. From now on. You're to sit here and.

Jay 2   What? And watch telly? Sit in silence and stuff ourselves silly on cakes just so long as we don't have to talk to each other?

Annie   Jay don't love, please. What's got into him Tony?

Tony   I'm telling you boy. You'll not go crackers on me.

Jay 2   Flick through the channels till it's time for Mum to put the hoover on so she can't hear you sneak out the back and shut the door behind you?

Tony   *You!* –

Annie   Tony! That just isn't true, Jay. Where's he getting these ideas from, Tony?

Jay 2   And then hoover the whole house for the fifteenth time so she doesn't have to think about where you might be all night long?

Annie *lets out a stifled shriek and covers her ears with the packets of biscuits – one in each hand.*

Tony   James, that is enough!

Jay 2   Had enough? Is this not how it goes, Dad? You're like a pair of zombies, you are, saying things from out of a book. Your mouths are flappin but it's just dust is coming out. Dust from an old book you never even read. No wonder the hoover's always on. Mum. I feel sorry for you. I really do but no wonder he goes off with Auntie Pauline. Praps all that crying she does makes her more of a human. Praps it gives them something to talk about. What have you got to say? You don't even like housework. Or biscuits. Why do you waste all your money on bloody biscuits? All he ever does is moan on about this or that but none of it means nothing. Come on Dad, when was the last time you actually *did* something or *said* something real?! Something that means something? You're pathetic, the pair of you. Straight talking it's called, Dad. And you don't like it.

Annie *is sitting, stunned, silent, staring ahead with her mouth open. It is as though dust might escape from there.*

Jay *goes to door.*

Tony (*icy quiet*)   James, you will not go up that damn lightning tree ever again.

Jay   Why? Who's gunner stop me?

Tony   I am. I already have. I'm having it chopped down.

Jay   You're what?

Tony   You heard. Tonight. Some of the boys. I'm doing it for Pauline. She's asked me to do it and I'm doing it. Hear me son? Does that 'mean something' to you son? Hm? Does it?

Jay   But –

The doorbell rings. **Jay** *opens it, still stunned. A journalist rings the bell and stands in his way on the doorstep.*

Journalist (*over* **Jay**'s *shoulder*)   Mr and Mrs Jones? Are you joining the campaign to end the curse and chop the tree down? James? How are you feeling as this tragic anniversary approaches? What drove you up that tree, James? Can we have a comment, James?

Jay 2 *roars and pushes past the journalist. Lights down on the Joneses' home. Behind the journalist are many more. A whole crowd has gathered in the street.*

Jay 2   You want a comment? How's this? (*All three* **Jays** *pull the finger at the crowd from where they are.*)

Crowd Chop it down! Rip it down! Out of sight, better for the town! (*Repeated, and then:*)

Chop it! Chop it! Chop it! (*This is repeated underneath next speeches.*)

Jay 2 *pushes through the crowd, wild and upset.*

Jay 2 Leave me alone leave me alone leave me alone!

The crowd is still chanting.

Jay 1 (*to audience*) I push my way through the crowd and it's like a forest of arms and legs and I'm kicking out and lashing a scramble full of scratches in all directions cos I gotter get up that tree and protect it.

As the crowd's chanting continues, **Jay 1** *climbs up into the tree. From the noise of the crowd, individuals call up to* **Jay** *and plead with him.*

Annie Come on sweetheart. You're right. Of course you're right. Your Dad and I, we – (*To* **Tony**.) See what you've done? See?

Tony Lad! Now, now lad. No need to take on like this. We'll make amends, son. I – I only ever want the best for you son.

Annie Jay, love? Please! I've made your favourite . . .

Pauline Don't put us through this, Jay, please. It's Danny's memorial tonight. He'd want you there Jay, not stuck up here in this terrible place –

Pauline *starts to cry,* **Tony** *puts an arm round her, pats her on the back, awkwardly, aware that* **Annie** *is by his side.*

Terry Come on Jay! This isn't like you! You should be at home . . . playing . . . Scalextric . . . or whatever it is boys of your age get up to . . . Come on lad!

Jay 2 (*to audience*) Scabloodylextric? I'm sixteen for God's sake!

Jay 3 (*shaking his head*) Haven't. Got. A. Clue.

Miss Owen I'm all ears, James. As I said in assembly. If you want to talk. *Any* time.

Tania   Come on Jay. You're famous enough already!

Lisa   Yeah, what a hero!

Miss Owen   You'll not be suspended you have my word.

Tommi   Can borrow my Xbox!

Pauline   James, please! Tony, tell him we'll leave the tree alone. If that's what it takes. We'll leave the tree where it is.

Terry   There, there love. (*He tries to comfort* **Pauline**, *but she ignores him.*)

Tony   But I'm doing it, Pauline. I told him. Told him straight.

Annie   Well un-tell him, then, for God's sake. Do as she says, Tony.

Pauline   Just get him down.

Tony   Right. Lad, Lad?! Now you listen to me. It's off, lad. The tree. Tonight. I'll tell, the boys. Right? You hear me? Now you get down from there right now and get your sorry arse to mass or you're grounded! For life!

Annie   Come on love. Just for the service. We can go together. Just you and me. You can go as you are. No one'll mind –

Jay 2   They're all at it, they all have a go, except good old Morris Muggins of course, who's minding his own, as per. Anyway, I'm not budging. I just block my ears and sits tight like a right regular Swampy.

Jay 1   You'll not pull the tree down with me up in it!

Jay 3   I think I get a glimpse of Pritti in amongst them all, and it makes something leap up in my chest and rattle on the door of my throat it feels like an age since I seen her and for all I knew she could of got sent to India and I try to call out to her but my voice just gets lost in all the shouting below.

Pritti   And I am there alright, but trying to keep a low profile cos if my mum saw me I'd be dead for a third time for sure. But then –

She is led aside by **Jenny**.

Jenny   You're James's girlfriend aren't you?

Pritti *appears very shy*.

Jenny   Pritti Patel?

Well. I've done my research. I know you care about him.

I've seen you together.

I want to help you.

To help him.

What's he doing up that tree? I know it's *something* special, but I need to know what exactly. I didn't get a chance to find out. Not properly.

Pritti *looks down . . . unsure of what to say*.

Jenny   Why is it so important to him?

I can see he's not planning on throwing a rope around his neck.

I can see that. I could make others see that too if you'd help me.

You want them to leave him alone, don't you?

And the tree.

Pritti *is starting to be persuaded . . .*

Jenny   So. Help me get a chance to show them what it's really all about.

I just need a bit of time . . . at that tree . . . on my own.

Pritti's *not so sure . . . sounds dodgy . . .*

Jenny   I can be honest with you Pritti. It'll help me too. I'll get my exclusive. That's true. But more importantly, I'll get a scoop that will help you to help Jay and put an end to this whole affair. I'll make the world listen, you'll see. We can make something positive out of all this. We *can* make it work, I know we can.

Pritti *isn't really following . . .*

Jenny You do care about him, don't you Pritti?

Pritti *nods.*

Jenny So you will?

Pritti's *still unsure . . .*

Jay 2 I'm still sitting there as it starts to get dark and people begin to drift off and go home for their teas.

The crowd disperse, on their way home; we see **Annie**'s *crying.*

Tony Don't let the boy think he's beaten us, Annie. We'll ignore him for a bit. He's bound to get bored and give up, you'll see.

Annie *shrugs him off and moves away from him.*

Jay 3 And at last I get a bit of peace and quiet and there's just the faint swish and rustle of people pulling suits out the cupboards and giving them a brush down, as slowly, the town gets dressed in black.

Jay 1 Peace at last. Thank God. Cos I've got work to do.

In the tree, **Jay 1** *turns his back on the audience. He is busy at something. A flurry of sawdust falls to the floor like snowflakes.*

Lights fade.

Scene Eight: The General Pause

A light in one of the miniature houses downstage. Lights up on the Patel home. **Pamela** *is watching TV in the living room.* **Pritti** *is in her bedroom, putting an anorak on over her pyjamas. She turns to the audience and puts a finger to her lips.*

Pritti *Sssh.*

She then climbs out of her bedroom window, away from her mother, who is watching TV.

Jay 3 (*speaks to audience as* **Jay 1** *is busy working away at something up the tree*)   And you don't need to worry. I'll not get sleepy and nod off for a nap. Nothing. I mean nothing! Will. Move. Me.

Jay 2   Except. Well, except maybe –

Pritti *appears at the base of the tree, knocks on the trunk.* **Jay** *looks down and sees her.*

Jay 1 (*grinning*)   You never went to India then?!

She shakes her head – no.

Come up?

She shakes her head – no. She goes over to his BMX, which is lying on its side near the tree and sits on the saddle. She dings the bell.

What is it Pritti? You wanner go somewhere?

She nods.

But you're scared of bikes.

She shrugs, she smiles at him.

Oah, I dunno Pritti . . . I – I would, but – This is important. It's best I stay . . .

Pritti   Come on. I want to show *you* something.

Jay 1   Oah . . . Well OK.

He jumps out of the tree.

Jay 1 (*to audience*)   Well. I mean. Wouldn't you?

They both get on the bike – **Pritti** *pedalling and* **Jay** *on the back.*

Where we going?

Pritti   You'll see.

Music. **Pritti** *pedals faster and faster . . . the headlamp comes on, music lifts . . .* **Jay** *stands up on his pedals . . .*

Chorus   *Go go go go!*

As the music plays, and **Pritti** *stands up on his pedals, individual chorus members take the lines:*

Chorus   – They bike along the back of the hill

– The ridge

– Spinning out the cliff edge streams

– Tearing through the gathering dark

– Pedalling mad fast feet feet fast and hearts pounding

– Hard on ribs his beats against its cage his chest doing its best to leap straight into Pritti's.

– He can feel her own beating bird batting its mad wings crashing against her back. He can feel where lurks a storm thrashing in an anorak and jammies.

– He can hear it. The air crushing in and out those almighty lungs

– As they glide and gasp and swallow whole the giant night among the stars they are

– Slowing

– The town falling out of sight, just showing until

– The twinking lights drop off behind the ridge

– And all you're left with is

– An orange glow glooming up the sky.

– The path unravels further

– And then.

– Skid. Stop. Listen.

Silence.

Pritti   There.

They scramble off the bike and take a couple of steps forward, look out.

Jay 1   And there it was. Just. Nothing. Silence. Where the mountain finished and dropped down into the far end of the valley. Opposite way from the town. A giant, stretching, soundless nothing.

Pritti   Look.

They look up to the sky at stars.

Jay 1   It's so quiet.

Pritti   You spend all your time listening to people talking. And as far as I can tell, it's always the gloomy stuff you're interested in.

Jay   But – Well – It's the messed up ones is most interesting, isn't it?!

Pritti   Well *I'm* not messed up. I don't think.

Jay   You're different. (*Beat.*) People just talk for the sake of it. Talk a load of rubbish. Don't say what they really want to say. Most people can't do it. You're –

Pause . . . silence.

Pritti   In music, when the orchestra stops and goes completely silent it's called '*Tacet. The General Pause.*' It can be deafening sometimes.

Pause.

Always makes me shiver.

Pause. Standing closer still. Looking out.

Jay 1   You're shivering now. And your heart's beating, I can hear it.

Pritti   That's lucky!

Jay 1   Listen.

They stand looking out, listening to their hearts beating.

Pritti   I like you Jay.

Jay 1 (*grinning*)   Well. I mean. (*Shrugs.*) Who wouldn't?

Jay 2 (*to audience*)   I say, and I get back on the bike and I go –

Jay 1 (*to* **Pritti**)   Righto. Best be gettin back then.

Jay 3 (*to audience*)   But what I really mean is something much, much bigger and I'm busting and all I can think is how I STILL haven't clocked her eye to eye, not quite, not one shot. And how I wanner give her everything, everything I've got!

Jay 2   But like I say, mostly people don't say what they really want to say. Can't do it, most people, and who said I was any different?

Jay 1   It's coming ten o'clock by the time we come back round the corner of the path, and – Hang about! What's that I see? And there they are. The vultures. Hundreds of em. All flocking round my tree.

Jay 1, 2 and 3   No!

Jay 2   Not my tree! And they're slinging a great big chain around it, and flashing gnashing cameras taking great chunks out of my world with their snap snap snapping.

Jay 3   And I can't believe it! That Pritti. Who now, I see, is white as me, and has her hand clapped over that tiny, quiet, secret mouth of hers.

Jay 1   You – You tricked me! You –

Pritti   No! I – (*She clambers off bike and runs off.*)

Jay 1   Porky Poppadom! I shout after her, but she's off. Ripping towards the crowd and tears my heart out with her. (*Shouts out.*) Porky Poppadom!

Jay 1 *is very distressed and fighting back tears.*

Jay 3   She stuffed me up good and proper. Took me for a ride alright and I just fell right in like the prize one idiot.

Pritti *is fighting her way through the crowd to get to the tree. We see her bump into* **Jenny** *on her way through.*

Jenny   Pritti, wait.

Pritti *struggles to get by her.*

Jenny   Pritti. I'm so sorry. I didn't mean for –! I thought I had them on side – they just wouldn't listen, Pritti. Nobody would listen.

Pritti *shakes her head violently and pushes* **Jenny** *away, shoves past her, towards the tree.*

Jay 1   And then I see the crowd is moving in closer on my tree and they're shouting and waving and fussing at something I can't quite see.

Jay 1 *drops the bike and moves towards the crowd, curious.*

They've got the chain on now and I hear someone yell –

Crowd   One, two, three!

Jay 1   – before someone else shouts

Crowd   Stop!

We that see **Pritti** *has got through the crowd and is beginning to climb the tree.*

Individual **Crowd** *members take the lines.*

– What's going on?!

– Somebody stop her!

– She'll fall!

– Somebody get the girl down!

– Wait! Look this way! (*Snap.*)

– Over here love! (*Snap.*)

– She going to top herself or what?!

– You got your camera switched on haven't you?! You dare miss this and you're fired!

– Is this the moment we've all been waiting for?!

– Somebody help her!

– You! Up there! Will you get down?!

Pritti *is clearly terrified. She shakes her head – she won't come down. She clings on for dear life.*

Crowd   – We're going to pull the tree down, dear! Do you understand? It's got to come down!

She shakes her head even more.

– Do you have a comment for us miss?!

– Smile!

Snap.

Pritti (*to audience*)   My God, my Mum'll kill me all over again. (*Looking down into crowd, shouting down to* **Jay** *over hubbub.*) Jay? Jay? I'm sorry. I'm sorry. I didn't mean for this to – I won't let them –

Woah!

Her foot slips, the crowd gasps, **Jay 1** *pushes to the front and tries to get up there after her.*

Jay 1, 2 and 3   Pritti!

But the **Crowd** *hold* **Jay 1** *back and restrain him so he can't climb the tree.*

Jay 1   Pritti!

Crowd   Don't worry son, we'll get her down.

Jay 1 (*struggling*)   But she's scared of heights! She's scared of –! Get off me! (*Calls up to her.*) Pritti! Just put your feet where the notches are. It's safer higher up, see?

Pritti *climbs higher.*

Jay 1   That's it, Pritti.

Pritti   Oh Jay! Oh, Jay!

Jay 1 (*speaks to audience, over the hum of the crowd, who are still babbling*)   And she's seen what I been doing. All the carvings I've made. Of all the people in the town. In the branches of the tree. And then. (*Calls up to her.*) Go on a bit. A little to the left. More. Got it? There.

Pritti *has seen what* **Jay** *has made for her up in the tree. She is amazed.*

Pritti (*gasps*)   *Jay!*

Jay 1 (*to audience*)   And I know now that she never meant me no wrong and to see her clinging to that tree trying to save it – for me – well! – And by God I hope she likes it!

Pritti   It's beautiful!

Jay 1   Play it Pritti. Play it! Go on! I made it for you. Just one step more –

Pritti *takes one more step. She slips and nearly falls again. The* **Crowd** *– and* **Jay** *– gasp and stare in silent anticipation and fear.*

Some way off, we hear a ding-ding of a bike bell. We see **Jenny** *has climbed onto* **Jay**'s *abandoned BMX and is pedalling towards the town, the headlight on.*

Jenny   I'm sorry. I'm sorry. I'm sorry, Prittiiiiiii . . . (*She speeds down the hill, dinging the bell all the way. She reaches the street where* **Jay** *and his family live.*)

Scene Nine: The Listening

All the lights are on in the miniature houses downstage. Nearing the houses **Jenny** *clambers off the bike and dings the bell.*

Jenny   Please! Please! You must listen to me! (*Ding ding ding.*)

Tony (*coming and peering out of the front door*)   What in God's name is this now –?

Annie   What is it Tone?

Jenny   Please!

More and more people come to their doors.

Pauline (*calling to* **Terry**)   Love? Love? She wants us to listen, love.

Terry   Who's that?

Miss Owen   What sort of time is this to −

Others   What's going on?

Pauline   She says she wants us to listen to −

Tony   I will not listen to another bloody −

Annie   No, Tone. *Listen.*

Tony   I've told you −

Annie   Shut up, Tony!

There is quiet at last and the air fills with the most magnificent sound they have ever heard.

Terry   What the −

Pauline   Sssshh.

Annie   It's −

Miss Owen   Beautiful.

Jenny   Please. I realise that you are all on your way to a memorial service but please. Follow me. There's a young boy and a young girl up there − alive and well − who need your attention *now*. Please −

(*She turns to speak directly to the audience.*) But it didn't matter what I said. The people were filing out of their houses and drifting up the hill towards the sound. It drew them in like so many black breaths. They formed a slow but sure procession of shadows. And up they went.

As she says this, and the people leave their houses, they each take the light from their corresponding miniature house at the front of the stage and carry it with them, up towards the tree.

Jay 2   Up on the top, the press pack was still holding its breath. Pritti had found what I made for her alright and she seemed to like it, right enough.

*The **Crowd** from the town has joined the crowd beneath the tree, and all stand back, looking up.*

Jay 3   And it was like fantastical.

Crowd (*individual crowd members take the lines*)

– Like every sound, every voice –

– Every story or meaning or message gone wrong that tree ever picked up in its branches

– Was being swirled around and mixed about

– And put in some sort of perfect order so it all made sense

– And, if you just . . . listened . . .

– You could all breathe easy again.

Crowd   And we just stood. The whole town. And let it wash over us like it was raining down. And everyone –

Annie   Mam,

Tony   Dad,

Terry   Terry

Pauline   and Auntie Pauly,

Miss Owen   Miss Owen,

Jay 2   the lot,

Tom   even Tomos –

Jay 3   the prize – . . . Well, let's just leave it that –

Tom   was all just stood, agog.

Jay 1   Except for good old Morris Muggins of course – who was busy – not minding his own this time, but swizzling his latest contraption – a- a-

Morris (*turning a dial on a machine with speakers and wires and whatnot*)   One, two, three, four . . .

Jay 2   He's amplifying Pritti's tree music! Right out into the stratosphere – right out into that big black empty sky and beyond. Good old Morris Muggins.

Pritti   I got my concert, Mum.

Pamela   Oh, Pritti! It looks like we have a future after all!

Jay 1   And they weren't the only ones.

We see **Tony**, **Annie**, **Pauline** *and* **Terry** *moving closer towards each other as they listen* . . .

Jay 2   And I have to admit, I did feel a tiny, incy itch of pride come up on me when I let myself think just for a tic –

Jay 1   That was me! I made that!

Jay 3   And I give my knife, snug in my pocket, a tight little squeeze.

Jay 1   And I have to admit, I do feel a tiny, incy itchy bit of glee come upon me, when I let myself think, just for a sec –

Jay 2   You lot – you lot all thought I was a waster. A loser. A looper. A loner. A total no-hoper.

Jay 1   But I'm not. And do you know? I never was.

Jay 3   And I have to admit, I do feel a tiny, incy, itchy bit chuffed, when I let myself think, just for a mo –

Jay 2   The tree won't get pulled down now. I know it won't. It'll be left. Minding its own. Allowed to just be. It won't be ripped out of sight to try and hide things that can't be hidden, chopped to try and lop things that can't be forgotten.

Jay 3   It stood there then and it'll stand here now and it'll stand here for a lot longer still, through thick and thin, sad, happy and grim, if we let it.

Crowd   And we will.

Jay 2   And it's about then. Stood with my family, friends and neighbours, the sound of the tree music ringing in my ears, that I start to feel, for the first time in . . . for ever.

Jays 1, 2 and 3   Like one person.

Jay 1   One me. Just one me, allowed to just be. Myself.

Jays 2 *and* **3** *take their caps off, looking up at the tree, respectfully.*

Jay   And it's then I catch Pritti's eye. And she catches mine back.

Pritti   And then I stopped playing the tree – the most magical flute – and the very best thing anyone ever made, for me.

I stopped.

And.

Silence.

Tacet. The General Pause.

And I swear the whole earth shivered.

Jenny *comes forward to speak to the audience. As she does so, the members of the crowd each hang the lights they've brought from the miniature houses on the branches of the tree.*

Jenny   And do you know, the silence continued. A nice, peaceful, respectful silence. Even from the media. Because *that's* a story that's just unbelievable. There's not an editor in the land would buy that! And anyway, I got it wrong. My editor was right after all. It's the messed up ones is the interesting ones, isn't it? People don't buy happy stories. Do they?

Silence, the twelve strokes of midnight begin to fade up. **Jay** *takes his hat off, respectfully. Lays it on the ground before the tree. Stands.*

The strokes of the church bell get louder, then finish. A silence as the lights fade to black, leaving seventeen candles glowing in the tree.

Oedipus/Antigone

D. J. Britton

from the Theban plays of Sophocles

About the Author

Since the success of his first Australian stage play *Landlovers* (West Australian Theatre Company, 1987), D. J. Britton's many theatre works have included *Cargo* (Swy/Perth Theatre Company, 1993; Swan Gold Play of the Year) and the epic *Plainsong* (Black Swan/Perth International Festival, 2000; Equity Production of the Year). He now lives in Wales, where he lectures in Dramatic Writing at Swansea University. A former head of radio drama for ABC Australia, he writes extensively for radio, recent works ranging from the first drama on the global financial crash *When Greed Becomes Fear* (BBC R4) to his acclaimed imagined conversation between Dylan Thomas and the Chelsea Hotel *Chelsea Dreaming* (BBC R3, now released as a BBC CD). His two seasons of the children's classic *Old Peter's Russian Tales* were broadcast as Christmas specials. David Britton is a board member of the National Writers' Centre for Wales, and worked with the National Theatre of Wales in its inaugural season. Other plays for young people for Sherman Cymru include *Waves in the Chatroom* (2005) and *The Matthew Files* (2007).

About the Play

The cumulative tragedies faced by generations of the royal family of the city-state of Thebes have found their way to us from ancient Greece through thousands of years of telling and re-telling. The best-known accounts of the life of King Oedipus and his daughter Antigone are the three Theban plays of the great Greek dramatist Sophocles, written around 440–401 BC. They also appear in Homer's *Iliad*, in a version by the Roman writer Seneca, and in many other tellings, some of which recount more about the final humiliation of the great city. In the centuries since Western Europe rediscovered the classical tradition, there have been numerous fine full translations and interpretations of Sophocles' Theban plays and if you enjoy this new version of *Oedipus/Antigone*, those complete translations – they are about four times as long – will provide a further rich experience. Two of Sophocles' tragedies,

Oedipus the King and *Antigone*, form the basis of this new script, with a fleeting reference to his third play, *Oedipus at Colonus*. Sophocles' plays were not written in order and it is unlikely they were ever intended to be grouped as a trilogy; they contain too many inconsistencies.

So one aim of this *Oedipus/Antigone* is to draw the key events together, creating a fast-moving performable script that tells the big story economically in a single cohesive drama. Although its style stays close to those elements of classical convention that distance it from modern naturalistic dialogue and provide a sense of mythic timelessness, this *Oedipus/Antigone* is not bound by the formal rules of Greek drama. Rather, the intention is to leave scope for the wide range of physical and visual metaphors through which modern performers can explore the far-reaching questions of human existence which lie within these great myths.

The script has few stage directions and is divided into scenes only for convenience. It is intended to be played with no built set, and for the action to be continuous. There is an optional act break between the *Oedipus* and *Antigone* sections. A straight read of the play, without physical additions, is about one hour.

Producing the Play

The first production to use this version of *Oedipus/Antigone* was an ambitious promenade event involving 130 young performers and taking its audience on a journey through the empty spaces of a desolate and deserted theatre building in Cardiff, capital city of Wales. In February 2010, the Sherman Cymru company was in the final stages of vacating its Senghennydd Road building so that the theatre could undergo a major refurbishment. To mark the closure, the Sherman Youth Theatre, under the direction of Phillip Mackenzie, took over the entire building, using both stages, the offices and dressing rooms, and the labyrinth of corridors to create a combination of installation, theatre-on-the-move and powerful set-piece physical drama to tell the story. *Oedipus* itself was performed on the main stage, *Antigone* in the studio theatre, with a chanted version of events at Colonus delivered as the audience passed through the passageways between the theatre spaces. Performance installations based on elements of the text provided an overture to the main action.

The central text was delivered by members of the Sherman's senior youth company, with the choral work divided between other groups from the youth theatre. The script was written with this initial large-scale production in mind, but also with an eye to further productions using a smaller core company in which the central characters would also become chorus members.

Central to the success of the production was the rich and subtle aesthetic used by Mackenzie on the two main stages. There was no built set and costume was contemporary/ageless. Combining rhythmic and disciplined physicality, a powerful sound-scape and dramatic horizontal lighting and avoiding conversational dialogue delivery, the production played to the timeless metaphors of the Oedipus myth. Roles were not entirely gender specific – notably Teiresias was played by a young woman dancer who was brought on stage in an ancient bath chair.

Further Reading

Modern full-length translations include *Sophocles Plays 1* (introduced by Don Taylor and Michael J. Walton, Methuen Drama, 1986) and two in Penguin Classics (by E. F. Watling and Robert Fagles). Older, but also accessible, are the classic rhyming translations by Gilbert Murray. Duncan Steen's translation of *Oedipus the King*, with Michael Sheen as Oedipus, is available as a Naxos CD.

Characters

Chorus Leader
Oedipus (Ee-dipus)
Creon (Cray-on)
Teiresias (Tie-ree-see-us)
Jocasta (Jock-asta)
Corinthian
Shepherd
Antigone (Ann-tig-on-ee)
Ismene (Is-may-nee)
Guard
Haemon (Hay-mon)
Boy
Chorus/citizens

Scene One

Thebes. Outside Oedipus' Palace.

Citizens of Thebes (the **Chorus** *and their* **Leader***) plead with their king,* **Oedipus***, over the plague and famine gripping their city.* **Oedipus** *has with him his two daughters,* **Antigone** *and* **Ismene***.*

Chorus Leader
Oedipus. Our king.
Look on our suffering
and do something. Thebes,
our city, is stricken with plague.
Crops wither,
houses stand like tombs.
Babies die in mothers' wombs.

Once before you saved us.
You broke the curse of the Sphinx;
solved its riddle. For that
we gave you the crown.
Now again it's to you we turn.
We pray to the Gods:

Chorus
To Athena, virgin warrior.
To Artemis, goddess of childbirth.
To Dionysius, Bacchus,
god of many names,
for wine and fertile crops.
To Zeus himself,
that he might smite
the slayer who lays us low.
We pray to Apollo
beloved of Thebes
bringer of light,
bringer of music,
the healer, the killer of snakes.
Apollo hear us. Draw your golden bow.

Oedipus
Citizens young and old.
Children.
I stand before you with my
daughters, Antigone and Ismene,
to show that – with my own – I feel
what you feel, and more. For
you feel it each for yourselves.
I feel the weight of the crown.

Many years have come and gone
since you made me your king.
By taking as my wife Jocasta,
the widow of your dead King Laius,
I have brought you harmony,
unison, prosperity.

But this plague on us all
is beyond my knowing.
To outwit such wickedness
requires a higher wisdom.

My wife's beloved brother
Creon is to meet me here.
He has been to Delphi
to the Oracle, whose truth
is ever wise; whose wisdom
never lies.

Leader
Then with all my heart
I plead; take these words
and make them deeds.
Make Thebes again
a city of men.

Chorus
Creon comes:
Bearer of news,
holder of hopes,
messenger of wisdom.

Creon *enters.*

Creon
Citizens, friends,
beware. Prepare.
The Oracle has spoken!

Oedipus
Then tell us! Our hearts are
open; our hopes lie in your words.

Leader
Thebes lies bleeding and broken.
Nothing you can tell us
could be worse.

Creon *gestures to the ailing city.*

Creon
This, what you see, is a curse.
A blight, brought upon us
by a failure to do what was right.

Oedipus
These are the words of the Oracle?

Creon
Yes. And more.
Brother in law,
brother in love,
you came to Thebes unknown.
You defeated the Sphinx
which held us in fear.
We offered you the crown.

Our King Laius had been killed.

Leader
Murdered by assassins, yes.

Creon
In despair at the curse of the Sphinx
we sat on our hands.
We did not find his killer.

You arrived and, like a captain,
took the tiller; steered us to
prosperity. But, says the Oracle,
the murder remained unsolved,
unavenged. This is why the Gods
have cursed us. Our city must
remain plagued until just
revenge is done for the death
of King Laius.

Oedipus

Then it shall be done.
I did not know
that so little sweat had
been spent in pursuit of this
crime. We'll get to the heart
of this, and free our city from
its living death. Someone must
know how Laius breathed his last breath.

Chorus

Oedipus, Oedipus,
favoured in fortune.
Oedipus, Oedipus,
seizes his sword.
Oedipus, Oedipus,
hero of heroes.
Oedipus, Oedipus,
admired and adored
Oedipus, Oedipus,
Oedipus, Oedipus,
Oedipus, Oedipus . . .

Leader

. . . our Leader and Lord.

Oedipus

Creon, bearer of this news,
speak on. Did the Oracle
say more? Where shall
we seek the bloodied hands?

On distant shores? In
foreign lands? I shall show no pity.

Creon

My king, the Oracle was clear.
Our dear city of Thebes
hides the mind behind the crime.

Oedipus

Here? In Thebes? Then
we need have no delay.
Tell me all you recall of
the death of Laius; how he fell.
How Thebes heard of the murder.

Chorus

There were robbers.
Thieves struck him down,
sword in hand,
on the road to Delphi,
to the Oracle,
to learn of life and fate.
All his party slain but one
who returned to tell the tale.

Chorus

Oh Apollo, Lord,
come to us now.
Help find the hand
that held the sword.

Oedipus

You pray. I say
the Gods help those
who help themselves.

Here is my word.
If any person here in Thebes
knows who it was killed
King Laius, let him come
forward. He need fear no harm
for his secret story. Peaceful

banishment shall be his punishment.
But if someone in this city knows
and fails to speak, then he shall feel
the full force of a furious city.

Chorus

In his dying prayers we shall give no pity
but turn away. No shelter, no food, no water.
Through him we are cursed. Let him die of thirst.

Oedipus

As for the killer, I say this.
A torment on his soul.
A curse on his whole existence.
Were such a man to stand in my home
I should wish every foul curse
on my own head.
Those who refuse me help
I deem lower than dogs.
Indeed, whom, then, shall I turn
to in this hour of need.

Creon

It is said the blind Teiresias
sees at once both nothing
and all things.

Oedipus

Then send for him;
we shall hear his dreams sing.

Creon *leaves, to fetch* **Teiresias**. **Antigone** *and* **Ismene** *leave.*

Chorus

Oh Teiresias,
Man of second sight.
Through your inward eye
may we see the darkness,
and the light.

Scene Two

Thebes.

Oedipus, **Chorus** *and* **Leader** *remain.*
A boy leads in the blind mystic Seer, **Teiresias**.

Oedipus
Teiresias, have no fear.
You have heard the word from
Delphi, and I swear that
Laius shall be avenged.
Tell us what you see,
what you know.

Teiresias
What I see and hold in mind
cannot be shared. Be kind,
O King. Spare me from
your demands. I am not
the one to call upon.

Oedipus
What?
Would you let the city bleed
and die? We need
no lies. Only your advice.

Teiresias
Oedipus. I cannot.

Oedipus
You will not.

Teiresias
Aye. I will not. For what
I know, I have known long
and have long feared this moment.

Oedipus
You defy me?

Teiresias

Aye.

Oedipus

Then you must die.

Teiresias

Do not try to frighten me.
I have seen a sight, here
within, that would make the
skin creep; mothers weep,
and you, Oedipus,
would seek sweet mercy.

Oedipus

This blind fool of empty eyes
threatens me. Me the king.
I rule, old man. No-one defies
me. Now speak!

Teiresias

Oh Oedipus. You have eyes
but cannot see. The curse
is with you!

Oedipus

What is this drivel?
Did your tongue shrivel
along with your eyes?
Speak simple. No riddles.
What do you mean?

Teiresias

A lost temper, a lost history,
and a lost future. King
you may be, but what has been
has been; what will be, will be.
It's not of your making
nor mine. When you have heard,
do not say I did not warn you.

Oedipus

Tell me what you know!

Teiresias

Oedipus, I say this:
You are the killer of the king.
Ask me no more.

Oedipus

What blind madness is this?
No, not madness, treachery.
Who told you to say these things?
Who is it seeks my downfall with
these jealous lies?

Teiresias

Blind I may be; but I have the gift of sight.
Blind to the truth you are,
and blind and helpless you shall be
before this day turns night.

Oedipus

Of course! It's clear! There's only
one in line to take my throne.
Creon made you speak out,
paid you, no doubt, to poison
my name in front of my people.

(*To* **Chorus**.)

Fetch him. Bring him here.

Two of the **Chorus** *leave to fetch* **Creon**.

Teiresias

Fear drives men from the
fate they must bear.
Oedipus, I do not serve you.
Neither do I serve Creon.
I serve only Apollo,
The bearer of light.
He alone gives me sight.

Listen:
Your past is stained.
Your sweetest love is tainted.
Your children, without blame,
are cursed. You will collide
with such horrors you will wish you had died
and not King Laius. Poor proud man,
you shall grope your way towards
damnation.
Now, do your worst.

Leader

Oedipus, stay your hand.
The man is blind, yet bound to the Gods.
Let him leave, and pray his riddle
has some kinder meaning yet unseen.

Oedipus

Yes, he may go. But the meaning
is clear to me. These hideous
lies are a plot, meant to lower me
in the eyes of the city.

The boy leads **Teiresias** *out.* **Creon** *is brought in.*

Oedipus

And here's the mind behind
the words. Creon. My wife's brother.
Lover of intrigue. Traitor.

Creon

Oedipus, calm your fury.
I don't want your crown,
I'm content as we are,
a perfect symmetry.
Yourself, Jocasta and me,
with Oedipus at the head.
I am happy to be led,
yet still enjoy our shared nobility.

Oedipus

> Liar! Snake. Driven by greed
> you betray me, and all Thebes,
> at our time of need. You shall die.

> Take him. Do the deed.

Creon *is seized.*

Creon

> Wait! Think of your wife.
> My sister. Jocasta.
> Would you deprive her of a brother
> on a judgment born of anger?

Leader

> Oedipus, the fate of the city
> is in your hands. Do not be hasty.
> The Gods are easy to offend.
> If you intend to put this man to death,
> first breathe a slow breath.
> Take time to pray. Do not paint as black
> what may only be grey.

> Consult Jocasta, your beloved.
> Hear what she may say.

Oedipus

> Very well. Hold him fast.

Creon *is restrained.*

Oedipus

> Lead us in prayer.

Leader

> As you say,
> we pray. To Athena/

Chorus

> /virgin warrior.
> To Artemis,
> goddess of childbirth.
> To Dionysius, Bacchus,

god of many names,
for wine and fertile crops.
To Zeus himself,
that he might smite
the slayer who lays us low.

Leader

We pray to Apollo,
beloved of Thebes/

Chorus

/bringer of light,
bringer of music,
the healer, the killer of snakes.
Apollo hear us.
Draw your gold-strung bow.

Scene Three

Thebes.

Oedipus, **Chorus**, **Leader** *and* **Creon** *remain.* **Jocasta** *enters.*

Chorus

See here the beautiful Jocasta,
Queen of Thebes,
widow of King Laius,
wife to King Oedipus,
mother of his children;
two boys,
Eteocles and Polynices;
two girls,
Antigone and Ismene.

Leader

Jocasta, Queen.
Your husband and brother seethe
in spiteful argument.
Oedipus makes claims of treachery
against Creon, which Creon denies.

    Stop their fight that they might
    stand shoulder to shoulder against
    the common foe which has
    cursed our city.

Jocasta
    Husband. Brother. Make an
    end to this jealous squabble.

Creon
    He's condemned me to die.

Oedipus
    Aye. That or banishment.

Creon
    I swear. I did not do the things he says.

Jocasta
    Oedipus, if he swears so,
    you must believe him.

Oedipus
    I fear his survival means my downfall.

Leader
    Look to the past. This man never did you
    any harm.

Jocasta
    Look to the future. Our house must stand
    united against the storm.
    Free him. Let him go home.

Reluctantly, **Oedipus** *makes his decision.*

Oedipus
    As she says. Free him.

Creon *is released and leaves.*

Jocasta
    And leave us alone.

Chorus *and* **Leader** *withdraw to the shadows.*

Scene Four

Thebes.

Oedipus *and* **Jocasta** *are left in their own space.*

Jocasta
Now husband, what's this?
Creon is your friend. Always has been.

Oedipus
Then, if a friend, why say it was I
brought Laius' life to an end.

Jocasta
He said that?

Oedipus
As good as. I believe it was he
who framed the words which the
Seer gave shape.

Jocasta
What Seer was this?

Oedipus
Teiresias.

Jocasta
Trust your own eyes and ears my love.
Take guidance from the Gods above.
To chase your tail in a search for
the source of a rumour is futile.
It was the Seer who spoke; the Seer who
must be chided. These men are fools,
misguided prophets who see shadows
where others see the glorious sun.
Listen: Just such a Seer once plagued
my life, when I was wife to Laius.
He prophesied that the king would die
at his own son's hand.

Oedipus
But you have no son.

Jocasta
I had one, briefly. My husband,
in fear for his life, ordered our baby,
his feet pierced with iron spikes,
cast out on the mountain top
and left to die. And so, by taking his
fate in his own hands, Laius made
a lie of the prophecy.

Oedipus
A cruel course.

Jocasta
But right. Fears and rumours
make poor rulers. So let
Teiresias say what he will.
He is a blind fool. Apollo alone
has our life-path in clear view.
Let my words bring courage to you.

Oedipus
They do bring some relief, but other
shadows darken my mind.

Jocasta
What kind of shadows?
What troubles you?

Oedipus
These tales of Laius' death.
Attacked by robbers, they say.
On the road to Delphi.

Jocasta
Aye. Driven from the road and
run through with a sword.

Oedipus
How many in his party?

Jocasta
Five.

Oedipus

Five. As I feared. How tall was
Laius?

Jocasta

Your height.

Oedipus

His beard? Tinged with grey?

Jocasta

Aye. The years had had their way.
What are your thoughts. What do you say?

Oedipus

When first I came to Thebes my journey
was broken by a skirmish on the road.
Five warriors, wealthy and well-armed
blocked my path; I could not pass.
We fought. My sword-hand did its work.
One by one they fell until I faced their
leader, grey-bearded, of size and strength
similar to my own. I was younger, faster.
He went to Hades; I went on to Thebes.

Jocasta

My love, this is but two horses of
similar hue. It was not you who
killed Laius. One of his party
– a shepherd – did not die but
returned to tell us of the murder.
He made it clear. A band of robbers,
many in number, had made the attack,
not a lone swordsman fighting for his life.
It was sworn; the words he said
cannot be taken back.

Oedipus

This is good news. We'll find this shepherd
and bring him before the people to speak.

Jocasta

Yours is a brave story of strength against odds.
But why were you at the mercy of the Gods
and prey to swords of warriors on the road?

Oedipus

Another prophecy, this time about me.
My home was in Corinth as you know,
of royal blood, son of the king of that city.
One night, a noble, full of drink and
foul of tongue, sneered a slur on my parentage.
I tried to dismiss it but could not.
So I sought out a Seer, that he
might put my fears to rest.

Jocasta

And did he, this man of shades?

Oedipus

No. Rather he condemned me to Hades
should I stay in Corinth, for his prophecy
was as foul as it was fearsome.

Jocasta

What did he say that turns you
grey-skinned at the thought?

Oedipus

That I would kill my own father
and wed my own mother.

And so I fled from Corinth
that these hands, outstretch
them as I might, cannot reach
my parents. But each
night I sleep, the fear, the dread,
invades my dreams.

Jocasta

These fears in the night
are like a dog
snarling in the dark.

A bark there may be.
There is no bite.

Oedipus
Your are my comfort and my love.

Jocasta
Then be a man, be a king.
Speak with the Gods, not their underlings.

Oedipus
First I shall send for the shepherd.

Jocasta
My love, he witnessed and gave
his word. Let it lie.

Oedipus
No. I would hear it
with my own ears.

Jocasta
Then leave me.
Let me pray in peace.

Oedipus *leaves.* **Jocasta** *is in silent prayer.*

Scene Five

Thebes.

Jocasta *remains. A* **Corinthian** *enters.*

Corinthian
Lady,
I have a message for your
King, Oedipus. His life
will be changed by what I say.

Jocasta
You are welcome here,
though as you see

our city staggers under
its own sadness.
Speak to me. I am his wife.

Corinthian

The King of Corinth, the man
who raised Oedipus,
gave him life, is dead.

Jocasta

How? Was there some crime?

Corinthian

No. The passage of time,
the steady steps of old age.
He died in peace.

Jocasta

Then Oedipus is released from
his curse! *(Calls.)* Oedipus!

Oedipus *enters with the* **Leader**. *The* **Chorus** *steps from the
shadows.*

Jocasta

My love. It is as I said.
Prophecy is no more than
a fool's imagining.
Our fate is for ourselves to fashion.
Your father, the King of Corinth
is dead. And was this by your hand?
No. This messenger tells us how
the old man died peacefully,
gifted with the gentle release of old age.
Your curse has been lifted.

Oedipus

Then I am both sad at his passing
and glad for how it was he passed.

Corinthian

This is a strange response to my news.
I am confused. What is this curse?

Jocasta
A foolish prophecy had said
that Oedipus would kill his father
and share his mother's marriage bed.

Oedipus
This is why I fled from Corinth.

Corinthian
Had you asked I could have said.
There was no need.

Oedipus
What do you mean?

Corinthian
Those you call your parents:
Your mother the Queen of Corinth
and your father, the King,
are no such thing. Legally,
yes, for you have their name and rights,
but not in birth or blood. So you may
return to Corinth when you will
and fear no ill between yourself
and the Queen through this prophecy.

Oedipus
Not in blood? What do you mean?

Corinthian
Oedipus, you were a foundling.
It was I who carried you
to Corinth and to the king.
He and the Queen had no child of
their own. No-one to inherit the throne.

Oedipus
I was not my father's son!
Nor my mother's!

Corinthian
Oedipus they had no others.
They raised you in noble love.

Oedipus

But not of noble blood!
If this story is untrue
you will die!

Jocasta

You say you found the baby
and took him to the King of Corinth?

Corinthian

Yes and no. I took him to the King
but the child came to my hands
on the grazing grounds in the
mountains between our two lands.
Given, not found.
A shepherd from Thebes passed him
to me. Asked me to take pity.
I did. The boy's feet were bound
in iron. I removed the shackles.

Jocasta *groans in realisation.*

Jocasta

No!

Oedipus

Who is this shepherd? Is he
still alive?

Jocasta

Oedipus, my love!

Leader

One such old man does survive.
I know where he lives.

Jocasta

Oedipus, I beg you.
For all that you and I
are together. For our children,
for our future and their
futures, do not reach any

deeper into this darkened pit.
My mind leaps into the gloom
and sees ahead to the horror,
while yours lags behind.
My love. This will be our doom!

Oedipus
Strange to see you quake with fear.
The truth is near. Your words were
clear: 'our fate is in our own hands'.
So. We defy prophecy;
we may not deny history.
Why you are so aghast
I do not know. The past holds the key
and so I go to face it.

(*To someone from the* **Chorus**.)
Take her. Take her inside.

Jocasta
Oedipus! Oedipus. I did not know.
Until now I did not know!

Jocasta *runs into the shadows.*

Scene Six

Thebes.

Oedipus, **Chorus** *and* **Leader** *remain. A* **Shepherd** *is led in.*

Leader
This is the man I had in mind.
A servant-shepherd to King Laius.

(*An afterthought.*)

Also, I believe, the man who saw
that good king die.

Oedipus
The same man?

Leader

Aye.

Corinthian

Do you remember me, old friend?

Shepherd

Yes . . . or no. Whichever makes the better end.

Oedipus

No need to fear. The truth is all
we need. I swear no hand will harm you.
Stand tall and speak. Do you know this man?

Corinthian

In our youth, in the mountains among the trees . . .
I from Corinth, you from Thebes. We tended
flocks. You remember?

Shepherd

Some things are better forgotten.

Corinthian

He remembers.

Leader

This man of Corinth says you handed him a baby.

Shepherd

It's true. A boy.

Oedipus

Was he your son?

Shepherd

No.

Corinthian

Did you find him, abandoned?

Shepherd

Again, no.

Oedipus

Then what was he doing there?
Why was he living in your care.

Shepherd

> Good . . . great . . . king. I am nothing.
> A poor man. I showed you mercy once,
> thinking it to be a kindness.
> The blindness of men darkens
> the path we tread. Silence has been
> my protection for many years.
> There will be tears when I speak,
> bitter and angry. I beg you,
> in your turn, show me mercy.

Leader

> Oedipus has given his word.
> Your words are what we wait for.

Shepherd

> Old King Laius carried a curse.
> It was foretold that
> he would be killed by his son.
> So when his wife bore him one
> they made me take the boy
> to the mountains, irons on his feet,
> and leave him there to die.
> No son, no killer. No killer no curse.
> But I was weak. I could not kill
> the boy. Instead, I gave him
> to this man. (*He indicates the* **Corinthian**.)

Leader

> Who removed the irons and took him to Corinth.

Corinthian

> Where he became Oedipus.

Shepherd

> Whose name means 'He who walks in pain'.

Suddenly, all becomes clear to **Oedipus**.

Oedipus

> No! No!

Chorus
> Oedipus, Oedipus,
> son of King Laius
> Oedipus, Oedipus,
> son of Jocasta
> Oedipus, Oedipus,
> murdered King Laius
> Oedipus, Oedipus,
> married Jocasta
> Oedipus, Oedipus
> fathered her children
> fathered his sisters
> fathered his brothers,
> Oedipus, Oedipus,
> Oedipus, Oedipus,
> Oedipus, Oedipus . . .

Corinthian
> . . . cursed as no other.

Oedipus *runs off. A messenger arrives. Whispers in the* **Leader***'s ear.*

Leader
> Let all be silence!
> The Queen is dead.
> Sensing what was to be said,
> She ran to her room,
> locked the door, and with
> a rope cast off the ties of life.

Corinthian
> You must prepare her body for the Gods.

Leader
> Yes. Where's Oedipus.

Shepherd
> Gone to her.

Corinthian
> Then we must hurry.

Corinthian *leaves.*

Chorus
    Oedipus, Oedipus,
    mired in misfortune.
    Oedipus, Oedipus,
    seizes her pin.
    Oedipus, Oedipus,
    Seeks out the darkness
    Oedipus, Oedipus,
    plunges it in
    Oedipus, Oedipus,
    Oedipus, Oedipus,
    Oedipus, Oedipus . . .
    again and again.

Oedipus *reappears, led by the* **Corinthian***. His eyes have been put out.*

Scene Seven

Thebes.

Oedipus, **Chorus** *and* **Leader** *remain.* **Creon** *enters.*

Creon
    Have the Gods no heart?
    I heard. I came and find
    my sister hanged and Oedipus
    blinded by his own hand.

Leader
    How did he do this?

Creon
    Pushing everyone aside
    he threw himself into her room.
    Seizing the golden brooch
    from her breast, he grasped
    the pin and pierced his eyes
    crying:

Creon/Oedipus
Darkness for ever. Cast out the light.
Never more would I look on myself,
or my sins, or the lives I have blighted.
Darkness. Darkness.

Leader
Poor man. Where are his riches now?

Chorus
Gone, all gone.
All delusion.
All illusion.
Pride pricked.
Love, honour, respect,
gone like the passing
of a long-held breath.

The words tail off like a diminishing wind . . .

Oedipus. Oedipus,
Oedipus, Oedipus
Oedipus, Oedipus . . .

Leader
Death would be a mercy.

Creon
What fate he must face
the Gods shall command.

Leader
The crown is yours Creon.

Creon
Wordly power alone
cannot judge what must be done.
What would you seek, Oedipus?

Oedipus
Two things I beg.
First, set me from the city,
that no-one shall set their

eyes on this eyeless man.
Second, take care of my
children. They bear my
name, but share no blame.

Leader
They are here Oedipus.

Antigone, **Ismene** *and two sons* (**Polynices** *and* **Eteocles**)
step forward from the shadows. **Oedipus** *touches their faces.*

Oedipus
The boys will soon
be men themselves.
But my girls, my little
ones, Antigone and
Ismene, treat them as
your own, Creon.

Antigone
Father!

Oedipus
Father, yes, and brother too.
It will be hard for you, Antigone,
Ismene. Look to the Gods.
Be noble. Hold your honour above all.

Creon. Will you grant me banishment?

For pity's sake. Cast me out man.
Have done with it.

Creon
Your time giving orders is over Oedipus.
You are nothing.

Chorus
Nothing. Nothing.
Oedipus is nothing.
Oedipus is nothing.
Nothing. Nothing.

Repeat as required.

Creon
  I hear no words from the Gods,
  Oedipus.
  Where Apollo points his golden
  bow, that course I shall follow.

A moving light is Apollo's arrow. The **Leader**, *three children and*
Creon *step back into the shadows. The* **Leader** *re-joins the*
Chorus. **Oedipus** *and* **Antigone** *begin their long walk to*
Colonus.

Note: if required, an interval may be taken here.

Scene Eight

Towards Colonus.

Chorus *and* **Leader** *watch as* **Antigone** *leads* **Oedipus**. *Much*
time has passed.

Leader
  Banished and punished,
  years in the wilderness,
  Oedipus wanders,
  Despised and decried.

Chorus
  Led by Antigone,
  faithful Antigone.
  always Antigone,
  his eyes and his guide.

  Comes to Colonus,
  close beside Athens,
  city of Theseus;
  death breathes in his breast.
  Sword-hero Theseus.
  Honourable Theseus
  Wise-minded Theseus
  grants shelter and rest.

Now comes Ismene,
riding from Thebes.
Word from that city
of flesh turned to ash.
Gentle Ismene.
Fear-filled Ismene,
Soul-scarred Ismene,
brings news of the clash.

Scene Nine

Colonus.

The **Chorus** *steps back into the shadows.* **Oedipus** *and* **Antigone**
remain. **Ismene** *enters.*

Ismene
Thebes is in turmoil.
Our brothers do battle.
Eteocles has thrown in
his lot with King Creon.
Polynices is banished
and raises an army
in Argos. They fight
for your crown, father.

Creon, once calm, has
become full of fury.
He has seen the Oracle
and fears your banishment
will curse his cause.
He would have you return
as a slave to his mission.

Oedipus
Never. If naked ambition runs
wildly through Thebes, if
Creon finds cruelty his master,
if brother and brother
would slay one another,

then let it be so.
Antigone, my eyes,
my guide, my comfort,
what do you say of
this news from your sister?

Antigone

I say this my father.
You deserve rest.
What honour is left
to our family, I pray
to the Gods that we may
seize it and hold it.

Ismene

Creon is convinced.
He fears the curses
of our poor blind father.
He would seize him
and hold him. When
death comes, Creon wants
to be the one to bury
Oedipus. In this way
the favours of Zeus
fall on Creon's head.

Oedipus

He is too late.

Death walks beside me,
behind me, before me.
Death shall not bind me
to more mindless
slaughter. Let brother
kill brother; for I favour
neither. I seek only peace and
an end to my torment.

Dearest daughters,
I step towards destiny's door.
Walk with me no more.

He begins to walk, unaided, into the shadows.

> Misfortunes have plagued me.
> I did not design them.
> The father I killed, the
> mother I slept with,
> the babies she bore me,
> I never intended; they were
> not of my knowing.

> Enough of this life.
> Sacred Colonus
> has granted me succour.
> Farewell my daughters.
> Be kind to each other;
> do what you can to
> outdistance dishonour.

Gradually, **Oedipus** *fades from sight.*

Ismene
> He walks without guide,
> as if he has eyes.

Antigone
> Sure steps towards destiny.
> His path towards peace.

The sisters watch him disappear.

> *Our* path leads to Thebes,
> where the battle is raging.

Ismene
> But our father . . .

Antigone
> Our father has found his fate.

> Our own fate is our family.

> I am long betrothed
> to heroic Haemon,
> son of King Creon.

Our bond shall
bind up the wounds
of our families.
Thebes is our destiny,
sister Ismene.

They walk together into the shadows; from there the **Chorus** *call swells
from whisper to shout:*

Chorus
Antigone
Ismene
Antigone
Ismene
Antigone
Ismene
Creon
Thebes!

Scene Ten

Thebes – After the Battle.

Sound: The aftermath of battle/crows/dogs. **Ismene** *and* **Antigone**
re-enter.

Antigone
Our brothers Eteocles and Polynices
both dead in the battle for Thebes.

Ismene
One fighting beside King Creon,
one against him. Death is cruel.

Antigone
Dishonour is crueller still;
See how the victor seizes the story.

Ismene
Antigone, sister, why the fury?
Sadness, yes. But anger

walks us only into danger.
Our brothers are dead.
We must live.

Antigone

When you know what I know
sister, you may change your song.

Ismene

Then tell me. What is it? What's wrong.

Antigone

Creon has spoken from on high:
To die for *him* is noble.
To die an enemy is to die
no better than a beast.

Ismene

Creon says this?

Antigone

Aye.
Eteocles has been buried with honour.
But Polynices lies still where he fell.
Outside the walls. Undressed, unblessed
unburied. Food for animals. Creon
denies him the rites and rituals of death.
And so he lies. Open to the skies.
No pathway to the Gods for Polynices.
The dogs shall have his heart.
The crows his eyes.
On pain of death he has ordered
that no-one must touch the body.

No man, king or common,
should deny another his heaven.
Polynices is Creon's kin;
he is our kin, Ismene.

Ismene

Antigone, you should rest.
Calm your mind. From wild thoughts

come wild deeds. We need,
you and I, some refuge, some respite.
Too many of us have died.

Antigone

Polynices cannot rest and nor shall I.
Come with me sister. We shall creep
from the city and bury the body.

Ismene

Antigone, no! Our duty is to Thebes,
and Thebes is Creon. Believe me!

Think sister. Think of your flower-scented
marriage to Creon's son, heroic Haemon.
Once that is done, our families are bonded and
branded in one.

Antigone

I love Haemon. But Creon has no right
to leave our brother lying in the light,
cut off from ancestors, from Hades,
and the God-given path through shade.
Creon is a man, not a deity.
If I must die, then so it be.

Ismene

I beg you.

Antigone

You may beg all you like, Ismene.
Beg of Creon, but not me.
I do not beg.

Ismene

Sister!

Antigone

What kind of kin is this,
that cries 'sister' yet denies her brother?
My way is duty and family.
Your way defeat and ignominy.

I offered honour.
You chose to decline.
Go your way; I shall go mine.

They depart in opposite directions; the **Chorus** *and* **Leader** *step forward.*

Scene Eleven

Thebes.

The **Chorus** *and* **Leader** *become* **Creon**'s *victory crowd.* **Creon** *stands before them.*

Chorus
The king!
King Creon,
victorious in battle;
The king!

King Creon,
our only strong Leader,
The king!
King Creon,
now lead us in peace.

Creon
The battle was won because the
Gods were with us. Because they
were with us, we won the battle.
In war, we were firm, decisive.
In peace, the same. A king's
word, when the Gods are with him,
is not a sapling twisting this way
and that in the wind. It is an oak,
unbending, strong. Polynices
was a traitor, prepared to see
Thebans die in the name of his
ambition. A traitor is not a man.
His treachery denies him the
rights of his mortality. And

so, out there he must lie.
Unloved, unhonoured, unburied.
Let scavengers pick at his remains.
Let other men look on and see
that treachery has its price.
Those who bring comfort to traitors
are themselves traitors. Lest
any man defy me on this, let that
rat – for so he be – lie in the same nest.
Defy me on this and die.

Leader

Soldiers have been sent to
guard the body, to see
that no-one gives honour to
Polynices where he lies.

Chorus

Is it fortune,
or fate,
or a twist of the wind,
that makes a man happy?

Whatever the answer,
whatever the cause,
we envy him, the lucky man.

Such a man may
stand alone.
He feels the wind.
He feels the tide.
His luck is his own.

Leader

But what of the family
stranded, feet in sand,
in the rising waters
of misfortune.

Oh Zeus! Watch how
the wind tears at their flesh,

year after year, on and on
through generations.

Chorus

No hope before them.
No honour behind them.
Is there nothing they can cling to?
A floating branch,
a rock, slippery, but with a hand-hold?

Leader

No. There is nothing.
Father, mother, brother,
son, daughter; on and on.
The world wreaks its endless retribution.

Chorus

Did the Gods do this?
Looking down from Olympus,
frowning on the forlorn efforts
of mortals to turn back the oceans?

Leader

Hope lifts our feet from the mud,
but in stepping upwards
hope becomes ambition,
ambition becomes glory-greed,
and Zeus, ever watchful,
swirls the turbid seas
and draws us down again.

Chorus

And should a family thus cursed
escape the rising waters, what then?
The fate which awaits them is fire.
The funeral pyre.
Cinders and dust.

Leader

For some, a covering of dust,
funereal formality,

the final rites of passage,
would be a blessing.

Scene Twelve

Thebes.

The **Chorus**, **Leader** *and* **Creon** *remain. A* **Guard** *enters, initially beyond the notice of the King and his entourage. The* **Guard** *addresses the audience.*

Guard
   Who could be more miserable than me?
   A poor soldier, placed on guard duty.
   'Not a hard task,' you may say.
   'There are worse fates.' Maybe.
   I deserve your pity. Me,
   the man who closed his eyes
   for a second and opened them
   to find disaster.
   Guard a body. Easy to say.
   Bodies don't run away.
   Bodies don't stab you when you're sleeping.

   It did stink a bit,
   I'll own up to that
   and we did drink a bit,
   to drown out the smell.
   But now, here I am,
   The one who has to tell
   Creon that his body has
   been buried. Behind our backs.

Creon (*spotting the* **Guard**)
   Who is that man? What does he want?

Leader
   One of the soldiers my Lord,
   sent to stand as guard

over the body. Speak man,
what's your news?

Guard

Such news, sirs, as I would
not tell. Except I will.
I must. The others put their trust
in me. We drew lots. I lost.

Creon

Then out with it.
What word do you bring?

Guard

The word sir is *dust*.
Not much more than that.
Sand and dust. Just enough
to cover the body. We don't
know who did it, nor how it was
done. But one of our number
whose watch it was must have been
resting his eyes a moment.
When we all saw the body,
covered from head to toe,
dusted, as it were, with sand,
we had a go at each other
saying 'it was your fault',
'no it was yours', but the truth
is sirs, we know what you'll say:
The blame is all of ours.

Creon

Traitor!
D'you think I was born yesterday?
There are those, in this city,
determined to unseat me.
What was the price
to have you say such lies?
Listen, all of you, I made it clear
the man who betrays Creon, dies.

Leader

Sir. King Creon. Send this man
back to his watch.
Let him catch the man who
did you this dishonour.
By doing so, he will show
his innocence.

Creon

Very well. Let him go.
But know this, Guard.
Come to me with lies on your breath
and you will wish for death,
such pain will I bring to you.

The **Guard** *leaves.*

Chorus

A fearsome Lord
a fearful Guard.
Two men set apart
by worth and birth
yet men they are, both.
Mortal beings. Masters
of the oceans and the earth.

The living spirit of dead **Oedipus** *enters.*

Oedipus

What a wonder is mankind
who has tamed the wild beasts,
and tilled the rocky soil
into a furrowed and submissive land.
In ships of wood and iron
he crosses stormy seas,
taking fish as he fancies, taming birds to his
delight. Oh mankind, mankind.

And speech! No other beast
has the gift of tongues, and more:
to take the words and write them

down, for those who follow to learn from;
words and wonders known before.
With words come laws, the rules
of living side by side in safety.
And best of all, the city. Humanity
together, life beside life,
a subtle harmony of hope.

One sickness alone he cannot cure.
Death. And because all must end,
when the road bends, a path
is chosen. All depends
on this: Choose honour and honesty
and the city, the gods and all humanity
below them, will hold a man
kindly, with an open hand.
Steer your steps on the wrong road,
the path that veers from honour
and into arrogance, to pride and
pointless power, and see how
fate repays a man.
Doors slam.
Eyes turn away in distrust
and dismay.

Oh mankind,
what a wonder you are.
How brilliant.
How blind.

Oedipus *leaves.*

Scene Thirteen

Thebes.

The **Chorus**, **Leader** *and* **Creon** *remain. The* **Guard**
reappears, leading **Antigone***. He pushes through the* **Chorus***.*

Guard
    Make way, make way!

(*To the audience.*)
    What kind of a world is this?
    Sent away in fear, all a tremble,
    Only to find the culprit right
    there. Beside the body.

(*To* **Antigone**.)
    Come along miss. Don't stumble
    on your chains.

(*To* **Creon** *and* **Chorus**.)
    Citizens. King Creon. Look
    what I have! Caught red-handed,
    attempting to make a grave
    for Polynices.

Creon
    This woman? Antigone?

Guard
    It was she who buried the body.
    Tried to do it again, in our sight;
    no denials, no escape, no fight.

Leader
    Your own sister's child.
    So wild; so determined.

Guard (*to the audience*)
    I don't like to see
    this girl in misery.
    But better her than me.
    That much I know.

Creon
    Antigone. You heard
    my ruling? Say.

Antigone
    Yes, every word.

Creon
    And yet you disobey?

Sensing trouble, the **Leader** *dismisses the* **Guard***.*

Leader
Go, Guard, while you may.

Guard *leaves.*

Antigone
I obeyed custom, decency;
the rights of my family.

Creon
But not me. You did not obey me.

Antigone
You are a man, not a God.
I know what you said.
And I did what I did.
I prefer to die with honour
than leave my brother dishonoured.

Creon
Who put you up to this?

Antigone
No-one. I was alone.

Ismene *has been watching from a distance. Now she bursts in.*

Ismene
She lies. It was I. I stood beside her.
If she dies so must I.

Antigone
Liar. Do not try to claim
honour second-hand.
You refused to stand beside me
as I covered our brother.
As we decide, so we must bide.
You made your choice. Live with it.

Ismene
In the name of Athena,
Goddess of love,

do not turn from me
when I turn to you.

Antigone

I turn from all that is not true.
Uncle, you mocked the dead
who have no voice.
My choice is to join the dead
rather than mock them.

Creon

This is madness. Polynices
turned on the city, turned on me,
turned on his own brother Eteocles.
By honouring one dead brother
you dishonour the other.

Antigone

Polynices would never
deny his brother
the rites of the dead.

Creon

Oh the words of woman's heart!
So now we honour the good
and the bad in equal part!

Antigone

Those who have died share one quality:
their lack of life. What do we
know of their land and their laws?
The dead may honour the dead equally.
Love is a constant. It favours
neither loser nor winner.

Creon

This is the philosophy of fools.
The world, thank the Gods,
does not run by women's rules.
Since you love the dead so well,
join them. Do not talk to me of love
or law. I am the law; and the law

of Thebes says those who defy
must die.

Antigone
Then make it soon.

Ismene
And take me too, Uncle.

Antigone
No. You would not help
when I asked. You may
not help me now.

Ismene
But to live in the shadow
of your name! To live only
with shame and regret!
Sister I cannot. I will not.

Creon
One mad in her very making,
the other mad in the moment.
While others crave life and breath,
these women, these daughters
and sisters of Oedipus, these
offspring of my own unhappy sister
crave death. Take them inside,
out of sight, make them silent.
I want no more of these women.
Bring me my son. Let me talk with a man.

Antigone and **Ismene** *are taken away.*

Chorus
The path branches.
Creon has made his choice,
sealed his fate.
His steps veer one way.
Arrogance the trap; power its bait.

Oh, Antigone.
Oh, Ismene.

Young hearts are full of fire,
moved easily to fury.
Right and wrong,
foul deed or noble,
they see these clear and plain,
like a bloodstain on a linen robe.

Not for them, the woven
cloth of politics; strand upon
strand, subtle patterns,
blended colours; woven words,
embroidered promises;
the silken threads of vanity,
clothed in the lacework
of rules and legality.
Oh mankind. Oh Creon.
This girl, this Antigone,
is betrothed to your own son.
She is his love. His happiness.
Would you take this
from him. And life from her?

Creon
Too late. My mind is set.
It shall be done.

Leader
But Haemon. Your son . . .

Creon
There are other women.
I shall find him one.

Scene Fourteen

Thebes.

The **Chorus**, **Leader** *and* **Creon** *remain.* **Haemon** *enters.*

Haemon

Where is my father?
Where is Creon?

Creon

Haemon. You have heard?

Haemon

Father, I cannot deny
that you are my elder
and my better. I hold
your judgement high.

Creon

And so you should.
A father's word
should be the good
son's guide.

Listen, I know about women.
They're full of tricks and traps.
We lust after them and
think we can trust them. But
what they do in bed
can turn the head of a young man.
Let this woman disobey,
let any woman disobey,
then see the price that we must pay.
For those who would rule a kingdom
must first rule their own home.

Haemon

Father, you have the wisdom
of years. I bow to that.
But my ears and eyes hear
and see the cries of the city.
The people say Antigone
has acted in honour; that
to bury a brother killed in
battle is an act of duty,
not of treachery. Father,

no-one wants more than me
to see you happy. But hear me:
Surely the man who listens
to the world and weighs wider
wisdom alongside his own
is wise, not weak.

Creon

Enough. This is baby-talk.
You're as weak as a woman.
Forget Antigone. She is as
good as gone. You shall never marry her.

Haemon

You speak as if *you* are the city;
as if you are Thebes in person.
Father, you are mistaken.
If she dies, I die too.

Haemon *leaves.*

Chorus

Passion
Love
Hate
Desire.

Wisdom cannot quell them,
or rule them.

Leader

Find the loneliest island
or a busy alley;
a rocky peak,
a grassy valley.
Passion lies there,
everywhere,
waiting for the human soul.

Chorus

Aphrodite, rising from the sea,
seeks us out, puts passion

into places where reason
was once secure. The free
citizen, the slave, woman,
man, poor or rich, each and every
one of us may be prey to
this madness. Aphrodite,
God of love and passion,
pity us lovers,
as we love to destruction.

Creon

Haemon is wrong. I hear the city.
Antigone's fate shall be sealed
by the Gods, not by me.

Leader

How can this be?

Creon

She shall be taken to a rocky cave
and sealed within. She shall have
time to think and food for a time
and the Gods may steer her mind
to whatever end they are inclined.

Leader

This is still a death sentence.

Creon

Aye. But she docs not die
by my hands. Take her away.

Antigone

Wait! Citizens, remember me,
crossing the silent river.
Fate had promised me marriage.
Now I shall be a bride to death.

Chorus

Death.
But death untouched by dying.
No disease or illness.
No sword-thrust or axe blow.

Neither struck down nor cut down.
The death of the living.

Leader

My child, this had to be.
Your own strong will
has willed it so. The shame
of your father goes before you.

Antigone

Is this how it must end?
No friend to mourn me as I die.
Fate may be fixed,
but in life I had a voice.
I made my choice.
Honour over obedience.
Honour me, at least, for this.

Creon

Such words in the face of death.
Guards, take her. You know the
the place.

Antigone *is taken away.*

Creon

Thebes,
citizens, if mercy is in your hearts
then hear my mind.
I *shall* spare the other girl,
Ismene. We must be kind
to our kin. She asked to die.
She shall remain behind;
life shall be her destiny.

Scene Fifteen

Thebes.

The **Chorus**, **Leader** *and* **Creon** *remain.* **Teiresias** *enters, led by his* **Boy**.

Teiresias
> Creon! Where is King Creon?

Creon
> Who is that?

Leader
> Teiresias, the blind prophet.
> He who sees when others cannot.

Creon
> You are welcome here.

Teiresias
> Not so welcome I fear
> when your eyes are uncovered
> by my words.

Creon
> Our battle is won, Teiresias,
> Traitors judged, enemies slain,
> and yet again the frowning brow!
> The city celebrates, while you
> worry for all of us.

Teiresias
> I have cause Creon. Listen:
> As I sat at my sacred seat,
> where I read the heavens
> and seek to complete
> the picture of what is to come,
> from the skies above I heard
> an unholy, unnatural sound;
> death cries, feathers flying, birds
> tearing each other to shreds.
> Shuddering, I had my boy lead
> me to the place of sacrifice.
> I lit the fire, but the flesh
> would not burn; the dripping fat
> gave off such a stench that
> it seemed death itself was
> moaning in the flames.

The boy took fear. All heavenly
hopes seemed to fade away.
Throughout the city, other
supplicants suffered in similar
fashion. Creon, the angry Gods
refused our offering.

Leader

What does this mean?

Teiresias

Only this:
The sacrificial flesh was no less
than that picked by dogs and crows
from the unburied body of Polynices,
son of Oedipus, whose curse he carries
in his unblessed blood.

Chorus

Polynices son of Oedipus.
Polynices brother of Antigone.
Polynices dishonoured.
Polynices unburied.

Creon

You mean to frighten me old man?
You don't.
You want me to bury Polynices?
I won't.

Teiresias

You hold in your hands two souls.
One from a body unburied, unblessed,
one from a life entombed, undead.
In payment for these, your own son shall die.
The Gods shall have their justice.
More. The rank flesh infecting the altars
of Thebes shall infect the altars of your
neighbours. City on city shall fall upon
Thebes to avenge this curse.

Take me away boy. Madness makes a mockery
of judgement here.

Teiresias *and the* **Boy** *leave.*

Leader
Creon, Teiresias has been right
too often to be ignored.

Creon
He is a man like any other.

Leader
No. He has the gift of sight.
He sees within and without.
He speaks for the Gods.
Only a fool clings to self-will
in the face of higher evidence.

Creon
Then advise me! What should I do?

Leader
Release Antigone and give Polynices
full burial honours.

Chorus
To make mistakes is the fate of men.
Yet all men may make amends.

Creon
Very well. Very well, let it be done.
Come, I'll do it by my own hand.

Creon *and the* **Leader** *leave.*

Scene Sixteen

Thebes.

The **Chorus** *remains.*

Chorus
> Bacchus, Dionysius,
> come to us now.
> Joy-giver, vine dancer,
> take away care,
> take away pain.
> You of the many names,
> come from Parnassus,
> come here to Thebes,
> seven-gated city,
> Thebes which loves you,
> which gave you birth.
> Let our stars, in our sky,
> dance for you, Bacchus.
> Son of the thunderer,
> dancer who skips from
> the dead to the living,
> Joy-giver, pain-taker
> dancer and wine-bearer,
> come to us now,
> to the city that needs you.

*The **Leader** returns. The spirits of **Antigone** and **Haemon** speak from the shadows.*

Antigone
> Too late.

Haemon
> Time. Fate.
> All was against us.

Antigone
> They buried Polynices;
> all that the dogs and crows
> had left of him.

Leader
> Creon himself shovelled
> soil on the sad remains.
> We said our prayers and hurried

to the cave where Antigone
was entombed. The stones
had been rolled aside and sounds
of great anguish came from within.
Creon knew the voice. It was
his son, Haemon. He pushed us
aside and went first into the cave.

Slowly, **Antigone** *and* **Haemon** *emerge from the shadows.*

Antigone

There, they found me, hanging
quite dead. When Creon tried
to comfort his son, the boy
drew his sword and drove him away.

Leader

Then, standing beside Antigone,
he thrust the sword into his own side,
and as he fell, embraced her in his arms,
his blood making red her pale, pale cheeks.

Creon *enters.*

Creon

Fool! I am a wilful fool!
I am the slayer; my son the slain.

Chorus

Creon the king.
Creon the king.
Brother to Jocasta,
Dead.
Brother in law to Oedipus.
Dead.
Uncle to Eteocles.
Dead.
Uncle to Polynices.
Dead.
Uncle to Antigone.

Dead.
Father of Haemon.
Dead.
Creon the king.
Creon the king.

Leader
One more.

Creon
No. No more!

Leader
One more dead.
Eurydice, your wife.
When she heard of Haemon's death,
Quietly she took her own life.

Creon
Oh Gods!
Must we learn only through sorrow?
Everything has gone. Only emptiness now.
No more light for me. Only night.
Let it come soon. Let it come!

Antigone
Onward and onward.
Fall after fall.

Haemon
A family fatefully driven
to fashion its own destruction.

Leader
Poor man!
We live only in the present
and his present is intolerable.
Yet he *is* a man.

Leader/Chorus
Did the Gods do this?
Looking down from Olympus,

frowning on the forlorn efforts
of mortals to turn back the oceans?

Hope lifts our feet from the mud.

The **Leader***, with a flicker of hope, realises there is one yet alive.*

Leader
Ismene. Where is Ismene?

Leader/Chorus
Hope lifts our feet from the mud.

End.

Tory Boyz

James Graham

About the Author

James Graham has been Playwright-in-Residence at the Finborough Theatre in London since 2005 when he was just twenty-two. His plays for the Finborough have included *Albert's Boy* (2005), *Eden's Empire* (2006; winner of the Catherine Johnson Best Play Award 2007), *Little Madam* (2007), *Sons of York* (2008) and *The Man* (2010). His other plays include *Tory Boyz* (Soho Theatre, 2008); *A History of Falling Things* (Clywd Theatr Cymru, 2009); *The Whisky Taster* (Bush Theatre, 2010); and *Huck* (The Theatre Chipping Norton, national tour, 2010). His television work includes *Caught in a Trap*, ITV1's primetime Boxing Day drama in 2008. His radio plays include *How You Feeling, Alf?* and *Albert's Boy* (both BBC Radio 4, 2009).

About the Play

I think politics and theatre can suffer from similar challenges when it comes to engaging with young people. Many feel excluded from or disillusioned by both. Not to mention frequently bored.

I was still starting out as a 'playwright' when Paul Roseby of the National Youth Theatre approached me about writing a piece on Ted Heath. I'd tackled Prime Ministers before, and had developed a passion for trying to make political histories less stuffy on stage, more young and fresh, for younger, fresher audiences.

But Ted Heath? Not a PM to instantly get my pulse racing, I have to admit. But that was probably because no one had ever properly explored him before. What we found was a very unconventional politician who, as a young man, had doubts and insecurities and questions about himself that would resonate with a young audience (and anyone) today. Questions about his sexuality, his social adeptness, about who he was and where he belonged.

I had a friend in politics that didn't fit into traditional 'categories' either. He was young, from the North-East, gay . . . and a Conservative. 'Northern' and 'gay' were not traits I traditionally associated with Tories. He introduced me to his peers within the party and Parliament – parliamentary researchers, interns, and so on. All of them young, some gay, some straight, from different regions, ethnicities, wealth brackets . . . and *Tory Boyz* was born. A play for young people about the energised, bright young things behind the scenes in British politics.

There are still, and always will be, uncertainties surrounding the sexuality of this former Prime Minister – but I hope the question that *Tory Boyz* asks is less 'Was Ted Heath Gay?' as opposed to 'Does it really matter?'

Producing the Play

Tory Boyz premiered at the Soho Theatre in the summer of 2008. The cast size was approximately twenty. It can, of course, be less by doubling parts, such as the schoolchildren with the Broadstairs kids and so on.

The play shifts focus and location quite rapidly. Our set was a flexible space where furniture was wheeled on and off 'suggesting' a specific place. Worlds frequently overlapped around the stage. A screen at the back projected changing images to suggest locations. Lighting and sound transitions contributed to the kinetic feel of the show. The only blackout came at the very end.

For the orchestral opening our director, Guy Hargreaves, placed Ted within the audience where he 'conducted' a musical montage of the different characters passing through the stage, performing different actions, as gradually the world of Sam's office was assembled around them, and the play began.

Tory Boyz was written when the Conservatives were in Opposition. At the time of publication they are in power. No doubt this will change again one day, and then change again. This shouldn't matter, as hopefully the themes and ideas are universal. However, I think it's entirely acceptable for future productions to modify the detail within the text where appropriate – for example, the term 'Opposition' being swapped with 'Government', 'Shadow Minister' with 'Minister' and all knock-on effects, if directors want to suggest the Tories are now in power. The same goes for Sam's speech to Michelle about small policies that go unnoticed – newer ones can be discovered. Equally, feel free to keep it as is.

I think we were all overwhelmed by the reaction from our audience every night. It was a funny, frolicking show thanks to a great cast and team. So my final advice is to have as much fun with it as possible.

Characters

Sam, *Parliamentary Researcher. Male. Twenty-three. North West.*
Nicholas, *Chief of Staff. Late twenties. South East.*
Nina, *PA. Twenty-two. London.*
Robbie, *intern. Nineteen. London.*
James, *Labour Parliamentary Researcher. Twenties.*
Douglas, *librarian.*

Tommo, *male. Fifteen/sixteen. GSCE student.*
Shayne, *male. Fifteen/sixteen. GSCE student.*
Muznah, *female. Fifteen/sixteen. GSCE student.*
Heather, *female. Fifteen/sixteen. GSCE student.*
Michelle, *female. Fifteen/sixteen. GSCE student.*
Ray, *male. Fifteen/sixteen. GSCE student.*
Adam, *male. Fifteen/sixteen. GSCE student.*
Teaching Assistant

Ted Heath, *Joint Deputy Whip. Male.*
Mrs Heath, *Ted's Mum. Twenties/thirties.*
Miss Locke, *Ted's piano teacher. Seventeen.*
Timothy, *Junior Whip. Male. Twenties.*
Frank, *Junior Whip. Male. Twenties.*
Kay, *Ted's friend. Female.*

Young Teddy/Teenage Teddy
Young John
Young Kay
Kids

Many of the roles can be doubled – for example, the modern-day GCSE students can become the younger children of the 1950s (as indicated in the text), Librarians can be Junior Whips and so on, or alternatively just cast one actor per individual part.

Notes on the Text

A slash mark (/) indicates the character with the next line should begin speaking, overlapping with the preceding character.

(Text within a bracket) indicates that the line is spoken softly or internal.

Spotlight on a music stand, holding song sheets.

Ted Heath *enters to applause. He bows to the audience. The applause dies. He turns to face the dark stage.*

As he flicks his baton, individual parts of the scene light up, accompanied by a musical instrument – for example, one flick lights a desk lamp, accompanied by a flute, before darkness again. Another lights a phone, which sounds a ring. Another, a spot on the filing cabinet accompanied by a tuba, etc. – as though the 'scene' were an orchestra warming up.

Objects and areas begin to light up of their own accord, interrupting each other. **Ted** *taps the stand for silence, regaining control.*

He lifts his arms grandly . . . and begins. Characters enter and are 'conducted' by **Ted**. *Parliamentary researchers answer phones, open filing cabinets; schoolchildren fight, dance, play . . . the music reaches a climax,* **Ted** *drops his arms, the music cuts out, and he disappears.*

Sam*'s office, the Houses of Parliament.*

Two desks. Computer, phone, papers scattered around. A few chairs. A closed door to an adjoining office. A flip chart with a handwritten list of secondary schools (some crossed off), unions and associations including NUT, NASUWT, NAHT, GTC, ASCL and ATL. **Sam** *is at his desk, on the phone, in mid-flow . . .*

Sam   . . . so in principle, yes, just concerns over implementation. And resources, of course.

Nicholas*, Chief of Staff, enters slovenly, sighing, holding a packet of crisps, a bottle of water and a tabloid newspaper, which he tosses onto a nearby desk.*

Nicholas (*yawning*)   Well that was a bag of wank. (*Sees* **Sam** *on the phone.*) Sorry.

Sam   And what about our proposal for money to follow the pupil rather than it going direct to the school?
Great. Well. Thanks for your time. That's been really useful. Thanks. Bye.

Nicholas (*stretching, referencing the flip chart*)   Ticking them off, Sammy boy?

Sam (*puts the phone down and stands, crossing a name off the list*)   Yep.

Nicholas   The hell is NASUWT again? National –

Sam   National Association of Schoolteachers' Union of Women Teachers –

Nicholas   La-lah la-lah la-lah. NUT, GLT, ABC, one two three. Jesus Christ, I'm bollocksed, man. Never a good night's sleep, Sundays, is it. And I've just had (*dramatically*) 'the morning from hell'. So. (*Slumps into a chair. Swivels.*) Fucking. 'N-U-T'. Urgh. Laugh a minute, it was not. If you can, do, if you're a cock, teach. (*Opening his crisps. Looking at his paper.*) Usual moans. Micromanagement. Short-term thinking bla bla bla. Heading to the Village drinks tonight?

Sam   Offered to do a stint at the press office.

Nicholas *laughs, shaking his head.*

Sam   Fuck does that mean?

Nicholas   Means you make me laugh, Sam. Bout Humphrey's civil what's it thing this afternoon? Partnership. Upstairs. What are they called if it's . . . ?

Sam   Called weddings, Nicholas. And I'm at the school, aren't I? And why would I be going? Don't even know him.

Nicholas   No, but I . . .

Sam   What do you . . . ? Why . . . ? It's not some club, Nick. You don't just go along because –

Nicholas   All right, Tetchy Von Sensitive. (*As 'street'.*) Take a chill pill, in'it. (*Beat.*) Well. Have fun at your school today (*chuckles*). What is it, one of the goods or the bads?

Sam   Uh, middle.

Nicholas (*referencing the adjoining office*)   Is he in?

Sam   No he's still in committee.

Nicholas   Oh, Shizer Chiefs. Well he'll be a delight this afternoon then. (*With the paper.*) Urgh. Questions, questions, since when was the front page about asking questions instead of just reporting the fucking news? 'More Poles in Britain than British?' No.

Phone rings. **Sam** *answers.*

Sam   Hello?

Nicholas   'Is there a paedophile in your son's bedroom right / now?' No, it's all fine, actually, thanks. Just carry on.

Sam   Four o'clock. OK. Bye. (*Phone down.*)

Nina *enters.* **Nicholas** *stands to greet her with mock-adoration.*

Nina   Afternoon.

Nicholas   Ah, there she is. How are we, how are we? What's that?

Nina   Baguette.

Nicholas (*imitating*)   'Baguette.' What kind? / What kind of baguette?

Nina (*handing to* **Sam**)   Here, OFSTED. Rest are online.

Sam   Ta.

Nina   Tuna Niçoise.

Nicholas   Tuna Niçoise, très bon, très bon. (*Taking her hand and holding it out, looking at her outfit.*) Like this little number, today, Nina. (*As Jim Carrey.*) 'I like it a lot.'

Nina   Worn it before, dead old.

Nicholas   First time I've seen it, though.

Nicholas *spins her as he sings.* **Nina** *laughs and groans, not fully cooperating.*

Nicholas   'The first time . . . ever I saw your face.'

Nina   Do you mind?

Nicholas (*looking at her hand, gasping playfully*)   And what is this, Nina, Nina, ballerina, no ring, no ring, on your pretty little finger, oh no! Weekend in the Cotswolds not go quite to plan, this is terrible. Time you moved on, ey Sam?

Nina   Look, it's fine, yeah? Just –

Nicholas   Sam's in one of them, today.

Sam   In what?

Nicholas   In one of them moods.

Sam   I'm busy, if that's what you mean.

Nicholas   No, that isn't what I mean, but never mind. (*Sympathetic groan.*) Oh Nina.

Nina   Genuinely don't want to talk about it, and I'm gonna get annoyed in a sec. So.

Nicholas   Well *I* . . . (*wanders, opening his bottle of water*) . . . I had a fabulous weekend, children. I went to that guy's restaurant, near the 'rents house, in lovely Berkshire, and I cannot quite describe to you this menu. / It had –

Sam   Whose restaurant is it?

Nicholas   What's his face's – (*the baguette*) that absolutely stinks, Nina.

Nina   Deal with it. Whose restaurant?

Nicholas   Thingy McShit. Cries over chickens, curly hair. Blooming . . . Bloomingdale.

Nina   Blumenthal.

Nicholas   Blumenthal.

Sam   You're thinking of Whittingstall. Curly hair.

Nicholas   No, this is Bloomingdale.

Nina/Sam   Blumenthal.

Nicholas   Blumenthal! Fuck's sake! Right. Listen to this. (*Holds out his left hand.*) Bacon. (*Holds out his right hand.*) Ice cream. (*Puts his hands together as 'one'.*)

Nina   Bollocks.

Nicholas   Na-ah. Na-ah. Bacon ice cream. (*As Peter Kay.*)
'I've tasted it, it's the future.'

Sam   Sounds ridiculous.

Nicholas   You're ridiculous.

Nina   I don't believe you.

Nicholas   Don't care if you believe me, I'm not saying it to
impress you, I'm saying it to inform you. Whether or not you
learn and grow is up to you.

Robbie *enters, apologetically.*

Robbie   Nina, sorry. You've got a, um –

Nicholas   Ah-ha! And who's this? Our next intern
extraordinaire?

Nina   Robbie, Nicholas; Nicholas, Robbie. Don't listen to a
word he says.

Nicholas   'Don't listen to a . . . ' (*Tuts.*) Hi Robbie. (*Shaking.*)
Nicholas. And you know Saint Sam-u-el over here?

Robbie.   Uh, yeah, we, we briefly. Met. Uh, Nina, sorry,
there's a photographer from the *Observer* outside.

Nicholas   A what? Why?

Robbie   He says he's here for something else, some cere-
mony thing.

Nicholas   Oh, yeah, Shadow Health, civil partnership. This
afternoon.

Robbie   He wants to quickly nab a pic of the office if he
can?

Nina   Why? / No, he can . . .

Nicholas   Ah! (*Mock 'ner-ner' childish.*) 'I know what it is.'
It's thingy. Ted Heath again. Fella gossiping on the *Today*
programme this morning. Dredging it up.

Robbie   Saying what?

Nicholas   Saying he was gay again.

Sam   (Fuck's sake.)

Nina   What's that got to do with us?

Nicholas   This used to be his office.

Nina   Did it? I didn't know that.

Nicholas   One of them. Once upon a time. (*Making to leave with* **Nina**.)

Nina   Why didn't I know that?

Nicholas   Jesus Neen, every office used to be someone else's and these have been offices for centuries, we're probably breathing in about twenty dead Prime Ministers.

Nina *and* **Nicholas** *leave.* **Robbie** *watches them go, unsure whether or not to stay.* **Sam** *has a glance at him before continuing to shift, staple, move, sign, etc.*

Robbie   So. You're not your average Tory.

Sam   Really.

Robbie   You've got an accent.

Sam   Ah. *You've* got an accent.

Robbie   You've got a northern accent.

Nicholas *has re-entered.*

Sam   / Yes. I do.

Nicholas   Shame, he's buggered off. Do what?

Sam   Yes I do have a northern accent.

Nicholas   Yeah, sorry about him, he's like a genetic deformity. And there's no cure, unfortunately. Me, though, I'm true blue. Home Counties, cricket and rugger, father in the military, huzzah. That more what you expected?

Robbie   Pretty much. (*Beat.*) So. Ted Heath was gay, then?
God.

Nicholas   Who fucking knows? No one, that's who. Just talk,
mate.

Sam   Why 'God'?

Robbie   Dunno. Gay Prime Minister. You'd think you would
have heard. And Conservative as well.

Nicholas   Lesson one, Robert, the Tory Party is the gayest
of them all. Reckon we've more gay party members, staff,
councillors, etc. than anyone else. 'Specially in London.

Robbie   I've never met a gay Tory.

Nicholas   Sam's gay.

Robbie   Are you?

Sam (*shoots* **Nicholas** *a look; short pause*)   If it matters.

Nicholas   Oy, no one's saying it matt – . . . fucking, the boy
was only asking, Mr Prickly. He might be gay, all we know.
Are you?

Robbie   Uh. (*Pause. Shrugs.*) Dunno. A bit.

Nicholas (*laughs*)   What?

Robbie (*pause. Laughs, embarrassed.*)   Sorry. That was a weird
thing to . . . I don't . . . know what I meant, sorry, it – I . . .

Nicholas (*pause, unnerved he may have crossed a line*)   No, that's
. . . don't – sorry, I shouldn't have . . . (*Pause.*) No, there's a, um
. . . isn't there, Sam, a, like a Westminster gay night. Tonight.
Monthly gay – well, it's not just Westminster any more but,
you know, lots of . . . very popular. Even the straight ones feel
obliged.

Robbie   God, never would have imagined.

Nicholas   And you should see the gay disco at the end
of the party conference. Something to, uh . . . behold. So.
Anyway, how, how you finding it, all right?

Robbie   Yeah, just been, you know. Coffee and photocopying, but –

Nicholas   Well it doesn't get much more exciting than that, I'm afraid *The West Wing*, this ain't. You had a tour of the place?

Robbie   Yeah, a brief one. It's weird. Loads of cafés, and gyms and bars. / So many bars.

Nicholas (*laughs*)   Did you see the Sports and Social? Where the old school Labours meet to guzzle down their real ale. We tend to go Bellamy's, don't we?

Sam   (*busy*)

Nicholas   Well, Sam doesn't have a life but you'll likely find a lot of us lot there.

Robbie   Yeah, and that's what's . . . I can't – you're all so young.

Nicholas   Hire that man! (*Laughs.*) No, it's because, in all seriousness, the pay's pretty rubbish. Just to warn you. The MPs, they nab us as graduates desperate to get on any ladder as researchers, PAs, dogsbodies, and by the time we hit our late twenties, we're bored and underpaid and so we leave or get headhunted and off we pop to earn some real money. I'll be leaving soon, God willing. But Sam here, he's been told he could have the pick of the bunch if he stays. CRD. CCHQ.

Nina *re-enters.*

Nina   Those reports are ready for binding, Robbie, if you want.

Robbie   Uh, yeah. Cool. Sorry. Thank you. (*Exit.*)

Nina *perches on her desk, eating her baguette.* **Sam** *still busying around them.*

Nicholas (*raising an eyebrow at* **Nina**)

Nina (*chuckling*)   What?

Nicholas   Nice, your boy there.

Nina   Piss off. Just nice to have someone being keen for a change.

Nicholas   Oh God, he's not one of these that 'believes' in things, is he?

Sam   I believe in things.

Nicholas   That's what I mean.

Sam gets a text message on his phone. He reads it.

Nicholas   (Can't be doing with two fucking Gandhis, drive me nuts.)

Sam   It's him.

Nina and Nicholas stand into 'work' mode. A distinct sense of efficiency now.

Nicholas   What's he need?

Sam *(reading)*   'Trust school, Hertfordshire question mark, parent co-op, name and results asap. Can't find.'

Nicholas *(moving to computer but pointing behind him to files as he goes)*   In there?

Nina *(retrieving them)*   No, he took them up, I'm sure.

Nicholas *(sits at computer, pointing to the flip chart)*   And not one of them on the board?

Sam   No, they're all comps and old ones at that.

Nicholas *(typing)*   I'll get the name, then Sam you phone for results.

Sam *(with a BlackBerry)*   They'll be listed on the website./ (What was the name?)

Nicholas   Ah Wikipedia, what would we do without you?

Sam *(searching her files)*   I wanna say St Mary's, St M-m-m –

Nicholas *(reading the screen)*   Actually, I'll check local newspapers.

Nina (*with lists, running her finger down*)   Hertfordshire schools, here.

Nicholas   Good.

Sam (*found it*)   Got it. St Mary's-in-the-Field. Local resident trust school established '07.

Nicholas   Eureka. (*Begins typing.*)

Nina   Got it as well. (Phone number . . .) (*Dialling on the phone.*)

Nicholas   Here we go. (*Searching screen.*) Results, results. Come on. Shit, shit, shit.

Sam (*pointing to the screen*)   There. (*Texting as he reads.*)

Nicholas   Well done, well done.

Nina   We good? (*Putting the phone down.*)

Nicholas   Sam?

Sam (*sending the message*)   Yep.

Nicholas (*reading*)   And doing very well. Seventy-two per cent grades A–C, blimey.

Sam   OK. Sent.

Nicholas   Weuw! (*Standing.*) Well done, ladies. (*Stretching.*) Fuck, think that's me done for the day now, Jesus.

Robbie *enters again.*

Robbie   Nina, sorry, there's / a –

Nicholas   Stop apologising, Robbie, this is the House of Commons for Christ's sake.

Robbie   Oh. OK, sorry. Nina, there's a call for you.

Nina   Thank you. (*Exits.*)

Robbie (*to* **Nicholas**)   Sorry. (*Exits.*)

Nicholas   'Sorry.' 'Sorry.' Jesus. Apologises more than Boris.

Sam   Thanks for that.

Nicholas   What?

Sam   Earlier.

Nicholas   What the fuck is your fucking problem today? Go get some lunch.

Sam   He's still in there, might text down again.

Nicholas   I'm on it. (*Drinking some more water. Watching him.*) Oy.

Sam   What?

Nicholas   Be happier.

Sam   Be . . ? I don't know what that means. What does that mean?

Nicholas   You know what that means. Be nicer. He was only trying to be nice.

Sam   I was only trying to be nice.

Nicholas   Try harder. (*Beat. Drinks.*) Sam? (*Serious.*) Try harder. When you get this busy you get distracted with people. Forget minor courtesies.

Sam   Like what.

Nicholas   Like smiling. Remember what it was to smile, Sam?

Sam   I'm smiling now.

Nicholas   Smiles have teeth, Sam. See. (*Smiles.*)

Sam *smiles a grotesquely 'teethy' grin.*

Nicholas *mimics him, more grotesquely, and* **Sam** *mimics him back. They stop, and smile genuinely at each for a sec over the silliness of this, before returning.*

Nicholas   Oy.

Sam (*sighs, looking up again*).

Nicholas   He isn't a threat. He's just a boy.

Sam (*beat, stops what he's doing*)   Now I'm really sure I don't know what that means.

A moment, **Sam** *and* **Nicholas** *looking at each other,* **Nicholas** *swigging from his bottle.* **Robbie** *enters and smiles, waiting, as though to continue whatever it was they were doing before.* **Nicholas** *makes to leave.*

Nicholas   Sam, as you're clearly not going to lunch, why not give Roberto here a whirlwind tour of the life of a parliamentary researcher. I'll be upstairs.

Nicholas *leaves.* **Sam** *continues with his work for a while.*

Robbie   So he's your boss.

Sam   He's the Chief of Staff. Michael One has four –

Robbie (*pointing to the adjoining office*)   Michael One?

Sam   No. Two Michaels. Michael Pritchard upstairs, Shadow Secretary of State for Schools Children and Families. Michael Two is Daikens, the minister underneath him. I'm Michael Two's Researcher, Nina his PA and Nicholas is Chief of Staff.

Robbie (*momentarily stunned by the sharpness of the answer*) 'K. And what do you do?

Sam (*confused*)   You a first year undergrad?

Robbie   Will be. Just done my A Levels. Dad's Honorary Chairman of Reading West association. Thought it'd be good me getting some experience.

Sam   PPE?

Robbie   Yeah. In Hull. Wherever the fuck that is. Didn't even go to the open day.

Sam   End of the M62, east coast. After you pass (what is it?) Pontefract, it's like the only thing left at the end. So by that point all the cars on the road have to be going to Hull or else drive straight on into the North Sea. Which to be fair, when they see Hull, a lot of people actually do.

Robbie *laughs.*

Sam   Hmm-hmm. (See. Happy, Jokes . . .)

Robbie   So, why, like, do the government listen to you lot and, you know, table your amendments into the Bill?

Sam   If the government wants a Bill to become law it might need MPs from *our* party to vote for it. Which we're more likely to do if we've amended it to our liking at committee stage, currently under way. Plus, God forbid we may actually have some good ideas.

Robbie   Gotcha. OK. Uh. So. Do you reckon he was gay then or what? Ted Heath.

Sam   I don't think it changes anything, do you?

Robbie   Why do you think he kept it hidden. If he was, I mean.

Sam   Well I would have thought that was obvious. He wanted to be Prime Minister. But things have moved on.

Robbie   Cool. Cool. What things?

Sam   ('What things.') People. The country, the party, those things.

Robbie   So it's never been a problem? For you, I mean. Being here.

Sam   Hasn't yet – is that everything? Or . . . ?

Robbie   Oh. Um. (*Beat.*) Well. Maybe I'll see you at that drinks thing tonight. Maybe.

Sam   No I'm doing a stint in the press office. Always got to be someone on late. 'Case the Queen dies or something.

Robbie   Right-oh. Oh well. (*Beat.*) I'd better . . . get back to it, then.

Sam (*smiling, dryly*)   Okey dokey.

Pause. **Robbie** *leaves.* **Sam** *has gathered his things and closes up his bag.*

Ted Heath *appears, faintly, almost an apparition, on the phone at the opposite desk. His voice like an echo, hardly distinguishable.* **Sam** *watches before exiting.*

House of Commons library.

Douglas, *an assistant librarian, is collecting some papers.* **Sam** *enters.*

Douglas   Hullo.

Sam   Hi. Erm. I just have . . . (*unfolding a note and handing it over*) . . . couple of extra reports for Michael we need pulling, if that's OK.

Douglas   Roger, roger. Pick up tomorrow morning, all right?

Sam   Thanks. (*Making to leave. Stops. Awkward*). Douglas, you . . . you've not been . . . you haven't heard anything about this new, uh . . . new Ted Heath stuff? Have you?

Douglas   Oh I don't pay attention to gossip, Sam. I'm surrounded by one of the most comprehensive banks of knowledge imaginable. Why waste time with rumour when I can make a withdrawal of hard facts? (*Laughs.*)

Sam   OK. Cool.

Douglas   Course I will say this. My Granddad always used to speak very highly of him.

Sam   Oh yes of course, 'cause he –

Douglas   Nearly thirty years here. Left when the Lady came to power. Now, he did say he was a very private man, hard to know unless he . . . you know, unless he let you in. Nice enough. But . . . you know. One of them. Bit funny.

Sam   Right. (Right.) Uh, thanks, Douglas. (*Exiting.*)

Douglas   I could give you a couple of interesting exhibits, mind. If you were . . . interested.

Sam *stops. Turns. Considers . . .*

A music classroom. Secondary school.

Some chairs, a couple of tables. A piano, keyboard, drum kit, other instruments dotted around. Noise approaching from outside. **Tommo** *bursts in and tosses his rucksack in anger. He's followed in by* **Ray**, **Shayne** *and* **Muznah**, *laughing.*

Tommo   Just fuck off, yeah?

Ray   Shit, man, that was fucking ace!

Muznah   No lie, that is the most hilarious thing I / have ever seen. Fact!

Ray   Serious, bruv! You gotta come see, he's still down.

Tommo   I ain't going back out there, no way, no fucking way.

Shayne   Why not, he can't hit for shit, man. Clearly. / You had him.

Tommo   He'll knock me out next time, swear.

Muznah   Don't be a fool, he just knocked himself out, innit.

Ray (*laughing, clapping his hands and hopping around*)   I cannot believe, cannot believe.

Shayne (*joining him and slapping hands, pissing himself*)   Shit man . . .

Tommo   Yeah, you laugh, it's all right for you, innit.

Tommo *sits down at a drum kit and begins bashing, kicking it.* **Heather** *and* **Michelle** *enter.*

Heather   What just happened?

Muznah   / Tommo, yeah –

Michelle   Why the fuck is Trip lying / lying on the ground?

Heather   Tommo?

Ray   No, he didn't do nothing, he didn't get a chance. Trip punched *himself* in the head!

Michelle   What?

Ray   Swear to God. He squares up to Tommo, yeah –

Tommo   Ray, leave it!

Ray   Proper up in his face, giving it all sumfin about
Tommo's brother and Trip's sister –

Shayne   Bruv, / is it true? Your Mark and his sister?

Ray   Tommo pushes him, and we're all like, 'fuck man'.

Michelle   Serious, / you pushed Trip?

Ray   Tommo's gonna die, yeah? Trip pulls his arm back, like
this, ready to go in, but he, obviously didn't reckon on Rocky
having knocked him so hard, wobbling, right? And he goes in . . .
(*laughing, imitating*), punches *himself*, back of the head.

Michelle *and* **Heather** *burst into hysterics. Even* **Tommo** *smiles
now.* **Michelle** *heads over to a stereo player and takes a CD from her
bag, still laughing.*

Shayne (*slaps* **Tommo** *on the chest*)   Fuck, man, you're like,
the only person to ever knock Trip to the ground, you should
be high / as a kite.

Tommo   He knocked himself to the ground!

Muznah   Man, you gotta get back out there, take a bow. (*As
a boxing call.*) 'The undefeated champion of the / woooorld!'

Tommo   Fuck that, no way.

Heather (*looking out through the door*)   Ey, he's up, walking
around now.

Tommo (*pacing, afraid*)   Awh shit, man. *Shit.*

Heather   Smedley's with him.

Shayne (*calling out*)   'Fattie.' / 'Fattie Smeders!'

Muznah   Ah, Trip looks well embarrassed. / He's bright red!

Ray   He fucking should be. (*Imitates punching himself again.*)

Heather   Adam's here.

Ray (*running over*)   Wait. Ssh.

Michelle   Heather, how did we miss that? Gutted!

Ray *has run to hide behind the door.* **Adam** *walks in.* **Ray** *jumps him, playfully but aggressively, from behind, trying to mount him.*

Ray   Yo Adam, man!

Adam   Argh, fuck off Ray!

Ray   Oh come on, you know you like it, don't lie. You've gotta be true to yourself, innit.

Adam (*scrambling free*)   Fuck off! Serious. Takes the piss. Why does he do it, why? Gay.

Ray   You're gay.

Adam   You are.

Michelle *has selected Dizzie Rascal's 'Dance Wiv Me' on the CD player, which now plays. Everyone except* **Tommo** *and* **Adam** *jump and whoop as they begin to dance around.* **Michelle** *skips forward in the song and turns it up loud before joining them.* **Shayne** *sits at the drum and begins bashing.*

Sam *enters with a* **Teaching Assistant**. *One by one* **Adam**, **Heather**, **Michelle**, **Tommo**, **Muznah** *and finally* **Ray** *clock him and stop.* **Michelle** *stops the music.*

Teaching Assistant   5b?

Michelle   Yeah.

Teaching Assistant (*to* **Sam**)   5b. The clip-boards over there and, uh . . . (*handing him marker pens*) keep hold of these. I'll leave you to it. (*Exits.*)

Sam   Thank you. (*Pause. Surveys the scene.*) Hey.

Shayne   Hey.

Michelle   Hello.

Sam   I'm Sam. How you all doing, all right?

Michelle   All right thank you. How are you?

Ray   Are you our politician man?

Sam   I am your politician man, yes. Except I'm not a politician.

Muznah   But you work for the Government, innit.

Sam   No, I don't work for the Government. I work for the Opposition. But I do work in the Houses of Parliament.

Ray   Like Big Ben?

Sam   Well, the palace where Big Ben is, yes. Big Ben is actually the name of the bell but –

Ray   The bell? Like Tommo, he's a bell. (*Laughs.*)

Shayne   Ey, you know the bottom of a bell, sir, do you call that the 'bell-end'?

Sam   I'm a researcher for the Conservative Party on schools and children. In fact I'm, I'm one of four people who knows more about Conservative educational policy than anyone else in the country. So . . .

Muznah (*sarcastic, mock-interested*)   Is it?

They all snigger.

Shayne   Wait, you're a Tory? Awh, man. I thought we was gonna get a Labour.

Ray   Aren't Tories all posh and old, sir?

Sam   No, I'm a Tory, do I sound posh or look old?

Tommo   No, you sound a bit like a pikey.

Michelle *hits him.*

Sam   I'm from Liverpool.

Ray   Ain't that a right shit hole?

Sam   No more than anywhere else.

Tommo (*trying to imitate a Liverpudlian accent*)   'Hello. I'm from Liverpool. Go on Redknapp. Go on Gerrard. Ay, ay, ay.'

Sam   Yes, that's. Very good. Erm . . .

Ray   So why'd you go pick the losing team, bruv?

Sam   I'm sorry?

Ray   Why didn't you choose to work for the Government, ain't that better?

Sam   I don't believe in the Labour Party's principles.

Muznah   My dad says that you're all the same, now. And that you're all shit.

Michelle   Muz!

Sam   No, don't worry, you can say what you like. I'm not a politician. That's the point. My job is to find the truth. It's why I'm here.

Michelle   So we ain't got to do music for a month, sir?

Sam   Please don't call me sir. Did Mrs Gillon not explain why I was here?

Heather   A little bit.

Tommo   It's cos Mr Lucas has got rabies, innit.

Sam   Your music teacher hasn't got rabies. But he is away for a couple of weeks. So we handpicked you guys to help us out with a little project. It's actually quite a cool thing, you erm . . . well you get to have your voices heard and input into things that could one day become law. So . . .

Heather   What about our music GSCE, we gotta pass it, haven't we?

Sam   Well that's why you were chosen by Mrs Gillon, as students who are excelling and could afford to miss three or four lessons.

Shayne (*spurts laughter*)   Not Raymondo. He needs all the help he can get.

Ray   Fuck you!

Sam   Oy, come on now.

Michelle   It's true, Ray, you is pretty shit.

Ray   Yeah, laugh it up, cause one day you gonna be seeing me spinning decks in the clubs you pay fifty fucking quid to get in to, innit.

Shayne   Yeah right, you can't even play Frère Jacques.

Everyone laughs. **Ray** *heads over to the piano and sits at it.*

Ray   Yeah, all right, fuck you all! Watch this.

Sam   OK, come on everyone.

Ray   I'll show you Frère Jacques. I'm gonna Frère Jacques the fuck out of this.

(plays a note) Wait.

(plays a couple of notes) Wait.

(plays a note) Wait.

(plays the first bit, goes wrong) Wait.

Ray *plays Frère Jacques on the piano, clunkily, slowly, but gets through it. Slamming down on the keys, and standing victoriously.*

Ray   Yes! Recognise.

Sam   OK, well done. / Now. Can we –

Ray   Eat your heart out Stevie Wonder. *(Imitates Stevie Wonder on an air piano.)*

Sam   All right, could we, like grab chairs and sit down please. Like . . . yeah in a circle, or . . .

The gang slovenly gather chairs and place them around, sitting.

Sam   Whatever. Cool. Thank you. So. Essentially. I'm here because, one, I'm interested in getting your opinions on a couple of matters, and, and two, because, as I'm sure you, you may or may not agree, that young people are often excluded from the political system or just, or feel disillusioned with the whole thing. More of you, when you reach voting age – you're like, what? Fifteen, sixteen?

Adam/ Tommo/ Michelle   Sixteen.

Ray/ Shayne/ Heather/ Muznah   Fifteen.

Sam   Right, so when you reach voting age, more of you will choose to vote in *The X Factor* than at the next general election.

Muznah   That's because what's the point, nothing changes.

Shayne   So what's your job then? What do you do?

Sam *goes to a flip chart and turns the sheet over. A drawing of a penis is there. The students burst into laughter, accusing and congratulating each other. They laugh into silence as they watch* **Sam***, waiting to see what he'll say or do.*

Sam *smiles slightly, and nods, as he draws a line from the 'slit' of the penis drawing, all the way down the penis, splitting it into left and right. He then begins to colour one side in red, half the other in blue, and the bottom half yellow.*

Sam   The House of Commons. The Government at the moment are Labour, because they have more MPs in the Commons than Tories, here, and other parties here. MPs from the government side form a cabinet with each of them taking on different departments, whether it be 'Health' (*writing, and so on*), 'Defence', 'Schools', 'Culture' and so on. But for every cabinet minister *they* have, we in the Opposition have what's called a Shadow minister. So we have our Shadow Defence Minister, Shadow Culture, to formulate alternative policies, challenge and also in some cases support their opposite numbers. I research for the Shadow schools minister.

Adam   What do you research?

Ray (*mock-gay*)   'What do you research?'

Sam   Hey. Please. So, um . . . so at this point in time, the Government has produced a pretty far-reaching Schools

Bill with things that will affect if not you then those slightly younger than you, their daily lives. Do you know what a Bill is?

Muznah   Not like a phone bill?

Ray   Idiot.

Muznah   I / was joking, dick head.

Sam   When ministers are formulating policies they'll normally submit a 'Green Paper' –

Michelle   What's that?

Sam   It's like a first draft of ideas. Then they get feedback from people within the industry in question, so like schools, hospitals, whatever, and then redraft the Green Paper into a White Paper. More consultation, until finally the minister in question will submit a 'Bill' to the House.

Ray   Not a phone bill, Muz.

Muznah   One more time! I / was joking, cock nose!

Sam   A Bill . . . OK, a Bill is a possible future law, but before the MPs can vote we go into committee stage. That's what we're in now. / Which –

Shayne   Which is?

Sam   It's where the Opposition MPs, i.e. my guys, can try and make changes to the Government's proposed law, based on what we want and what the people we've spoken to want. The idea being we all try and get the law as near perfect as possible before we all vote. If more MPs vote for it to become an Act of Parliament than not, then it becomes law. So –

Tommo   Sir, did you vote for the Iraq war?

Sam   I'm not a Member of Parliament, I'm just a member of the public. And please call me Sam. What I want to find out about is what *you* think to some of the things we're debating in this Bill. Lowering the voting age for you guys, reorganising the curriculum. Things such as raising the school-leaving age –

Muznah   What?!

Sam   So I was thinking we could form our own cabinet, if you like. To debate ideas. Like the real one. We each take a role. So someone will need to be Prime Minister –

Ray   I will!

Michelle   No way.

Sam   Which we'll vote on. Someone to be Education, Health, so on. And see how we go.

Ray   Michelle, why not me?

Heather   I think Tommo.

Shayne   No, he needs to be Defence, so he can protect us from Trip. (*Laughs.*)

Michelle   Is culture like dance and sport and all that? That's the one I want.

Sam   OK, so. Next week, why not come prepared with your top two preferred positions, uh, and we'll vote. Or something.

Heather   Are we gonna get like a certificate for this or something?

Sam   Well, you'll get to contribute to Conservative Party policy.

Heather   Yeah, I want a certificate.

Tommo (*to* **Shayne**)   Oy, get the fuck out of my bag!

Shayne   I need a pen, knob rash!

Tommo *tries to snatch his rucksack back, and* **Shayne** *stands, holding it out tauntingly.* **Shayne** *goes to get it, and a chase ensues, with the others leaping to their feet and running round in a circle after* **Tommo***;* **Sam** *trying to control them. The classroom fades as the shouts of the students turn into a nursery rhyme. They change clothes, taking off blazers, turning jumpers inside out, etc.* **Adam** *becomes* **Young Teddy***;* **Shayne** *becomes* **Young John***; the rest become* **Kids**. **Sam** *watches, before disappearing . . .*

Broadstairs, 1920s.

Kids (*singing*)   The farmer wants a wife; the farmer wants a wife,
Heigh-ho, Benjioh, the farmer wants a wife.
(*the* **Kid** *playing the farmer picks a wife*)
The wife wants a child; the wife wants a child,
Heigh-ho, Benjioh, the wife wants a child.
(*the* **Kid** *playing the wife picks a child*)
The child wants a dog; the child wants a dog,
Heigh-ho, Benjioh, the child wants a dog.
(*the* **Kid** *playing the child picks a dog*)
The dog wants a bone; the dog wants a bone,
Heigh-ho, Benjioh, the dog wants a bone.
(*the* **Kid** *playing the dog picks* **Young Teddy***, and everyone starts
patting him*)
We all pat the bone; we all pat the bone,
Heigh-ho, Benjioh, we all pat the bone!

The Kids pat **Young Teddy** *to the ground until he struggles free.*

Young Teddy   Ouch! Get off! John, tell them.

Kid   Look, over there!

Kid   An empty dinghy!

Kid   It must have floated away!

Young John   Come on, then, let's grab it.

Kid   Let's sail to France!

Kids   Yeah!

The **Kids** *exit cheering.* **Young Teddy** *follows but* **Young John**
pulls him back.

Young John   Teddy, you've got to stay here.

Young Teddy   What? Why?

Young John   They're *my* friends, and they don't even like
you, and you don't even like them anyway. And you wouldn't
like the way we play, so . . .

Young Teddy   Yes I would, why wouldn't I like it?

Young John   Cause you get wet, and you hate getting wet, and you get dirty, and you hate getting dirty, and you have to be a boy or a girl that's a bit like a boy, and you're just a girl so (*blows a raspberry*).

Mrs Heath (*calling, off*)   Edward!

Mrs Heath *enters.*

Mrs Heath   What are you boys playing?

Young John   Mum, can I go and get in a dinghy with my friends?

Mrs Heath   Yes, of course, John. Run along.

Young Teddy   Can I, Mother?

Mrs Heath   Teddy, why would you want to go and do a thing like that?

Young John   See.

Young John *runs off, scruffy and dirty, as* **Young Teddy** *gets fixed by* **Mrs Heath***, clothes straightened and face wiped, etc.*

Mrs Heath   Now Teddy, you know you've your lesson with Miss Locke. Don't you want to learn?

Young Teddy   I know, Mother. I do want to learn, honestly.

Young Kay *returns to fetch a hat. She looks at* **Young Teddy***, giggles, and exits.*

Mrs Heath   One of your friends, hmm?

Young Teddy   No, I don't . . . I don't even know her name.

Mrs Heath   It's Kay, Teddy. You know that. (*Sighs, wipes him down.*) You're ever such a bright boy, Teddy. Such a bright little boy. I'd hate you to get . . . distracted with . . .

Young Teddy   I won't, Mother. I promise.

Mrs Heath (*looks at him. Smiles. Stands.*)   Good.

Miss Locke *appears by the piano.* **Mrs Heath** *holds* **Young Teddy**'s *hand.*

Mrs Heath   Busy morning on the stall, Miss Locke?

Miss Locke   Yes, Mrs Heath, very busy.

Mrs Heath   What have they been going for today, I wonder?

Miss Locke   Geraniums today, Mrs Heath. We've had a run on them.

Mrs Heath   Geraniums? Isn't it funny? From one day to the next. Geraniums, you say?

Miss Locke   Hot cakes, Mrs Heath. Like hot cakes, I swear.

Mrs Heath   Well there you are. Geraniums, Teddy.

Miss Locke   Hello Teddy.

Mrs Heath   Say hello to Miss Locke, Teddy. He's been ever so keen to get started.

Miss Locke   I hope so.

Mrs Heath   Haven't you?

Young Teddy   Yes.

Mrs Heath   Ever so keen.

Miss Locke   Are you, Teddy?

Young Teddy   Yes.

Mrs Heath   Yes, ever so keen. (*Beat.*) Jolly good, well I'll be through here.

Mrs Heath *exits. Silence.* **Miss Locke** *wanders around, occasionally turning to look at* **Young Teddy** *and smile, until eventually just stopping and smiling at him.*

Miss Locke   Such a terribly serious boy, Teddy. You've always struck me as being a terribly, terribly serious boy; don't you ever have any fun? (*Pause.*) Why don't you ever smile Teddy; don't you ever smile?

Young Teddy *smiles.*

Miss Locke   That isn't a smile, Teddy; that's a terrible smile.

Young Teddy *frowns.*

Miss Locke   And that's a frown; what you're doing now, Teddy. That isn't a smile. (*Gasps.*) Look at that, that's one of the biggest frowns I think I've ever seen. You know, if you turned that frown the other way around, it would be the biggest smile I've ever seen. Don't you want to turn it upside down, Teddy. Like this.

Miss Locke *turns around and bends over, one hand on the floor, lifting her dress with the other and looking at* **Young Teddy** *through her legs.*

Miss Locke   As though you were about to stand on your head, Teddy. Turn upside down like this.

Young Teddy *suspiciously turns round and bends over, looking at her through his legs.*

Miss Locke   There you go. That frown's a smile now, Teddy. You've got a lovely smile.

They stay like this for some time. **Miss Locke** *stands.*

Miss Locke   Well I hope you're serious about learning to play the piano, Teddy, because quite honestly I haven't the time to ruddy waste, do you understand?

Young Teddy *nods.*

Miss Locke   Well let's get started then.

Miss Locke *goes and sits at the piano. Pats the seat.* **Young Teddy** *joins her.*

Miss Locke   Now. I'm going to teach you scales and I'm going to show you arpeggios and I want you to practise them every day. And I'll know, you know. I'll be able to tell if you haven't practised every single day. OK?

Young Teddy *nods.*

Miss Locke   Very good, Teddy. Very good.

Miss Locke *plays.* **Sam** *appears, away from this, sat cross-legged, reading a book. He turns the page as* **Miss Locke** *fades, and* **Young Kay** *appears, playing hospital. She has a stethoscope.* **Young Teddy** *joins her on the floor.*

Young Kay   Come on, Teddy. I need to check your heart beat. (*Lifting his shirt.*)

Young Teddy (*yelping*)   Kay! It's cold.

Young Kay   Look. Do you want to die? Because you will if I don't give you a check up.

Young Teddy   No.

Young Kay (*packing away*)   Fine. Go out and play with your friends then.

Young Teddy   You're my friend.

Young Kay   What?

Young Teddy (*beat. Shrugs.*)   You know. (You're my . . .) . . .

Young Kay *smiles, and puts the stethoscope on his chest again. They burst into giggly hysterics, clambering over each other in a play fight. They stop,* **Young Kay** *on top of* **Young Teddy**.

Young Kay   One day, we're going to get married you know.

Young Teddy (*scrambling free*)   Urgh, I don't think so.

Young Kay   Our mothers think so. I just heard them talking in the kitchen. You have to ask me, though. The boy always asks the girl.

Young Teddy (*putting on the nurse's hat*)   Why?

Young Kay   I don't know but that's just the way it is. I have to wait. And you have to ask.

Young Teddy (*beat. As a female nurse.*)   'Now young Lady. I am your nurse, Tedweena. And I need to check your heart beat. So lie down for me, there's a good girl.'

Young Kay *lies down as* **Young Teddy** *tickles her with the stethoscope on her stomach, as they laugh and fight some more.* **Sam** *closes his book and steps into Sam's office. Houses of Parliament.*

Evening. **Sam** *is by the entrance facing* **James**, *as though he's just got back.*

Sam   I'm sorry, who did?

James   I'm sorry?

Sam   Who let you in?

James   She did. Uh, the girl. She said just wait in here.

Sam   (*beat. Goes to his desk, dumping his things.*) Sorry, I . . . sorry, I just wasn't – I thought we said we'd meet downstairs.

James   Did we? Oh. Everything all right, though?

Sam   Uhuh. Yep. Sorry. Busy day. (*Busying himself.*) How, how's everything over at, uh . . . at Labour HQ?

James   Oh you know. Same same. How about you? Still mangling up our Schools Bill? Ha.

Sam   No, it was pretty mangled when we got it from you lot actually.

James   Not my lot, I've nothing to do with it. / And I was only joking.

Sam   No, you know, but . . . you know. Your side.

James   Right. (*Pause.*) Still got stuff to do?

Sam   Uh, I've, I'm in the, uh . . . the press office tonight, so . . .

James   You're . . . ? Sorry, you're . . . working tonight?

Sam   Later. Yes.

James   Oh. Oh. Sorry, are . . . are we not . . . ? Going out?

Sam   Uh, yeah. If you . . . for like a . . . drink.

James   But . . . (*looks at his watch. Beat.*) Right. So *one* drink.

Sam   Yes.

James   Oh.

Sam   Is that . . . ?

James   I just . . . I suppose because it was tonight, I had it in my head we were off to the, you know, the drinks. And then . . .

Sam   Oh. No, I . . . no, I never really . . . do all that.

James   No, I don't see you around, actually. You're not someone who I see around.

Sam *smiles, politely. Continues busily.*

James   Are you . . . ? Yeah, someone was saying, you've got some . . . (*laughs*), um, little. Project on or something? Using schoolchildren as witnesses to the Bill. That's . . . was that yours? Great gimmick, if it was. Well done.

Sam   Asking schoolchildren what schoolchildren want for their schools is a gimmick?

James   Well. Yeah. (*Beat. Takes out a note.*) I'm sorry, you did give me your number didn't you? That was you? 'Call me, 0-2-0 . . . ' etcetera etcetera.

Sam (*stops. Looks at him. Beat.*)   Um. Do you . . . actually, sorry, do you know what . . .

James   No, that's fine.

Sam   I'm just not . . . now is a bad time, sorry. I'm . . . not ready . . .

James   Well. Maybe let's try next week. Uh?

Sam   Yeah, sure, Give, give . . . drop me a . . .

James (*leaving the note on the desk opposite and nodding*)   Cool.

Broadstairs, 1930s.

Teenage Teddy *appears at the piano with* **Miss Locke**, *playing together.*

Miss Locke Very good, Teddy. I'm ever so proud, you know. Would you like me to continue coming round? Now that you're 'proficient'?

Pause. **Teenage Teddy** *shrugs.*

Miss Locke   Only I've plenty other things that need doing. If you don't need me anymore. (*Pause.*) I've a boyfriend now, you know. He's ever such a dish. Do you have a girlfriend, Teddy? (*Pause.*) What about that Kay, girl, hmm? I won't tell your mother, I swear it. Cross my heart and hope to die. (*Pause.*) You know, you really shouldn't spend so much time with your mother. (*Pause.*) Teddy?

Miss Locke *leans in and kisses him on the cheek. He doesn't move.*

Miss Locke   What do you make of that, hmm? How did that make you feel?

Pause. **Teenage Teddy** *shrugs.*

Miss Locke   Very well, Teddy. (*Stands.*) Very well. (*Exits.*)

House of Commons library.

Douglas *at work.* **Sam** *enters.*

Douglas   Ah, morning morning. (*Indicating a pile.*) Here we are, ready and waiting.

Sam   Uh. Thanks. Actually, I was wondering if I could . . . (*Handing over a list.*) . . . if you could maybe dredge up anything in addition to . . . your 'present'. Yesterday.

Douglas   Um. Okey cokey. But, uh . . . (*looking at the list*), you won't find anything, you know . . . 'revelatory'. If there was something, it would be out by now. Believe me.

Sam   Well I don't even know what I'm looking for, so . . . I know there'll be no, uh, 'lines' written down, but I at least want to *see* the lines that are, so that I may . . . read in between them. If you see my . . . (point).

Douglas   Of course. (*Makes to leave. Stops.*) I did meet him once, you know? I was here on work experience, years ago. He was the Father of the House, then. Longest-serving MP. My Granddad used to say that the Fathers haunt this place. Here for so long in life they can't leave it. Even in death.

Sam (*smiles politely. Gestures to the note.*)   See what you can do.

Kay *and* **Teddy** *appear, dancing a waltz in a light, the music distorted and ephemeral. They disappear.*

Sam *watches from the side. He leaves, as the music dies . . .*

Broadstairs, 1940s.

Kay *and* **Teddy** *walking home.*

Kay   I love dances. You should have worn your uniform. These military types can be so dapper and smart, I think. (*Beat.*) What was it like?

Teddy   What was what like?

Kay   The war. Being away. Fighting.

Teddy   Well. Can't say I really . . . you know, unlike some, really . . . fought. But . . .

Kay *skips forward a little, walking back to face him.*

Kay   You really are quite a good dancer, you know.

Teddy   Oh. Not really. I was just following you, Kay.

Kay *takes his hands and leads him forward as they twirl round together.* **Ted** *makes a show of resisting, before relenting. And laughing. They carry on walking.*

Kay   Back to London for you, then, tomorrow? Any word on vacant seats?

Teddy   No, not yet. It's simply a matter of waiting. Job keeps me busy. You? How's the school?

Kay   Oh fine. You know. Boys will be boys.

Teddy (*stopping*)   Well here we are, then. (*Beat.*) This is where we part.

Kay   Sorry?

Teddy (*indicating*)   This your road, isn't it?

Kay   Well. Yes, but –

Teddy   Ten minutes, you should be fine. I'm this way.

Kay   Uh. Yes, all . . . Gosh looks very muddy. Might even have to . . . (*takes off one of her shoes*) . . . get rid of these. Don't want to twist an ankle.

Teddy   Okey dokey.

Kay (*beat. Nods to herself, taking off the other heel. Beat.*)   You know, you're . . . don't – you're more than welcome to . . . see me all the way to my door, if you'd like.

Teddy   No, that's all right, thank you. My mother will probably be waiting up, anyway.

Kay   Right. Well. (*Waits expectantly. Small sigh. Kisses him on the cheek.*) Goodbye, Ted.

Teddy   Cheerio.

Kay *hobbles off one way, and* **Teddy** *strolls off the other . . .*

Sam's office.

Late. **Sam** *looking through books, lit by lamps.* **Nicholas** *enters slumping down at the other desk opposite, exclaiming dramatically.*

Nicholas   Why can't I escape!

Sam   How'd it go?

Nicholas   Well. If they *did* offer me a job I wouldn't take it because I couldn't work for a company so stupid they'd employ me based on *that* interview. (*Buries his head.*) Oh God. (*Looks at his watch.*) 7pm, Sam. Why you still here? What you reading?

Sam (*closing the book*)   Nothing.

Nicholas   Oh-oh . . . (*Off* **Sam**'s *look.*) Oh Sam. Sam-Sam. Why are you still here?

Sam   I'm just finishing up, I'll go / in a sec.

Nicholas   No, why are you *here*? I know why I'm here. I can't get a job combing old people's hair. But you. Michael has said he will recommend you for anything. I 'll . . . recommend you. (*With letters from* **Sam**'s *desk.*) Look. Just sat here. His reference. My reference. You could climb three, four rungs up the ladder. All you have to say is where. So Why Are You Still Here?

Sam   I'm not . . . I don't – I'm not sure that *this* is the ladder I want to climb. The . . . this behind the scenes stuff, I think I actually . . . I don't, that I actually might . . .

Nicholas (*laughs*)   Oh my God, I knew it. (*Indicating the adjoining office door.*) You want to be one of them, don't you?

Sam   I . . . (*shrugs*) . . . I, I don't . . . I'm not . . .

Nicholas   Hey, no listen. It's not like it wasn't obvious, even if it wasn't to you. All this . . . benevolent extracurricular stuff, like with the kids and shit. You're just, you're one of those that . . . you know. Want to. Make things better. I personally couldn't give a blind man's fuck and that's why I'm getting out. (*Beat.*) Sam. A 'politician'. (*Smiles.*) Ah, which now makes sense about the gay thing. I like your thinking.

Sam   What thing, what thinking?

Nicholas   You know. Keeping it on the down low. No parties, no . . . you know, no really 'gay' stuff.

Sam   I'm . . . I don't know what you mean. Sorry.

Nicholas   Well you know. Yes you do. Around here. On *this* ladder, it makes no difference. Does it? Diversity? Uh, 'yes.' But on that other ladder. Politics in public. Out there. (*Indicates window and 'real' world.*) You know? It's different. You can't . . . 'flaunt it'.

Sam   Flaunt it?

Nicholas   OK. I see you're getting . . . I was, I'm just trying to help. I've been in this party longer, I know what it's like.

Sam   OK, I'm – then tell me, I'm listening.

Nicholas   No, you're being passive aggressive, that's not the / same as listening.

Sam   OK, I'm sorry –

Nicholas   And now you're interrupting. (*Pause.*) Look. Just
. . . yes, of course, we have gay MPs. Humphreys. Married.
Yey. But they . . . they kind of have to wait till they're near the
top before they 'announce'. Just let your work do the talking,
and if you shine, you can be whatever you want. You like men,
women, old people, goats, hey. As long as . . . I'm saying they
don't . . . you know, they're not 'really' gay.

Sam   They're not – what? They're not –

Nicholas   They covered their tracks, is all. There are no
seedy stories, no pictures.

Sam   Why would there be seedy stories / just because
they're –

Nicholas   You might think the country has changed but it
hasn't all that. And you might think the party's changed but
you know that isn't true either. *We're* different, the new intake
are different. The young 'uns. And the front bench is different.
Hurrah. But behind them in the House and filling the hall
of the conference are party members as rooted in the Right
as they have ever been. And they will have a black, Islamic
wheelchair-bound liberal as Prime Minister before we see a
fella kissing his other half on the steps of Number 10. And
you know I'm right. (*Pause.*) Christ, I'm just saying if you want
to climb that ladder, don't make it an issue.

Sam   I didn't! You did! What are you actually telling me to
do, be less gay?

Nicholas   Is that what I said? / Is that what I said?!

Sam   I've no fucking clue what you're saying to be honest,
Nicholas!

Nicholas   Don't you speak to me like that, I am still your
fucking chief of staff! (*Pause.*) All right? Jesus H. I'm saying
keep on doing what you're doing, for Christ's sake! (*Pause.*)
Well now I'm in an even worse mood, thanks very fucking
much.

Sam (*bangs the desk. Pause.*)   I literally, I can't believe it's still . . .

Nicholas (*pause*)   Look, I didn't . . . things, they came out wrong, please don't . . . I'm – don't make this an . . . a thing. (*Pause.*) Sam? We cool?

Sam *nods his head.*

Nicholas *turns his desk lamp off – and that half of the room descends into darkness. He exits.* **Sam** *reads at his desk, lit by a lamp. His phone rings.*

Sam (*answers*)   Yes?

Ted*, on the phone, flicks on a lamp at the desk opposite, holding* **James***'s note.*

Ted   Hello?

Sam   Hello. Who's that?

Ted (*looking at the note*)   Have I got the wrong number?

Sam *slams the phone down and stares at it. He turns his light off and disappears.*

Ted's office, House of Commons, 1950s.

Ted *looks confused at his note. He hangs up and begins to redial.* **Timothy** *and* **Frank** *enter slovenly and yawning, with cups of tea.* **Ted** *puts the phone down.*

Ted   Morning, gentlemen.

Frank   Well that's the understatement of the year, Mr Heath.

Ted   Lots to do, lots to do.

Timothy   You know, I never knew there was a six o'clock in the morning, Frank.

Frank   No?

Timothy   No. I knew there was one in the evening, I've seen it. Every day. Bang on at six o'clock. But I did not know until today that there was another one. In the morning.

Ted (*handing out lists*)   Frank. Tim.

Timothy   We were out late at that Kensington fundraiser, Mr Heath.

Ted   Your government needs you, gentlemen, time to set to work, all right?

Frank   We were working last night, Mr Heath.

Ted   You were drinking last night.

Timothy   You can drink and work at the same time, that's what fundraisers are, drinking and working; working and drinking, my God I think I could sleep standing up. I do, I really do –

Frank (*reading*)   A Three-line Whip for a Transport and Denationalisation Bill. Makes me want to cry.

Timothy   The Chief could have mentioned it last night when we were necking our gins.

Ted   He didn't know himself then, this comes straight from the top.

Frank   Oh well thank you very much, Mr Churchill –

Ted   Look. (*Serious.*) We are hanging on by a thread, do you understand? We are literally under attack in there every single day. It's a barrage. And whether or not it's a Bill to regulate the size of grass or a Bill to invade Canada, the Opposition will divide the other way every single time. All it takes is a handful of our chaps to get a cold, sprain their ankle, or miss the bus, and we couldn't pass the parcel, let alone a law. So be good chaps and get to it. (*Dialling.*)

Timothy   Five past six on a Monday morning. They're gonna be angry.

Ted   They are going to be loyal! Gentlemen. (*Gesturing to their phones.*) If you please.

(*on his phone*) Ah. Mrs Turnbull. Joint Deputy Whip, sorry to bother you so early in the morning. Could I just have a small word with your husband please?

He's where?

The House of Commons? (*Winces at* **Timothy** *and* **Frank**.)

No, no. I'm sure you're right. We obviously just keep missing him. Apologies again.

Ted *puts the phone down and stares at* **Tim** *and* **Frank** *with a 'whoops' look.*

Ted   Uh, Tim, pull the card on Turnbull, would you? Stockton-on-Tees.

Tim *opens a drawer. Inside is a vast system of index cards. He flicks through them, until he finds the one he needs.*

Tim   Stockton. Got it.

Ted   Write on it. 'Marital problems' stop. Brackets 'adultery question mark'.

Frank   Well. When we bump into old tearaway Turnbull later I'm sure we won't have to worry which way he'll be voting, now will we?

Ted   The information we record is not for the purposes of blackmail, Frank, it is to foresee the potential for scandal and to nip it in the bud before it blossoms. Make sure we get him in this afternoon, will you? (*Small beat.*) And incidentally, yes, make sure he does understand that he'll be voting with us.

Frank *salutes.* **Ted** *leaves with an empty cup in search of tea.* **Frank** *whacks* **Tim** *with his list,* **Tim** *whacks* **Frank** *with his, as they slowly begin to work.*

Tim   Watch it.

Frank   You watch it. How's your head?

Tim   Like an elephant is sat on it. (*Looking at the cards.*) God, look at this. A litany of misadventures and sins. Very proud of this system, he is. I don't care what he says, he loves the gossip. (*Reading*) Adultery. Alcoholism. Sodomy. If it's wrong, I can guarantee you that somewhere there is a Tory doing it. Awh. Look at this. 'Edward Heath, Bexley'. Completely blank. That makes me sad.

Frank (*dialling*)   I'm quite proud of the few black marks against my name, Tim.

Tim   As am I, Frankie boy. As am I.

Frank   Sign of a life lived, I always think.

Tim   I entirely agree with you, Frank. I do entirely agree. But not our Teddy here.

Ted *returns as* **Frank** *speaks on the phone* **Ted** *and* **Tim** *continuing over.*

Frank (*on the phone*)   Morning, Mr Whitehouse? / How do you do sir, Frank in the Whips' Office. Just sounding our boys out regarding the Transport Bill for this evening. Patrick's adamant it's a full house for this one. (*Pause.*) Right . . . (*continuing*)

Tim   Did you have a nice weekend, then, Mr Heath? Get up to any fun?

Ted   Oh. You know. You?

Tim   Oh yes, thank you very much, yes indeed sir. Met a lovely young thing out in Southfields. A dance that my brother helped organise. Lovely she was. You?

Ted   Oh. The usual.

Tim   And what's that then?

Ted   Sorry?

Tim   What's the usual, Mr Heath?

Ted   You know. Quiet weekend.

Tim   Go out anywhere? Meet anyone? Do anything?

Ted   Are you making your way through that list all right, Timothy? Time is ticking.

Frank (*putting the phone down*)   I am. Aldershot confirmed. (*Picking up the phone.*) Right, Altringham.

Tim   I was just asking Mr Heath what he got up to over the weekend, Frank.

Frank   Oh, and what did he get up to, Tim, anything?

Tim   I'm just trying to find that out, Frank. Mr Heath? Anything?

Ted *whips a baton out of his pocket, spins round, and begins. Music.* **Tim** *and* **Frank** *freeze. As* **Ted** *waves his stick, almost like a magic wand,* **Tim** *and* **Frank** *follow, reversing out of the office, as it begins to fade into the music classroom.*

Music classroom.

Ray, **Tommo**, **Michelle**, **Adam**, **Muznah**, **Shayne** *and* **Heather** *sat in a semi-circle with notes and papers.* **Sam** *pacing, distracted . . .*

Michelle   So as Education Secretary, right, it is my recommendation that we don't change the school-leaving age to eighteen, based on the fact that school and academics and all that, yeah, is not for every pupil, and it would be better for those for which it ain't to go out and get jobs and start earning. (*Beat.*) Sir?

Sam   Uh, sorry. Right. Yes. OK. Um. So you plan to basically keep things as they are?

Michelle   Ba-sic-a-lly, yeah . . .

Sam   Thoughts, Prime Minister?

Adam   I agree. I think we're old enough to make our own choices.

Sam   But what about skills? That means these guys and girls are leaving untrained.

Michelle   Train on the job, though. Won't learn to build a building in the classroom.

Sam   What about crime. Home Secretary?

Tommo (*pause*)   Is that me?

Ray *laughs.*

Sam   Surely keeping kids busy in school or on apprenticeships gives them aspirations, gives them hope. Education plays a very important social role.

Shayne   We aren't all criminals, sir.

Michelle   Well just give 'em more stuff to do, yeah. Youth centres and stuff.

Tommo   And more police. Kick 'em in line, innit.

Sam   So you're going to spend money on police for when they *are* criminals rather than in education *before* they get the chance? OK. Gonna need to raise taxes, Chancellor.

Shayne   Fine, I'll raise taxes.

Adam   No. We're not.

Shayne   Fuck off, it's my call.

Adam   Sir, is the Chancellor really allowed to tell the Prime Minister to fuck off?

Sam   No. Well. The last one used to, but anyway. If you want to raise taxes (*sucking in air*) that means families are going to struggle more, perhaps leading to an *increase* in crime. When you've just invested all this money in extra police. How can that be?

Shayne (*sighs*)   I don't know, sir.

The school bell. They stand and begin to pack away / get ready to leave.

Sam   Well. It's something to think about for next time.

Heather   Well why don't you just tell us the right answer, sir?

Sam   There is no necessarily 'right' answer, that's the point.

Muznah   He'd raise taxes. My dad says all they're ever after is our money.

Sam   Not at all. We believe in low taxes. In fact one of the traditional divides between Labour and Tory (*indicates two separate groups that have formed as the students pack away*), Left and Right, socialism and capitalism or whatever is just that.

Ray (*running over to the other 'Tory' group*)   Fuck, I'm voting Conservative then.

Sam   Well, it just depends where you stand. Both arguments are good ones.

Muznah   How can high taxes ever be good, it ain't fair, man.

Sam   Well Labour traditionally seek higher taxes because they believe in higher spending, and that if we all chuck into the pot, then we all benefit. Problem is that means the tax burden on families is high. Conservatives believe if taxes are lower, the individual, men, women and families are able to succeed on their own terms, and if you let individuals strive and achieve, they move everyone forward with them, with a strong economy and big growth etcetera. Tories believe in less interference, Labour in managing more, yet spending more. So it's difficult. It is. I've grappled with it. This country has always grappled with it, flipping from one side to the other. In the seventies, more Left, collective responsibility; in the eighties, more Right, the individuals. And that's what you need to decide. Your party, your government. Which way. Welcome to power.

Michelle   Sir? What if you don't believe your party has chosen the right way on something, do you still have to vote with them and stuff?

Sam   It's expected you will, yes. There's something called a Whips' Office to check you do.

Michelle   But you just said you believed in individual choice. How is that fair?

Sam (*beat*)   I don't know.

Shayne   Bye, sir!

Ray   'Bye sir'! Gay. (*Feeling **Adam**'s arse.*)

Adam   Oy! The fuck you doing?! Why / you always doing that?

Sam   Hey! OK, everyone else, off you go. Ray. Wait here.

Ray   What? Fucking hell.

*The others leave. **Sam** is packing away his things.*

Sam   What's your issue with Adam; why do you go around calling him gay? Everyone gay?

Ray Cos it's funny?

Sam Well, when you get a little older you'll realise sexual preference, just like race, isn't something you should be insulted with.

Ray I know that, yeah, it's just . . . when you say 'gay' you ain't saying, like '*gay*' gay, you're just saying, like . . . 'Uh, that's gay'. As in. A bit shit.

Sam Some of the people you call gay might actually be gay and you're not helping them.

Ray Yeah, I'm encouraging them to come out, innit. Why you so bothered? Are you gay, sir? (*Pause.*) Are you? (*Pause. Smiles.*) I won't tell anyone.

Sam I'll see you next week Ray.

Sam's *office.*

Evening. **Sam** *is at his desk.* **James** *stands facing him.*

Sam I'm sorry.

James I've been down there twenty minutes.

Sam Time just slipped / away from me, I –

James Like I was down there twenty minutes on Monday. Getting a bit silly, now, isn't it?

Sam I know, I'm not . . . it isn't / that I –

James You do know people, don't you? You have interacted with people before? Socially. You've not been . . . I don't know, in a cave somewhere for twenty years. You've had, do have, friends. Relationships. Boyfriends? You are gay, aren't you Sam?

Sam I've just been very . . . I'm not – and someone . . . said / something to me that –

James Only I know a lot of gay people, in here, and outside, and what I see in them is pride and acceptance, I don't see that in you. I see awkwardness and I see shame.

Sam And what have I got to be ashamed about?

James (*rolling himself a fag with tobacco and a Rizla*)   You tell me.

Sam   You can't smoke that in here.

James   I know. I'm just / getting it ready.

Sam   Don't want to break the law now, do you? Your law.

James   Not my / law.

Sam   Ah, the great party of the working class, my God.

James   What are you doing? What's this now? Are we arguing? Having a / political –?

Sam   The needs and aspirations of the everyday man.

James   Well, you know. It's the closest thing we've got. Just like yours is the closest thing the wealthy and elite have got. We all have to make do. (*Resisting the temptation to bite back. Beat while rolling.*) You are an enigma, Sam. Your family are working class, aren't they?

Sam   Just because they're northern doesn't mean they're working class.

James   Absolutely, no of course. But your home town, its background. Manufacture, industry, all that. Industries and communities that your lot destroyed when last in power; what do your family and / neighbours think about your choice of –

Sam   No, I agree, my home town *is* no longer full of factories and mines and quarries and mills, it is now full of business parks, and retailers, and offices –

James   Well, gain a business park, lose a community. It's all about balance.

Sam   Ah, yes, those mythical communities you like to pretend existed. Where nobody locked their doors and everyone knew their neighbours –

James   No they did exist. (They did.) Still do. Despite the best efforts of you and yours. Is it a coincidence, I often wonder, that in the Labour heartlands, people still say hello to one another in the street /, are polite, when in the . . .

richer, Tory south, they hide in gated communities with alarm systems and never –

Sam   Wow, and the award for Generalisation Of The Year goes to? Yes, all those things we took away, working in dangerous industries, and replaced them with, what, good nine to five jobs, and two cars on the drive, and holidays abroad / and a Sky digibox –

James   Ah yes. Money. 'The most important thing.' (*Smiles. Pause.*) Shall I try again? In a few days? Just to see 'where you're at'? One last time?

Sam *shrugs.* **James** *shrugs back. Pause. He approaches* **Sam***, who moves back away from him, until his back hits the adjoining office door.* **James** *is close* . . .

James   What are you so scared of, Sam? I'm not scary. What is it . . . ?

He moves in for a kiss. **Sam** *pushes past him and leaves.*

Sam   Wait, sorry I . . . just need a . . . glass of . . . (*Exit.*)

James *sighs. Pause. The door to the adjoining office opens, as* **Nicholas** *pops his head round to check the coast is clear. Seeing nothing, he opens the door fully out, hiding* **James** *behind it. He enters, closing the door to reveal* **James***.*

Nicholas   Oh. Hi.

James   Hi. You're . . . ?

Nicholas   Nicholas. You're . . . in my office.

James   You've been next door? In there?

Nicholas   Working late. You know.

Sam *comes back in.*

Sam   So, listen, uh . . . let's – (*Sees* **Nicholas***.*) Hi.

Nicholas   Hello, Sam.

Sam   This is James. He works over at, um . . . have you – you're popping in or . . . ?

James   No, he was –

Nicholas   Yes. Yes, I've just popped in now. Just arrived.

James   Well, I was just heading off. So. (*Pause.*) Bye.

James *exits. Silence.*

Sam   I'll be heading off as well then, Nick. See you tomorrow. (*Exiting.*)

Nicholas   Bye bye now.

Ted *appears at the piano, playing.* **Mrs Heath** *is in a chair, a blanket over her, eyes closed.* **Sam** *watches . . .*

Ted *looks at his mother and stops playing. Long pause. He reaches his hand over and touches hers. He flinches back. She doesn't move. He reaches out and touches her again, holding her wrist. Nothing.* **Ted** *turns back to the piano. Beat. He plays.*

Sam's office.

Nicholas *is on the phone as* **Sam** *enters, a bit annoyed* **Nicholas** *is in the office. He dumps his things on his desk and sits, working instantly.*

Nicholas   Very well, thank you, very well indeed. I got a message to call back.

Really? Well that's . . . oh my God, wow, I'm . . . I'm delighted, thank you so much, I don't know what to say. Huh . . .

Will do, no problem. OK. Thank you. Talk to you soon. Bye.

He puts the phone down and leaps up, punches the air.

Nicholas   Whoow! Yeah! Get in! Come on! You will never guess what Sammy-boy. I have been put on the candidate list to be (*drum roll*) . . . bam bam bah! A Conservative councillor for Wandsworth. Courtesy of the local Putney Association. Booyakasha!

Sam   You . . . when . . . you applied to be a councillor? Why didn't you tell me?

Nicholas   Well, case I didn't get it.

Sam   I thought that kind of thing didn't . . . that you didn't care / about . . .

Nicholas   Yeah, well. You know, these councillors, great offers and shit, jobs, all that. What with their connections. Whoow! And, ey, as a fellow Wandsworth resident, I trust I have your vote.

Sits. Spins. Swivels. Laughs. Looks at **Sam***, and sighs contentedly.*

Nicholas   Now. I know something that I know you don't know that I know about you.

Sam   What?

Nicholas   You know the other night. In here. When you came in. And I was with that boy. I hadn't just arrived. I'd been in Michael Two's office. Working late. So I know he hadn't just 'swung by'. Do you see? (*Pause.*) Who does your boyfriend work for? He's not one of ours.

Sam   Well now I'm confused. For you see I do not have a boyfriend, so I cannot tell you for whom he works, do you see?

Nicholas   Hmm. ('Do you see'.) Well, I knew you batted for the other side, Sam. I just didn't know you were batting *with* the other team. If I find out that you've been sneaking signals over the top –

Sam   How dare you . . . !

Nicholas (*bangs the desk*)   Do not interrupt me and don't presume to tell me / what I –

Sam (*standing, overlapping*)   I won't stay to listen to this.

Nicholas   – dare or dare not say. (*Standing.*) Oh yes you fucking will, sit down.

Sam   How dare you –

Nicholas   There's Those Words Again. I / won't tell anyone but –

Sam   There's no rules saying you can't have . . . between – and / anyway I'm not fucking –

Nicholas   But I will tell you this. You're on a timer with me now, boyo. So I don't want any fuss, any accusations about things you think I may or may not have said during our little chat the other day. I don't want any threats; I basically just don't want you around. We don't like each other. Sam. Do we? If we're honest? Or at least I don't think you like me and I can't stand people who don't like me. You've got your references. Get a position somewhere else. And leave. Make it soon, make it quiet, but make it quick. (*Pause.*) Would you like me to go over anything?

Sam   . . . no . . .

Nicholas (*smiles, rubbing his hair, over-friendly*)   Then get outta here. You big queen.

Long pause, **Nicholas** *holding and smiling at* **Sam**. **Nina** *enters and they break.*

Nicholas   Nina, hey, guess what? Sam's decided he's moving on.

Nina   Oh. Cool. So you've finally chosen where you wanna go?

Nicholas   Catch you lovers later. (*Exits.*)

Nina (*pause*)   You all right?

Sam *nods, unconvincingly.*

Nina   You sure?

The phone rings. **Sam** *answers.* **Ted** *appears, on the phone, holding the note.*

Sam   Hello?

Ted   Hello? Who's this?

Sam *slams the phone down and pushes away from the desk.* **Ted** *disappears.*

Sam   Did you hear that?!

Nina   What?

Sam   That phone! Did it ring?

Nina   Yes! Sam, what's wrong, are you OK?

Sam (*sitting. Pause. Tries to laugh, unconvincingly. Pause.*)   Nina. What . . . what do people think of . . . am I . . . ? Of me. What do . . . ?

Nina   Right now, I'm not sure. (*Smiles.*) Kidding.

Sam   No, but . . . am I – do people. Am I someone that it's. Quite hard to like . . .

Nina   Sam, of course not. No . . .

Sam   (God.) Why these? Ey? This lot. This side of the fence. Why did you pick these?

Nina   Blue brings out my eyes. (*Smiles. Beat.*) I dunno. I remember at uni, sharing a house. We'd have arguments about the washing up. I would just do mine. Another housemate would sometimes do other people's. Her point being if everyone chipped in, it's nicer. And fairer. I thought if everyone just did their own, it would always get done. I think that's when I knew. Or started to.

Sam (*pause. Half-smile. Nods. Stands.*)   I . . . I have to . . . get to class . . .

Sam *saunters out.* **Nina** *follows.*

Hampstead Heath, 1950s. A bright summer's day.

Kay *is sat on one of two swings hanging from a tree.* **Ted** *stands. Watching her.*

Kay   You used to push me for hours at a time. Too high. I thought I'd go over the top.

Ted (*smiles*)   Hello, Kay.

Kay   Hello Ted. It's been a long time. I'm . . . awfully sorry about your mother.

Ted   Thank you for your card.

Kay   I meant to telephone but . . . life takes up so much time these days. Still, thanks for *your* call. I just adore Hampstead Heath in the summer. You come here often?

Ted   Um. Now and again, yes.

Kay   You must struggle to find the time. I hear you're doing terribly well.

Ted   They're considering me as a replacement for Sir Henry as full Deputy Whip.

Kay   Wow. Well, Teddy, that's wonderful. You really are / on the rise –

Ted   Only 'considering', though. They have . . . there are concerns.

Kay   Concerns, surely not. What concerns?

Ted   There are . . . rumours. (Not completely unsub –) . . . Problem, uh . . . (*laughs, semi-tragically*), problem is, the rumours are all I have. In a void that other people fill with . . . I don't know what other people fill it with. 'A private life', I suppose. If the rumours disappears there's just a, a hole where . . .

Kay   Ted, are you all right?

Ted   I miss her. So much. I . . . have a, a . . . *pain* . . . here. And I need it to go. I need it to be . . . replaced. You wouldn't . . . believe some of the things I've been . . . trying to –

Kay (*stands*)   Oh Ted . . .

Ted *stumbles back with his hands up, not wanting to be touched.* **Kay** *stops. He slumps down on the ground.*

Kay   Talk to me, Ted. Please. Why did you . . . is there a reason you got back in touch?

Ted   A reason? (A reason . . . ah yes.) And the orchestra cease playing, the hall goes quiet, and all assembled are awaiting my cadenza. If you'll allow me a moment to prepare. (*He shifts. Looks at the earth beneath him.*) London clay, Hampstead Heath. Only really to be found in the south, you know. Tough stuff. Contains some pretty amazing fossils by all accounts, and crystals too, if one had only the inclination to dig. (*Pause. Chuckles, tragically.*) 'Heath.' Rambling. Desolate. Low-level plant life. Shrubbery and weeds. Can only grow so high, before its inferior nature causes it to be surpassed by those . . . stronger. A waste land. A waste space, waste *of* space, just . . . (*Trails.*) I always thought if I was ever going to marry, Kay, then it would be you. (*Short pause.*) If I ever was, that is. But alas . . . that boat has left the harbour. And I'm characteristically left standing alone on the dock.

Kay   A girl can only wait so long. Teddy.

Ted (*nods*)   How is Richard?

Kay   He's fine. Thank you. We're both happy. And fine.

Ted   I'm sorry, Kay. I don't know what I was thinking.

Kay   Do you remember that Summer ball, Ted? I was going to kiss you that night. Only you never found out because you said goodbye and . . . Not out of . . . it was simply that . . . (*sighs*) Truth is, Ted, you're not like other people. In that you don't need Other People. Not the way other people do. (*Beat.*) We all make sacrifices. You just have to make sure they're worth it.

Ted   I still have that photograph. By my bed. To remember you.

Kay   I think the fact that you need a photograph, Ted . . . I think, speaks volumes. (*Smiles warmly.*) Now stop sitting there all glum, and come play with me on the swings.

Beat. **Ted** *saunters over to the empty swing and sits. They start to swing together.*

Music classroom.

Shayne, **Tommo**, **Heather** *and* **Muznah** *are dancing around to music from the CD player, while* **Adam**, **Ray** *and* **Michelle** *sit scribbling notes –* **Ray** *standing to contribute his own moves occasionally.* **Sam** *enters.* **Tommo** *presses stop.*

Tommo   Oh-oh. That's detention for you, sir.

Sam   Sorry, I'm . . . so sorry for being late, I got held up, and . . .

Michelle   We've nearly finished our Green Paper, sir.

Tommo *turns the music on again and dances, turning it off when* **Sam** *shouts.*

Sam   Cool. Uh, let me take a . . . (*To* **Shayne**.) Could you . . . turn that off, please?!

Tommo   Why, we've done our paper, gotta get back into the music groove, you get me?

Michelle   This is more important, Tommo. Cut it out.

Tommo   Why, I ain't never gonna be a proper politician like this guy, am I?

Sam   I'm not a proper politician.

Michelle   Don't you wanna be though sir?

Sam   No, I . . . I don't know what I . . . (*Beat.*) You know, at your age . . . yours isn't the only age where you're going to find you have to make decisions about your life, your future. Your future isn't just something you decide upon when you're young and then one day, bam, it starts. It, it's something that is constantly . . . readdressed.

Shayne   You mean you don't know what you want to be when you grow up? (*Laughs.*)

Sam (*shrugs*)   No. I don't.

The bell rings. The students begin to leave.

Sam   OK. Uh . . . listen, sorry I was / late but I'm, I'm glad you got some work done.

Shayne   Fucking hell, that was a long lesson. Thanks sir.

Sam   I'll look over this and . . . and feedback as soon as . . .

The student all yell 'bye' as they exit, except **Michelle** *and* **Ray**, *who stays seated.*

Michelle (*with the 'Paper'*)   Will it make any difference though, sir? Does anything ever?

Sam   Yes, of . . . everything . . . (*Pause.*) I know it feels like things don't change or that, that politics doesn't . . . (*Pause.*) No one ever wants to make things worse, politicians don't want . . . we all just disagree on *how*. And amongst all the bad news that only ever gets . . . amongst the big stuff, there are a hundred little things that happen every . . . (*Beat.*) Like, £370 million set aside, for example, why? War? Speed cameras? No, to be spent giving carers who look after disabled relatives A Day Off. Six hundred thousand stair gates are to be bought and given to poor families in order to stop their children from falling down the stairs. You won't hear that. And there's no agenda there, it's just . . . because it's a Good Thing To Do. I know that there is shit, my God. Terrible, inexcusable things that have to be sorted out, that are Wrong. But I *have* to believe that every day, in little ways . . . I have to believe that things can get better. That tomorrow will be better than today.

Michelle   Maybe you should become Prime Minister, sir. (*Beat.*) Maybe I should . . .

Sam (*smiles*)   You would be an excellent Prime Minister, Michelle.

Michelle *smiles. And exits.* **Sam** *paces, fraught, seemingly forgetting* **Ray**.

Ray   Can I ask you sumfin? Do you hide that you're gay 'cause you're in politics and that?

Sam   I never said I was gay.

Ray   You never said you weren't.

Sam   Well. Um . . . in certain quarters of life, erm . . . tolerance advances slower. Not long ago, teachers couldn't be gay. I'm sure there's perhaps stigma still in, in industry, manufacture. The military, in . . .

Ray   And, like, some families, and that. My family, they're like, Jamaican and well religious, into traditions and all that. My mum would go skitz, bruv. If you get me.

Ray *reaches out and rests his hand on* **Sam***'s.* **Sam** *looks at it.*

Ray   So. Like. Despite what I do. And say. I'm basically asking if you is all right. I'm asking if you're OK. Because what I'm saying is I Get You. Yeah?

Sam *begins to tremble, breaking down as he stares at* **Ray***'s hand. Overcome.* **Ray** *puts his hand on* **Sam***'s face.* **Sam** *closes his eyes. Lost. He stands –*

Sam (*exiting*)   Um. Thank-thank you for your work today. Ray. I'm sorry I was late.

Ray   You weren't late, man. Far as I'm concerned, you came right on time.

Sam's office.

Sam *and* **James**.

James   Well?

Pause. **Sam** *shakes his head. Struggling . . .*

James   OK. I won't bother you again. I'm sorry things aren't easier for you.

Sam   And why do you find everything so pissing easy?! (Fuck.) I mean us lot, first Lady Prime Minister, shit, maybe even the first gay Prime Minister, / who knows, so –

James   I'm sure you're right about absolutely everything but I'm leaving, Sam, I'm –

Sam   And your guy didn't even vote to repeal Section 28, / he didn't –

James   We didn't make the law; don't take credit for repealing a law that *you* made. *Your* guy didn't / vote to repeal it.

Sam   Our guy voted *for* the equal age of consent, civil partnerships. When not under a three-line whip he's consistently / voted for equal rights, whereas dear Prime Minister, your leader –

James   Civil partnerships would not have happened under any government except Labour and you know that's true. / I'll stand back and let you criticise us on anything –

Sam   He didn't vote for any of those things, any of them! / Missed all those votes. Why?

James   You can criticise our record on anything, but the one thing, the One Thing you Cannot criticise us on is this!

Sam   We had Torch, we have LGBTory, / senior gay party members, cabinet ministers –

James   What are you doing? What are you hiding behind this – Exactly, Sam, exactly! So who the fuck is stopping you from being happy? Hmm?

The phone rings. **Sam** *and* **James** *stare at each other.*

James   You should answer that. I'll see you, Sam.

James *exits. Beat.* **Sam** *answers the phone. A light on the opposite desk flickers on to reveal* **Ted***, on the phone. They both sound exhausted.*

Sam   Hello?

Ted   Hello?

Sam (*beat, smiles tragically, shakes his head*)   Hello.

Ted (*looking at his note*)   My apologies, I've been requested to get in touch. Uh . . .

Sam   Where are you, I've . . . I've been trying to find you but I can't, I can't . . . *find* you, I . . .

Ted   Well. I'm just . . . I'm here. (*Pause.*) Is there something I can help you with, or . . . ?

Sam   I mean, you're, you're very hard to, to . . . *pin* – to . . . I mean I'm not even sure what I'm . . . what are you – what were you looking for?

Ted   Uh. I don't think I under . . . (*Beat.*) Well there was just an, an emptiness. That appeared. A few, a couple of . . . and I suppose I thought the right, the best, thing to do was try and fill it. With something. But we all have holes. Just a case of −

Sam   Can I ask you . . . what made you choose? When you first began. Why these?

Ted   Um. In truth, I don't think you pick it. I think it picks you −

Sam   Because I can see, I can see its potential for the . . . for it to *work*, and I, I wanna be a part of that. I want to make it work. But sometimes . . . sometimes. Just when you think they've moved on . . . when they're on the verge of being . . .

Ted   Well. A friend of mine. Quite the orator. He once said . . . that we have defended ourselves against our enemies. But who will save us from ourselves? So. Why don't you tell me? What made you 'pick a side'?

Sam   Um. I suppose . . . (*sighs*) . . . I just remember, even as a, as a young . . . man, not even man, just a boy . . . I remember even as a boy feeling so different, and strange, and alone and I suppose . . . that when nothing makes sense to you, and you're not sure who you are . . . the idea of − the strength of the person that stands alone, carves their own path, doesn't have to rely on any group or any community or any one − of it not being who you are or where you're from but What You Do, it was . . . I suppose it was like a language I could finally speak.

Ted (*nods*)   Well. Of all the things you should take from this lot, then, I think you should hold on to that. If nothing else makes sense, if everything else just seems like a mess . . . 'it's not who you are it's what you do'. You should hold on to that.

Sam (*pause*)   Thank you. (*Beat.*) I'm sorry, I have to − I have another call to make. I −

Ted   Yes. Of course. Well. (*Smiles.*) Lots to do, lots to do. Goodbye.

They both put the phone down and disappear. **Sam** *picks up his phone and dials.*

Sam   Hi, it's Sam, Michael Daikin's office, a guy called James is about to pass through the lobby, tall, blond hair, could you . . . could you ask him to wait there for just a second? And I'll be right down. Tell him I promise.

Sam's office.

Sam *stands facing* **Nicholas**, *alone moments before* **Nina** *enters.*

Sam   Can I have a word? Please?

Nicholas   Of course you can, Sam-u-el. Any time.

Nina (*entering*)   Morning, Nick. I've got two / messages for you.

Sam   A proper word. A formal one. It's about the little chat we had.

Nicholas   Yes, of course. Can I just have one minute with Nina, first, and then I'll be right with you.

Pause. **Sam** *exits, passing by* **Robbie** *as he enters.*

Nina   What's going on?

Nicholas (*hushed*)   Right. Here's the – ah, Rob. Perfect. Listen. Um. Listen. You know . . . Sam, I think, is trying to . . . how can I say this, um . . . forward his own agenda. Basically he's going, I think he's going to make a formal complaint. About us.

Nina   About us? What for? Who to?

Nicholas   I don't know, this has come from someone who told me in confidence what Sam told them, which is that he's essentially going to climb on top of us to get where he wants by grinding his axe on the whole 'I'm gay, you're prejudiced' bit.

Nina   What? No, that's bullshit?

Nicholas   I'm telling you. Me, you, Michael One, Two. Why would I lie? So if you wouldn't mind standing in on this little chat, just so . . . you know, a united front –

Nina   Erm. OK. Jesus, shouldn't we get Michael Two in, just to –?

Nicholas   No, let's . . . see what he's got to –

Sam *re-enters.*

Nicholas (*taking post-its off* **Nina**)   Thank you, Nina. Thank you, thank you. So. Sam?

Sam   Yes, I'd just like a minute please.

Nicholas   Sure. Shoot.

Sam   Alone.

Nicholas   No.

Sam   No?

Nicholas   No. Nein. Nay. C'est impossible. You see, if you're planning on making any formal statements regarding your position here, I feel like I need to have someone else in the room. Standard protocol, you know. Just in case you were about to say something of great weight. In case the whole process of your transfer gets held up while whatever you're about to say is investigated. It might temporarily put a stop on your transit, is what I'm saying. So. In light of that, what is it you would like to discuss with me today, Sam?

Sam (*pause*)   Um . . .

Nicholas   Sam? Anything?

Sam (*pause*)   The, um . . . (*Beat.*) I think we should, uh . . . en-enforce an office policy of turning our machines off. Not just on standby. At lunch. And meetings, to set an example. You know? I think that would be a good idea . . .

Nicholas (*smiles. Points at him.*)   For you, Samuel? Anything. (*Pause.*) Thanks, guys. If that's everything –

Sam   Oh, and there was a message for you from the selection committee. Your candidacy for local councillor is under review.

Nicholas (*laughs*)   What?

Sam   On the grounds of prejudice and discrimination towards a fellow colleague.

Nina   Sam, what are you doing? Is this about all of us?

Sam   No, just him. Rumour has it that he, as my line manager, advised me to seek work in another department on the grounds that I was 'a big queen'.

Nina   What?

Nicholas   He's lying. Thanks, Sam, all right. Who's 'reviewing my candidacy'?

Sam   The deputy fundraising and members chairman for the Putney Association.

Nicholas   Well they don't know what it was we spoke about do they, you fuck. It's just your word against mine, because they weren't there.

Sam   Yes they were.

Nicholas   How where they?

Sam   Because I was there.

Nicholas   And?

Sam (*unfolding a letter*)   And I'm the new deputy fundraising and members chairman for the Putney Association.

Pause. **Nicholas** *takes the letter and reads.*

Sam   You were right, Nick, with your reference I was able to get any job I wanted. Thanks for that.

Nicholas . . .

Sam   Course, they thought I was grossly over-qualified but with the incumbent taking immediate leave and what with the selection for new councillors currently in motion they thought I'd better start straight away. My first job is to assess the suitability of candidates. I'm fine on three of them, there's just a black mark against one. A claim of misconduct, doesn't look good. (*At* **Nina** *and* **Robbie**.) Of course it will have to be qualified by other colleagues.

Nicholas (*beat. Claps his hands.*)   Well bully for you, Miss Fucking Marple.

Nina   Nicholas?

Nicholas   I didn't do anything, OK Nina?! He's making it up! Come on. Rob mate, you're not going to go along with this are you, he's lying.

Robbie   I dunno. You are the guy that asked what my sexuality was on my first morning.

Nicholas   . . . (*gasps in disbelief*) . . . W-what? That was just . . . (*Looks at* **Nina**.)

Nina   And I just think you're a bit of a cunt.

Nicholas (*pause. Looks around. Laughs. Stops.*)   Sam, come . . . Sammy . . .

Sam *doesn't flinch. Silence.* **Nicholas** *nods his head. Grabs his stuff. Pause.*

Nicholas   Just remember. That I said those things . . . because I wanted to help you, Sam. Because I wanted you to do well. Please at least remember that . . .

Nicholas *leaves. Silence.* **Nina** *and* **Robbie** *break it, laughing.*

Nina   Shit the bed, Sam! I can't believe that. And what's this new job, deputy members −?

Sam   Oh, it doesn't matter, I'm quitting soon.

Robbie   You're what?

Sam   Yeah, just wanted to make sure the right people made it onto the shortlist, then . . .

Nina   And then what? (*Excited.*) You staying here?

Sam   Nah, I think it probably is time to move somewhere different, you know.

Robbie   I hear the Prime Minister's position might be vacant soon. You could do that.

Sam (*laughs*)   Well. I'd need to be an MP first.

Ted *appears, standing at his desk with the card drawer open.* **Ted** *and* **Frank** *nearby, watching.* **Ted** *takes out one of the cards . . .*

Nina   Well become an MP then, idiot. You'd be ace.

Sam   Mmmdunno. You kind of need more experience first. Like . . . I don't . . . (*Smiles knowingly.*) A local councillor?

Nina   For Wandsworth?!

Sam   Ah-ah-ah. Cards close to your chest in this game, Neen. (*Looks over to* **Ted**.) Cards close to your chest . . .

Ted *looks at* **Sam***. He smiles, and rips the card, tossing it into the air and exiting with* **Tim** *and* **Frank** *as music grows . . .*

Ray, **Tommo**, **Michelle**, **Adam**, **Muznah**, **Shayne** *and* **Heather** *enter, dancing over to* **Sam** *and tossing their own cards into the air.*

Lights fade down.

The Butterfly Club

Sarah May

About the Author

Sarah May has collaborated extensively with The Mayhem Company, which has been devising and staging boundary-breaking productions since 2001 and whose core members are young non-professional actors living and working in London. Previous work for the theatre includes urban fairytale *Hamelyn Heights* (Young Vic Studio); *100° Fahrenheit* (Southwark Playhouse), a study of corruption in the black religious community; *Deluxe* (Southwark Playhouse) about a fatal shooting in a south London school; and *See You Tomorrow* (Southwark Playhouse), the company's response to a former member's decision to join the British Army and serve in Iraq. '*Real Life Sex Makes Baby*' (Royal Festival Hall, 2009) was written to mark SE1 United's hosting The Mayhem Company at Royal Festival Hall, Southbank Centre, and her latest collaboration with The Mayhem Company, '*Elephant 21*', about the regeneration of London's Elephant and Castle, was performed in July 2010 at Unit 215, Elephant and Castle Shopping Centre. You can find out more about Sarah's work with The Mayhem Company at www.themayhemcompany. net. Sarah has also written the following works of fiction: *The Nudist Colony* (Chatto & Windus, 1999), *Spanish City* (Chatto & Windus, 2002); *The Internationals* (Chatto & Windus, 2003) and the *Rise and Fall* trilogy (HarperCollins): *The Queen of Suburbia* (2006), *A Domestic Diva* (2008) and *The Wonder Girls* (2009).

About the Play

By the time I started work on *The Butterfly Club* in July 2008 twenty-two young people had committed suicide in and around the Bridgend area of South Wales. Labelled 'the suicide capital of Britain' (*Guardian*), the deaths themselves actually took place across the 110-mile-square borough, the majority occurring on the fringes and outskirts of the town itself. The words 'fringes' and 'outskirts' are important – not only in a geographical context, but an emotional one as well – because the overriding image I had was of people on the outside, looking in.

At the time homelessness and unemployment figures were high in the Bridgend area and one in five people of working age had no qualifications, compared with a national average of one in seven. Yet the media insisted on heavy usage of the words 'cult' and 'internet', promoting the internet itself as the harbinger of endemic evil while absolving society of any sort of responsibility for the deaths. In reaction to this irreverent and sensationalist reporting, I wanted to talk about the effects of history and inheritance, in particular inherited 'hopelessness'. How can you talk about children without talking about their parents? The young people killing themselves were the children of a generation who had themselves been economically and socially disinherited by a country that had no further need of their skills. What kind of parenting is an adult already functioning outside of evolution capable of? And if self-sufficiency cannot be realised practically because there are no employment opportunities what sort of emotional self-sufficiency can be realised? *The Butterfly Club* is, I hope, an ultimately life-affirming exploration of the consequences of a generation of children brought up by adults who cannot conceive of any sort of future.

Producing the Play

The Butterfly Club was produced by The Mayhem Company in the autumn of 2008 and performed with long-time host, Southwark Playhouse, London. The play has a cast of six young people, seven adults and three children. We cast the play with actors that matched the age of the roles, and staged it in traverse, which had a powerful effect on both actors and audience members, endorsing the play's central themes of responsibility and complicity.

As a company you have to be aware of the worlds that co-exist within the play: female and male, children and parents, home and society, childhood and adulthood and real and imagined – the butterfly club. Each of these worlds has specific rules that have to be understood before they can be broken, and these were clearly and simply defined in our production – a white three-piece suite set on a white floor was used in each home with a slight variation for each family. The difference between the public and private can be easily defined with basic yet effective lighting, and the snow at the end of the play represents an important consolidation of these two different worlds in a way that we found was ultimately cathartic for the audience.

Remember each of the eleven scenes has a clear centre that relates to the central scene of the play, scene six, which asks the fundamental question: where are the adults in the world?

The language veers between the authentic and the artificial as characters struggle to define and articulate the implications of responsibility, ultimately empowering themselves by giving the words they use back their meaning.

The initial production was made possible by the JJ Charitable Foundation, Youth Opportunity Fund and the Jerwood Space.

Characters

Angela, *Caitlin's mother*
Caitlin, *seventeen*
Ben, *seventeen*
Alex, *eight, Ben's brother*
Michelle, *Ben's mother and Samaritans volunteer*
Paul, *Ben's father*
Kate, *Cass's mother*
Cass, *eighteen*
Doug, *Cass's grandfather*
Tony, *Lauren's father*
Lauren, *seventeen*
Dante, *sixteen*
Tasha, *sixteen*
Ruth, *a Samaritans volunteer*

Scene One

A London suburb.

A white three-piece suite and coffee table are on stage. There is also a Christmas tree – undecorated apart from some lights, which are switched on.

Enter **Angela** *dressed in a Sainsbury's cashier's outfit. She's in a hurry and trying to put a pair of earrings on.*

Angela (*calling out*)   Caitlin! (*Louder.*) Caitlin? Have you seen my scarf anywhere? The yellow one? (*Yelling*) Caitlin!

Caitlin (*yelling back*)   What?

Angela   I said – I'm looking for my scarf – my yellow scarf. Have you seen it anywhere?

Caitlin (*off*)   No idea.

Angela   You should be thinking about leaving for college.

Silence.

She gives up and starts to exit.

D'you want a lift? Caitlin?

Caitlin (*off*)   I'm fine.

Angela   You're sure?

Caitlin (*off*)   I'm fine.

Angela (*beat*)   OK, well – see you around six. (*She waits, but there's no response.*)

Exit **Angela**.

Enter **Caitlin** *dressed in a white beautician's training outfit, carrying her make-up bag. She stands in front of the mirror and works on her eyelashes and lips then stares at herself.*

Caitlin   Who you looking at, bitch? You ugly, ugly bitch. And you're stupid – you're stupid as well. (*Applies another layer of lipstick to her mouth.*) Think that's going to make any difference? (*She rifles, distracted, through her make-up bag, pulls out a packet and puts some pills in her mouth, watching herself all the time in the mirror. Putting on an officious accent.*) Call that make-up, Caitlin? Somebody with no arms could have done better. (*She's separating her eyelashes as her mobile starts ringing and as she opens her bag,* **Angela**'s *yellow scarf is temporarily visible. She contemplates the mobile, deciding whether or not to take the call.*)

Caitlin   Ben? That you, Ben, you creepy shit – breathing at me? You know, mobile-phone companies charge premium rates for heavy breathing. I've got nothing to say to you. Anyway – *you* phoned *me* so why should I do all the work? (*Beat.*) Can't think of nothing? (*Beat.*) So why d'you phone?

She puts the phone back in her bag and pulls out the yellow scarf, wrapping it carefully round her neck. To her reflection.

Blah – blah – blah – blah – blah. (*Beat.*) Blah. (*She smiles suddenly at herself and waves.*) Ta-ta.

While **Caitlin**'s *on the phone a forest starts to grow.*

By the time the call's ended, she's surrounded by trees – and it's raining. She uses the phone to film the forest, sky and her feet, walking, as she starts to move slowly among the trees.

Rain. (*Beat.*) All it ever does.

She makes her way towards the Pavilion door and hesitates.

Recognise it?

She pushes it open and goes in.

Exit **Caitlin**.

The rain continues.

Caitlin's *mobile starts ringing inside the Pavilion.*

It isn't answered.

Silence. The forest disappears.

Scene Two

Enter **Ben**, *wearing black and carrying a pad of paper. He sits on the sofa and starts to bang out a quiet, steady rhythm on the coffee table.*

Ben   Now this is a story straight and true –
Don't expect me to say sorry cause this shit ain't new –

He continues to beat out the rhythm.

You're spending all your money on the lottery –
When the economy's as fucked as Pete Doherty –

Breaks off to write this down on the pad, then starts the rhythm up again.

When the economy's as fucked as Pete Doherty –

Enter **Alex**, *wearing a* Dr Who *cyborg mask, holding a light sabre and singing the theme tune from* Star Wars. *He jumps onto the sofa.*

Ben   Alex!

Alex *ignores him and continues to sing the* Star Wars *theme while fighting an invisible enemy.*

Ben (*yelling*)   Alex!

Enter **Michelle**.

Michelle   What's going on here?

Ben   Him – making noise. Me – trying to think.

Michelle   Alex –

Alex   I can't help it – just trying to protect myself. (*Thrusting with the light sabre.*) Aah – aaaahhhh – he got me.

Michelle   Alex – get off the sofa. Way you're going on there that piece of furniture's got the life expectancy of a pygmy in the Congo.

Alex   What's a pygmy?

Ben   Little person.

Alex   How little?

Ben   Little as you.

Alex   I'm not little.

Ben   OK, imagine being as little as you at fifty.

Alex   I'm not little.

Ben   But if you were fifty –

Alex   Fifty's never.

Ben   What are you meant to be anyway?

Alex   I used to be human, but I was turned into a cyborg. It's OK – apart from the times when I remember being human. That sends me mad.

Ben   Are cyborgs from *Stars Wars*?

Alex   *Star Wars*? You know nothing, man. They're from *Doctor Who*.

Ben   So why you singing the *Star Wars* music?

Alex   Don't know.

Ben   And carrying a light sabre?

Alex   I got it for my birthday.

Ben   But cyborgs don't carry light sabres.

Alex   I'm not a cyborg, I'm Alex. (*Beat.*) Alex. I used to be Alex. Aaaahhhh. I'm going mad. (*Starts running round the room, crashing into furniture.*)

Michelle (*to* **Ben**)   What you doing here anyway – you should be at work. New initiative by Tesco, is it? Dressing their cashiers in black? Or did you get a new job you never told me about?

Alex   He's Darth Vader.

Ben   I changed my shift.

Michelle   Why you do that?

Ben   Cause I'm going to the funeral.

Michelle   We never talked about you going to that girl's funeral.

Ben   What's there to talk about?

Michelle   We never talked about you going to the funeral.

Ben   Everybody's going.

Michelle   Who's everybody?

Ben   You want the names? OK there's me, Lauren, Cass –

Michelle   You get an invite?

Ben   Nobody got an invite. It's happening. We're going.

Michelle   You didn't even know her.

Ben   I knew her.

Alex   Can we do the tree now? You said we were going to do the tree. (*Goes through the box of Christmas decorations.*) I got the angel – Mum? The wool's coming off.

Ben   So chuck it.

Michelle   But Ben – that's your angel. You made it at nursery.

Ben   Whatever. I don't remember.

Michelle   But, it's your angel. You remember –

Ben   No memory.

Michelle   I remember –

Ben   Whatsoever.

Michelle   It was snowing. I came to pick you up from nursery. You were wearing that shirt – the one with the blue aeroplanes on.

Ben   Don't remember. Don't remember the shirt. Don't remember the snow.

Michelle   You're just saying that.

Ben   Mum – I don't remember.

Michelle   We walked home – the snow blowing hard in your face, making you cry. But you wouldn't let me carry you. You wouldn't let me carry you so I shouted at you. (*Beat.*) I know I shouted at you. I can still hear myself shouting at you. The snow was making you cry and I was tired. (*Beat.*) I can't bear it that I shouted at you. I can't bear the thought of you running beside me trying to keep up, clutching your angel. I can't bear it. It's hurting me now just thinking about it.

Ben (*relenting*)   Mum –

Michelle   Put your angel on the tree with Alex. I want to see you put it on.

Alex   I got it first.

Michelle (*to* **Ben**)   Then go upstairs and change.

Ben   I'm going to the funeral.

Michelle   I want you to go upstairs and change.

Ben   Don't do this – Why are you doing this? I was listening to you – I was believing you – that stuff about me in my aeroplane shirt.

Alex   She's getting confused. I had the shirt with aeroplanes on it. I remember that day. I remember everything about that day – the crying and the snow. You're getting confused, Mum. (*Beat.*) Mum –

Ben   You always do this.

Michelle   What?

Alex   So that makes this my angel. The angel, Mum – it's not his, it's mine.

Michelle (*distracted, watching* **Ben** *pick up the pad of paper from the coffee table.*)   You're getting confused, Alex.

Alex   No, you're getting confused. It was me what had the shirt with blue aeroplanes on it.

Michelle   *Who* had.

Alex   What?

Michelle   It was me *who* had the shirt with blue aeroplanes on it.

Alex   That's what I said.

Ben   Don't waste your breath – she *ain't* listening. Paul Geller got to her. It's that hypnosis CD that came free with his book – How to Become Middle Class.

Michelle   Nothing wrong in talking properly.

Ben   Or living properly. More to the point.

Alex   All I'm saying is it's my angel. I remember painting the red shoes on it and making the yellow dress. I remember it all –

Ben   It's your angel, it's my angel. Who cares, Alex?

Alex   It's my angel.

Ben   Whatever. I'm going.

Michelle   Where you going?

Ben   Where *are* you going?

Alex   SAY IT!

Ben   What?

Alex   Say it's my angel. Admit it.

Ben (*laughing*)   Admit it?

Alex   Admit it. Say it.

Ben (*suddenly angry*)   Who gives a fuck?

Alex   He said the word.

Michelle   Ben!

Ben   It's your angel – it's my angel – it's a fucking loo roll wearing a dress and shoes.

Michelle   Ben!

Ben   I'm gone.

Michelle   I don't want you going.

Ben   I'm gone.

Michelle   Ben – wait.

Ben   What?

Michelle   I want you back by six. I've got to go out, but Dad'll be here. Ben –

Ben   Where you going?

Michelle   Work. You know that.

Ben   Why won't you just tell me what it is you do.

Michelle   It's confidential. For my sake and our sake. As a family.

Ben   You're a traffic warden. I know it.

Michelle   I'm not a traffic warden, Ben. (*Beat.*) Six! I want you back here by six.

*Enter **Paul**, in his security guard's uniform.*

Paul *and* **Ben** *look at each other. Exit* **Ben***.*

Michelle   He's gone. Paul – he's gone.

Paul   Yeah – I saw.

Michelle   He's gone to the funeral.

Paul   What funeral?

Michelle   That girl who hung herself – Caitlin.

Paul   I read about that. (*Beat.*) Didn't he know her?

Michelle   No, he didn't.

Paul   Oh. Hey – Alex.

Alex   Hi, Dad. I'm doing the tree. I'm starting with the angel. This is my angel.

Michelle   I saw her round here once – that's all. They were laughing about something. Maybe he knew her at primary school. (*Beat.*) He did know her at primary school. She lived in one of those blocks down near the river. I picked him up from there once. (*Beat.*) How did I forget that? There was a box of Lyserone on their dining table.

Paul (*distracted*)   Lyserone?

Michelle   Lice powder, Paul. They had lice powder out on their dining-room table. It was just sat there. A box of Lyserone. Ben ate there – Ben ate there, Paul.

Paul   So what d'you want me to do about it?

Michelle   I don't know.

Paul   You better go. You'll be late.

Michelle   Yeah. (*Beat.*) I didn't want him going to the funeral.

Paul   Well, he's gone. They're probably all going.

Michelle   It was like he couldn't keep away – you think somebody's putting him up to going?

Paul   Nobody's putting him up to it.

Michelle   It's the second funeral in a month.

Paul   I know.

Michelle   I don't want him going.

Paul   I know.

Michelle   I don't want him anywhere near that girl's funeral. Why don't you go after him – stop him.

Paul   I'm dead on my feet, Michelle. I'm not stopping nobody.

Michelle   Anybody.

Paul   What I said. (*Beat.*) We had some gang stabbing in A&E . . . police everywhere . . . all jumped up. Everybody all jumped up, on the look out – I didn't even know what we were meant to be looking for anymore towards the end of my shift. Then you start seeing things. I was down by the canteen trying to get something to eat and –

Michelle   What?

Paul   It doesn't matter.

Michelle   What?

Paul   I caught sight of this – thing – out the corner of my eye, running across the floor. I thought it was just a reflection – light bouncing off something. But it made me nervous.

Michelle   So what was it?

Paul   Well, I glanced up at everyone else, but – nothing. Whatever it was, I was the only one who saw it.

Michelle   Only one who saw what, Paul?

Paul   It doesn't matter.

Michelle   You can't start saying something like that and not finish it.

Paul   It doesn't matter.

Michelle   What did you see?

Paul   A rabbit.

Michelle   A what?

Paul   I saw a rabbit; a white rabbit – in the canteen. It ran across the floor.

Michelle   A rabbit –

Paul   Don't look at me like that.

Michelle   Where did it go?

Paul   I don't know. I saw it once – like I said – by the fire extinguisher on the wall. (*Beat.*) A rabbit.

Michelle   So – what was it doing?

Paul   When I first noticed it, out the corner of my eye, it was running. Then, when I looked properly, it stopped near the doors – under the fire extinguisher. I turned away, then looked again –

Michelle   And?

Paul   It had gone.

Beat.

Michelle   Did you talk to anybody about the rabbit?

Paul (*shaking his head*)   I was exhausted doing my own shift then the cover – I don't know, maybe I just forgot.

Michelle   Maybe –

Paul   But I need to get onto somebody about it. I mean, we've got – what – rabbits in the canteen? (*Beat.*) I should get onto somebody about it, shouldn't I?

Michelle   Sleep on it.

Paul   Michelle – I saw the rabbit. The rabbit was there on the floor – under the fire extinguisher, by the door.

Michelle   Did I say you didn't see the rabbit? (*Beat.*) All I'm saying is – sleep on it.

Paul   Yeah –

Michelle   You're stressed.

Paul   I'm stressed. (*Beat.*) I am stressed. Can't pass a newspaper or put on the TV without hearing something about those two kids.

Michelle   It's like something's arrived. It could have gone anywhere, but it came here.

Paul   Yeah –

Alex   You should of tried to catch the rabbit, Dad – brought it home.

Paul   The rabbit?

Alex   The rabbit you saw.

Paul   I didn't think. Yeah – I could have done.

Alex   I always wanted a rabbit.

Paul   You did?

Alex   Always.

Michelle   I got to go. Make sure Ben's back by six. I told him six. Phone him.

Paul   I'll phone.

Michelle   You're his father.

Exit **Michelle**.

Paul   What's that meant to mean?

Scene Three

Enter **Kate**, *in an open bathrobe, wearing a bikini. Her hair's wet. She kneels down by the coffee table and takes a sandwich bag full of cocaine out of one of the bathrobe's pockets, and does a line.*

Enter **Cass** *dressed for the funeral.*

Cass   Mum? What are you doing?

Kate   What the fuck does it look like I'm doing? Having a bikini wax? (*She tidies the sandwich bag, etc. away.*)

Cass   I thought you were going to stop the blow –

Kate   What? It reminds me of my youth. So I never grew up – so what.

Cass   Yeah, well try to stay alive till I'm eighteen – I don't fancy going into care.

Kate   What's up with you anyway?

Cass   What?

Kate   All the black.

Cass   Caitlin's funeral.

Kate   That today?

Cass   In about an hour's time. (*Beat.*) Do I look alright?

Kate   You look like you work at a Spearmint Rhino Club. (*Beat.*) Thought you didn't like her anyway.

Cass   I didn't. Not particularly. But everybody's going –

Kate   Might go myself. Something to do. Get dressed up. Have a cry.

Cass   You didn't even know her.

Kate   I did know her actually. She did the most amazing Brazilians. (*Beat.*) Know what a good Brazilian does for you? It reminds you of your mortality. God – maybe my Brazilian was one of the last she ever did.

Cass   Mum –

Kate   What?

Cass   Thought you were meant to be having lunch out today.

Kate   Yeah –

Cass   So?

Kate   He cancelled.

Cass   So did you re-arrange?

Kate   No.

Cass   But – he seemed nice.

Kate   Yeah. Probably why he cancelled.

Cass   When did he phone?

Kate   Can't remember. (*Beat.*) About an hour ago. I've been out in the hot tub ever since – waiting for George Clooney – who didn't show either.

Cass *goes over to the tree and takes the angel from the top.*

Cass   Can't think why.

Kate   Me neither. Especially when you think of the panoramic views over the Dartford Suspension Bridge we've got from our tub.

Cass (*distracted*)   Remember this?

Kate   No.

Cass   I made it at school when I was like four or something.

Kate   Cass, I don't remember. You were forever coming home with crap like that.

Cass   I made the dress out of yellow gingham so it would match that one I had – that one I wore all the time. (*Beat.*) Look, I even painted her shoes red.

Kate   Those are shoes?

Cass   I was four. (*Goes over to the window.*)

Kate   What you doing standing there?

Cass   Just looking.

Kate   What you expecting to see?

Cass   Nothing.

Kate   So come away.

Cass   Why?

Kate   Looks like you're waiting for someone and it's making me nervous.

Cass   So? It's only a window. (*Beat.*) All you ever used to do when I was little was stand by this window. I'd come back downstairs after you'd put me to bed and stand in that doorway there, watching you wait for Dad coming home. And you were always waiting because he was always late.

Kate   Yeah, well he's running about twelve years late at the moment so I wouldn't bother waiting if I was you.

Cass   I'm not waiting.

Kate   Well, you want to stay away from windows or −

Cass   Or what?

Kate   Or before you know it you've spent over half your life waiting for a dark-haired, brown-eyed man who walks comfortable in a size ten.

Cass   He took a size-ten shoe?

Kate   Yeah.

Cass   And his eyes were brown?

Kate   Actually I made that part up.

Cass   No you didn't.

Kate   I did. I don't remember his eyes.

Cass   Me neither.

Enter **Doug** *in his wheelchair.*

Kate (*watching him, mumbling*)   Christ, who'd be me. (*Beat.*) Alright, Dad?

Doug   My bloody hands are bleeding − look.

Kate (*without looking*)   How come?

Doug   Chasing bloody rabbits.

Kate (*uninterested*)   Really?

Doug   In the park − a white rabbit.

Kate   In the park − right.

Doug   I fell asleep. I'm forever falling asleep these days − must be narcoleptic or something. When I woke up − there it was, running past the tennis courts. I followed it all the way to the back of the hospital. Then it vanished. (*Beat. To* **Cass**.) You look cold.

Cass   I'm freezing.

Doug   Thin blood. Like your mother – and you need to eat more. I never see you eating.

Cass   I eat.

Doug (*to* **Kate**)   She's messing up her metabolism by not eating.

Cass   Grandad – I eat.

Doug   Not eating's why you're cold – that and thin blood.

Cass *turns away and looks out the window again.*

Doug   Is it snowing yet?

Kate   Come away from the window.

Cass (*ignoring her*)   No – it's not snowing.

Kate   Cass! Come away from the window.

Doug   I thought it was going to snow – the sky was looking so heavy.

Cass   Well, it's not snowing yet.

Kate   Cass!

Doug   Maybe later –

Cass   Yeah – maybe.

Doug (*to* **Kate**)   I did see a rabbit.

Kate   Jesus –

Doug   Where you off to?

Kate   Back outside – thought I might try drowning myself in the hot tub.

Doug   What about food?

Kate   Go talk to the microwave.

Exit **Kate**.

Doug   What's wrong with her?

Cass   She got stood up.

Doug   Can you get stood up at lunchtime?

Cass   Guy who was meant to be taking her out works nights.

Doug   Oh. (*Beat.*) What time's the funeral?

Cass   Soon – I should be going. (*Beat.*) It's weird. Last funeral I went to was Grandma's.

Doug   You get your hair from Elsa. You've got beautiful hair, Cassie. Especially in this light.

Cass   D'you remember?

Doug   What? If it happened decades ago – probably. If it happened recently – no chance. My short-term memory's been completely buggered by the medication.

Cass   D'you remember the summer Grandma made me that yellow dress – the one I wouldn't take off? Mum had to wash it at night while I was asleep so it would be ready to put on again the next morning.

Doug   I remember. She used an old tablecloth she didn't want anymore cause it had a raspberry stain on.

Cass   That's it.

Doug   Yeah – Only it wasn't Elsa who made you that dress. It was your mum.

Cass   Mum? Mum doesn't sew.

Doug   She used to. Sewed all the time. Made all your dad's shirts – even made her own wedding dress. It was definitely her made you the dress. I remember Elsa and her had an argument over the colour of it. Elsa saying there was no point putting yellow on you – it had to be blue to set your hair off – and Mum saying all she had was yellow. The tablecloth was yellow. Needs must, but Elsa was right mind; she was always right. She was a queen in blue, Elsa was. A beautiful woman in every colour, but a queen in blue.

Cass   You miss her –

Doug   Course I miss her. What do any of you expect? She was my queen, and I'm tired of doing this without her. Bloody exhausted, in fact.

Cass   You've been on them sites again.

Doug   So, I've been on them sites. It's a human being's right to die. (*Beat.*) When they've had enough.

Cass   When they've had enough. Yeah –

Doug   Now's good for me – ten years without Elsa's enough. (*Beat.*) It's got to the point where I can't wait at the traffic lights without thinking of slipping the brake on this thing and freewheeling into oncoming traffic, but some cheery fucker would only end up scraping me off the road and getting me to hospital just in time. (*Beat.*) See – I wouldn't have to think like that if I was in Denmark. In Denmark, you can check yourself into a clinic, decide on a time – a décor. You can choose a décor to die in, in Denmark. Civilised, see.

Cass   Grandad –

Doug   What? I could lie there at a time I chose, waiting and letting my head fill with good stuff . . . brushing Elsa's hair . . . I used to love to brush her hair . . . and us dancing.

Cass   Where did you used to go dancing?

Doug   The Pavilion.

Cass   The Pavilion?

Doug   Yeah – haven't been there for years. There was an airstrip running down beside it then from the war. Most Fridays that's where we went. Place used to be packed – too much smoke and dust to breathe – faces running and everybody dancing. (*Beat.*) It doesn't last long enough; doesn't last near long enough, Cass. You got to catch it because it goes. God old age is a nightmare. One you know you'll never wake up from. Only thing you need to know about old age is you think it'll be bearable cause you'll feel old when the time comes – only you don't. The time comes – and you don't feel old.

Cass   I can't ever imagine being old.

Doug   Me neither. Every time I pass a mirror it's a total bloody shock. I expect to see something else – something better – only I don't, and I can't quite believe it. People pass me in the park, wrapped in my plaid, mumbling to myself and they think – he must be enjoying the sunshine . . . and the flowers. They smile at me and I smile back and nobody's any the wiser to the fact that I'm not mumbling to myself about the municipal planting – I'm composing elegies under my breath on the demise of my erectile tissue.

Cass   Grandad –

Doug   I'm serious, Cassie – a woman in a white t-shirt walks past thinking there's an old man out enjoying the sunshine and I'm thinking how much I want to grope her. The stoned sixteen-year-old under the chestnut sees me and thinks there's an old man out enjoying the sunshine and all I'm thinking is how much I want to get stoned under the chestnut.

Cass   Well, if you want to get stoned . . .

Doug   You can help with that?

Cass   What – now?

Doug (*insistent*)   Right now.

Cass *hesitates then takes a packet out of her trouser pocket, rolls a joint for* **Doug** *and passes it to him.*

You're on medication.

Doug   It won't kill me. (*Beat.*) How depressing.

They start to smoke.

This is good.

Cass   Yeah – it is good. (*Beat.*) You won't go without telling me, Grandad – will you? You won't just go – one-way ticket to Denmark or something? I couldn't stand that.

Doug   Not until I've taken that cruise down the Nile I promised Elsa I'd take. And not until I've seen you fall in love neither.

Cass   That'll never happen.

Doug   It'll happen.

Cass   I think about love – I see it dancing the jive.

Doug   The jive was the best – got the girls airborne – girls like to fly.

Cass   I see it wearing print dresses, lips painted scarlet – love's historical for me – it's you and Grandma; it doesn't happen anymore.

Doug   It'll happen. I heard the jive was making a comeback.

Cass   Yeah, well so's Valium.

Doug   It'll happen.

Cass   But it doesn't always – not to everyone. (*Beat.*) Look at Mum.

Doug   You're different.

Cass   Sleeping with Dad's toothbrush under her pillow still – a centimetre's worth of his stale cologne left in the bottle. Enough for her to sniff before passing out at night. I smell it on her sometimes –

Doug (*angry*)   You shouldn't talk about that stuff. There has to be stuff you don't talk about – you shouldn't talk about.

Cass   Nothing's ever going to change. It's always going to be like this. I know it is. It's like, some mornings I get up and open the curtains and can't ever imagine opening a pair of curtains and seeing anything other than that bloody bridge full of cars going backwards and forwards between nowhere and nowhere.

Doug   I don't know. I've been happy here – met Elsa here – had Kate here. I've been happy in Dartford.

Cass   Happy in Dartford – sounds like a bad indie movie.

Doug   You'll be leaving home after the summer.

Cass   Yeah, as loan bait for some fifth-rate university.

Doug   So don't go.

Cass   What else am I going to do?

Doug   I'd do anything to be your age again.

Cass   Yeah, well a day would be enough. (*Beat.*) It's funny, you spend your whole time as a kid trying to be just like everybody else; terrified of standing out. Then when you grow up you're desperate to be different, get noticed – but by then it's too late cause you're just like everybody else and nobody you really care about is ever going to notice you. You're just backdrop.

Doug   You'll never be average, Cass.

Cass   Grandad, you've got no idea how average I am.

Doug   You're unique – that's amazing in itself.

Cass (*to herself*)   I'm never getting out of here. Only way I'll ever change my view is to blow up that fucking bridge – or blow myself up.

Doug (*to himself*)   You'll never be repeated. Bits of you might re-surface in your children – grandchildren – but the combination that's uniquely you will never be repeated again.

Cass   Well, I'm never having kids. Not ever.

Doug   You will.

Cass   I won't. What's the point?

Doug   You will, Cass. (*Beat.*) This really is good stuff.

Cass   It gets you through. This and the Butterfly Club.

Doug   I never heard you talk about the Butterfly Club.

Cass   It's new.

Doug   Where is it then?

Cass   Anywhere you want it to be. Open to anyone, but totally exclusive. You only ever go to one meeting (*starts to laugh*) and never meet the other members.

Doug   Sounds Masonic. (*Beat.*) I don't like the sound of this Butterfly Club. Whose idea was it?

Cass   Nobody's.

Doug   Is it some internet thing?

Cass   Not really – no. But just knowing it exists keeps you company. And it's good to have something there – when it all gets too much. (*Beat.*) I'm going. Don't want to be late. (*Beat.*) Love you, Grandad.

Doug   Love you too.

She gives him her angel.

Doug   What's this?

Cass   My angel.

Exit **Cass**.

He goes over to the tree and tries to get the angel on the top. This could go on for some time.

Doug   Cass! Cass – wait. I can't get it on. (*Beat.*) Cass –

Exit **Doug**.

Scene Four

Enter **Tony**, *dressed as a magician.*

Tony   Lauren?

Enter **Lauren**, *dressed in black.*

Lauren   Dad? That you, Dad?

Tony   Alright, love?

Lauren   Yeah – you?

Tony   Not late, am I?

Lauren   We've got about ten minutes. I booked a taxi –

Tony   Shit. I tried to finish early.

Lauren   Dad, it's fine. How did it go? At the hospital –

Tony   Well, the good thing about working the terminal wards is the captive audience.

He trips up as he makes his way over to the table and puts the case down.

Lauren   Dad –

Tony   I'm fine – I'm fine.

Lauren (*watching him*)   Didn't you take Harvey?

Tony   Course I took Harvey. (*Beat – looks at the things he's put down on the table.*) Shit. Harvey. (*Beat.*) I think I left him at the hospital. (*Helpless.*) Lauren – What kind of a magician loses his fucking rabbit?

Lauren   Here. Sit down. (*Helps him into an armchair.*) We'll call in at the hospital after the funeral.

Tony   Harvey –

Lauren   It's OK – we'll go to the hospital.

Tony   I can't believe I left Harvey. Shit. (*Beat.*) I'm knackered, Lauren.

Lauren   I know you're knackered.

Tony   Did Angela ring?

Lauren   Angela? No.

Tony   I told her to ring if she needed to. I told her – Maybe we should go round to the house first before the crematorium.

Lauren   If she'd of wanted us, she'd of asked. She'll be fine.

Tony   She won't be fine.

Lauren   We'll see her there.

Tony   Yeah – (*Beat.*) Am I alright in this – if I change my shirt?

She nods. He starts to laugh.

Lauren (*worried*)   What? What is it?

Tony   Harvey. I was just thinking about Harvey and –

Lauren   What?

Tony   Maybe he's been planning this for years. His escape. (*Beat.*) Harvey's great escape. (*Beat.*) Dumb fucking rabbit.

Lauren   Taxi'll be here soon.

Tony   Right – right.

She starts to exit.

Tony   Lauren?

Lauren   What?

Tony   Don't hate me for saying this, but sometimes I think it would have been easier if we could have just buried Mum.

Lauren   I know –

Tony   It's knowing she's still here somewhere. Living a life with people who don't even know we exist.

Lauren   We don't know that.

Tony   D'you remember when she never came back that day and I knew she'd gone? We put those Missing Person posters all down Oxford Street – all the tube stations, bus stops. And about a month after that we got that phone call from a guy who reckoned he'd seen her on the westbound platform at Marble Arch.

Lauren   You made us spend a weekend underground.

Tony   On that platform – watching tube after tube go through the station like we'd arranged to meet her and were waiting for her to get off one.

Lauren   And then when there weren't any trains you stood on the edge of the platform peering down the tunnel like you expected to see her walking along it.

Tony   Yeah – I did.

Lauren   Like you were ready to give her a hand up.

Tony   I think I really did believe she'd just emerge from the tunnel, brush herself down and climb up and join us. Then we'd all laugh it off – go and have lunch somewhere . . . it was easier believing that than that she'd gone. Mad – but bearable.

Lauren   You're not mad.

Tony   I have been.

Lauren   Maybe there are some things you shouldn't have to get over. People expect you to, but you don't – can't. Maybe that's all you're going to do for the rest of your life – peer into the dark, waiting for her. Maybe that's OK.

Tony   It is?

Lauren   Maybe –

Tony   I don't know what I'd do without you.

Lauren   I'm not going nowhere.

Tony   Lauren?

Lauren   I know what you're going to say and I don't want you to say it.

Tony   Every time you leave the house – no the room. Every time you leave the room I can't do anything but wait till I know you're back.

Lauren   Dad – I don't know why Caitlin did what she did. I hope I never find myself in that place she was in where what she did felt like the best thing to do. (*Beat.*) Let's just get today over with.

Tony   Where you going?

Lauren   Upstairs. To get your shirt.

Tony   Don't be long.

Lauren   I won't.

Tony (*standing up suddenly*)   Lauren!

Lauren (*impatient*)   What?

He produces a bung of plastic flowers from inside his jacket and presents them to her.

Lauren   Magic.

Tony   Yeah. A bit left over. (*Beat.*) We should decorate the tree tonight. Get a pizza.

Lauren   We eat too much pizza.

Tony   Maybe watch some TV.

Lauren   There's never anything on TV.

Exit **Lauren**, *smelling the plastic bouquet.*

Exit **Tony**.

Scene Five

Enter **Angela**, *in mourning.*

Enter **Tony**, **Lauren**.

Angela   Tony – Alright, Lauren?

Tony   Where's Mark?

Angela   Inside. (*Beat.*) Crying. He hasn't stopped. He's been crying for days. I couldn't bear it any longer – that's what I'm doing out here.

Tony You want to go in now?

Angela No.

Tony Come on, let's get you in.

Angela I never wanted her cremated. I'm scared it's going to hurt her, Tony. I mean – it must, mustn't it?

Tony Come on, Ange.

Angela I can't go in. The idea of sitting there for the next half hour hearing everything that has to be said and – it's unbearable. It's unbearable, Tony. That's not Caitlin in there. Who am I doing it for? (*Beat.*) But you have to go to your child's funeral, don't you? There are rules even for something as unnatural as a child's funeral.

Lauren Caitlin wanted to be cremated.

Angela You talked about that? Why would you talk about something like that? That the sort of stuff young people talk about? I don't know – I don't remember. (*Beat.*) Why would you talk about something like that?

Lauren I loved Caitlin – so much.

Angela (*relenting*) I know you did.

Tony Come on. (*Beat.*) Lauren?

Lauren There's others coming.

Tony See you in there.

Exit **Tony**, **Angela**.

Enter **Cass**.

Cass That Caitlin's mum with your dad? They seem close.

Lauren So –

Cass So – Just saying.

She takes some tablets out her bag.

Lauren What are you taking?

Cass   Valium. All my mum had left. Organ music makes me panic. (*Beat.*) Where are the others?

Lauren   Coming.

Cass   Lot of people here. More people than ever came to any of her other parties.

Lauren   This isn't a party.

Cass   It's her last party.

Lauren   You're not even sad about it, are you?

Cass   Sad about what?

Lauren   Caitlin – dying.

Cass   No, I'm not sad. I've got respect for her. Never thought she'd do it. But I'm not sad, no.

Enter **Ben**, **Dante**, **Tasha**.

Ben   What – did you all get like an invite or something?

Dante   I didn't get an invite.

Cass   Nobody got an invite, Dante.

Ben (*wrestling Valium from* **Cass**)   Share.

Tasha   Where did all these people come from?

Ben (*looking around him*)   Dartford.

Tasha   This many people live in Dartford?

Dante   Shit. There's Frayne. What's Frayne doing here?

Lauren   She's giving the sermon.

Cass   Why?

Ben   Isn't she meant to be like a lay preacher or something as well as a teacher?

Lauren   Yeah – she just sort of inflicted herself on Caitlin's family. Honed in on them.

Cass   Predatory.

Ben   Yeah – look at her. She's like, running through them doors – can't wait to get her dose of tragedy and misery in the lives of others.

Cass   Guess –

Ben   What?

Cass   How many times Frayne said 'cancer' in assembly this term?

Ben   Cass –

Cass   What?

Ben   You – counting the number of times Mrs Frayne said 'cancer'.

Cass   You're a prime example of what's wrong with society, Ben. You don't think 'Mrs' Frayne's a freak for saying 'cancer' one hundred and fifty-two times, whereas I *am* a freak for counting . . . for bringing it to your attention. Well, she said it one hundred and fifty-two times – and I only started counting in September.

Dante   Who's that with her?

Ben   Where?

Dante   There. Guy in the glasses with the smoky lenses.

Tasha   That's her husband.

Ben   Never seen him before.

Tasha   Paedophile.

Dante   Yeah – everybody knows paedophiles wear glasses with smoky lenses . . . what I never worked out is – why don't paedophiles just stop wearing them then they'd be like undercover paedophiles and could go about their business un-molested.

Tasha   He's looking at you, Dante.

Dante   I'm too old for him.

Tasha   Yeah – so old, Dante. You're like ancient.

Dante   Fuck off, Tasha. I'm sixteen now – old enough to own my own chainsaw.

Ben   Look at everyone. They've come to see Caitlin – pay homage – because she did it; she actually did it.

Cass   I still can't believe it. She joined the club.

Tasha   Yeah – I always thought it would be you Cass, the way you go on about stuff.

Cass   What stuff? It's not like you never cut yourself.

Tasha   Yeah, but that's like a phase – something everyone does – like wearing Tinkerbell make-up and putting stickers on your nails.

Lauren   I never cut myself.

Cass   Cause you're still wearing Tinkerbell make-up.

Dante   I heard you tried it, Cass, with your dressing-gown chord from the banister or something. But then the banister broke cause you were like so fat. Is that why you went on that A-list diet? So you'd die thin and tidy.

Ben   Cass is too loud mouth – it's the quiet ones you got to watch out for.

Cass (*hurt*)   You think I'm loud mouth, Ben?

Ben   Quiet ones like Caitlin. (*Beat.*) And Lauren. (*Beat.*) Not thinking of surprising us any time soon are you, Lauren?

Lauren   No – cause it would make you too happy, and you're happy enough already.

Ben *gives her the finger.*

Ben   Been thinking about it though? You and Caitlin were close. Your dad worried about you?

Lauren   Yeah.

Tasha   I'd do it just to piss my dad off. Anyway when I heard about Caitlin – I thought it was to do with her being pregnant.

Lauren   She wasn't pregnant, Tasha. If she was – I'd of known about it.

Cass   So why did she go so quiet around the time those rumours started appearing on her Facebook Wall.

Ben   She went quiet because of the rumours.

Dante   And anyway, those rumours started up ages ago – before what happened.

Tasha   Yeah, but the details . . . rumours don't do details. Whoever it was said they saw her buying a Predict pregnancy-testing kit.

Dante   Didn't she have an eating disorder or something?

Cass   Dante, half of Dartford's got an eating disorder and just because you've got an eating disorder doesn't mean you can't get pregnant. Bulimia isn't a contraceptive.

Ben   Why does there have to be a reason for what Caitlin did? Maybe she was just fucked off because it was Christmas – or she got up that morning and the sky was the wrong colour.

Tasha   Or she looked in the mirror and remembered all over again how ugly she was.

Lauren   Caitlin wasn't ugly.

Ben   Or she got tired of seeing pictures of Amy Winehouse on all the front pages – like it's news she's going into rehab again.

Cass   Or she got tired of waiting for it to snow.

Ben   Never question why someone decides to join the Butterfly Club. Trust your own judgement. When it's your time you go.

Dante   You writing the rules now, Ben?

Ben   I'm not writing any rules – I'm talking about Caitlin.

Lauren   I saw you both once. In the art block. I saw you through the window, sitting at a bench and you looked . . . I mean, you looked like you were together in the art block. Not just in the art block, but together in the art block. Like – there was nothing random about it.

Ben   So we both did art. So I was sitting next to her.

Lauren   The room was empty.

Ben   So everyone knows I went out with her.

Lauren   You seemed really close.

Cass   Shame the Tribute he put on her Wall was so mediocre then.

Dante   It's weird her Facebook still being there. It's like part of her hasn't gone. (*Beat.*) How long's it going to be there for?

Tasha   Until someone takes it off.

Dante   Who's going to do that? We're talking about a real gap in the market here.

Cass   Dante!

Dante   Come on – think about it. People don't just need themselves laying to rest anymore, they need their virtual selves laying to rest as well. These days you've got to die twice. (*Beat.*) We could do it –

Ben   What?

Dante (*excited*)   Set up an online funeral service – laying people's virtual selves to rest.

Cass   That's a shit idea, Dante.

Dante   No, wait – think about it. Ashes to Ether virtual funerals.

Cass   I'm thinking about it.

Dante   And –

Cass It's shit.

Dante We could make a submission – to *Dragon's Den*.

Ben Forget it, Dante.

Dante What if I go ahead and make a submission and they call?

Cass They won't call.

Dante What if they do?

Cass They won't.

Dante What if I get to be on it?

Cass Dante – you won't. You're under age. You have to be eighteen.

Lauren *starts to exit.*

Ben Lauren! Lauren – where you going?

Lauren The music's started. I can hear it.

Exit **Lauren**, **Ben**, **Cass**, **Dante**, **Tasha**.

Lights.

Scene Six

The coffee table is strewn with paper plates, cups, etc.

Tony *is clearing the rubbish into a bin liner.*

Enter **Angela**, *still in mourning. She's barefoot and yawning.*

Angela Tony? What you still doing here? (*Watching him move about the room, tidying up.*) You don't have to do that –

He smiles but doesn't respond.

Angela I must have fallen asleep. (*Beat.*) We don't sleep at night. We can't – In fits and starts, maybe, but most of the time we just lie there pretending the other one's not awake.

When the moon's up it's unbearable. The sheets on Mark's side of the bed get drenched in sweat. They get stuck to him. When he turns over, the sheets, duvet – everything – all turn with him. Then I get so cold – It feels like my skin's being lifted right off me.

Tony   Come on, Ange, come and sit down.

Angela (*ignoring this*)   I gave Mark some of them sleeping pills the doctor prescribed – was that wrong of me?

Tony   Course it wasn't wrong. You were prescribed them.

Angela   People think Mark's grief's unnatural . . . nobody's said anything, but you can see it in their faces. I saw it today – even today. At the crematorium. When the coffin was there for everyone to see. It was there in the air – the traces of all the things that have been said about us – all the judgements that have been made.

Tony   No-one was judging you.

Angela   I saw them. (*Beat.*) I heard them. And it was incredible. Isn't it incredible? That people think to judge the way in which others grieve. As if there's a right way and a wrong way.

Tony   You got through it.

Angela   Day's not over yet. (*Beat.*) What did you think of the service?

Tony   I thought it was moving.

Angela   Did you? What else are you going to say – me asking you a question like that? I didn't believe a single word that woman – Mrs Frayne – said. And her tone – like what happened to Caitlin is what happens to people like us. Like it would never happen to her. Wasn't she enjoying herself.

Tony   You should go back to sleep.

Angela   How's Lauren?

Tony   Alright. Far as I can tell.

Angela   Only we can't, can we? Not after Caitlin. Bet you can't bear her being out of your sight at the moment.

Tony   That's cruel.

Angela   Maybe – There were so many of them at the funeral. I never thought there'd be so many. All those people – didn't recognise half of them.

Tony   You need more sleep, Ange – come and have a lie down here on the sofa.

Angela (*ignoring this*)   I offered her a lift – that morning. I offered her a lift, but she said she'd walk. I should have insisted. I should have climbed the stairs and insisted. There are twelve stairs. I should have climbed them. (*Beat.*) It was my scarf, Tony – She used my scarf.

Tony   You need to sleep.

Angela (*shouting*)   Stop saying that! (*Beat.*) You know how it is in the beginning – when they're so tiny you can hold them with one arm. There's this intimacy, isn't there? This intimacy you've never felt before and never get again – not with anyone. People go on and on about love, but it's beyond love. It's a sort of wonder that fills you up so that you only notice the hours passing. Then the wonder dies down, becomes love and you start to notice the weeks. Then things settle down and the months start passing again. By they time they start school, it's the years you're thinking of; years are the things that are passing, and you know you've started to lose them already. Stuff just goes – (*Beat.*)

I've been in her bedroom. I can do that now. (*Beat.*) But I can't touch her things. I can't touch anything in that room. Maybe there's something Lauren wants. She can come round and take a look when I'm at work. I'll leave the keys under the bin. She won't be offended, will she? I just can't bear to see her round here yet. I don't mind her being here – just not when I'm in. (*Beat.*) There's a photo – here. I meant to give it to Lauren. It's Caitlin and her on the beach at Ramsgate. D'you remember? We took them both one summer holiday – Caitlin's in that blue dress of hers with the rabbit on the front – the one she wouldn't take off – wore all summer.

Tony (*taking photo*)   I'll give it to her. (*Beat.*) Come on – come and sit down on the sofa here.

Angela *runs her hand along the back of the sofa then checks it. After this she goes over to the coffee table, recently cleared by* **Tony** *and runs her hand over this as well.*

Angela (*muttering*)   Filthy. Completely filthy.

Tony (*concerned*)   Angela?

Angela *picks up some polish and a cloth.*

Tony *watches as she goes over to the coffee table, circles it a few times then drops to her knees and starts to polish.*

Angela   Look at this dust. It's everywhere . . . must have happened while I was asleep (*Beat.* **Angela** *continues to polish hard.*) I can't believe I just fell asleep like that when there was all this polishing to be done –

Tony   Angela –

Angela   It's the dust. It won't stop falling. Look at this, Tony. I'm polishing – see – as we speak. (*Sprays more polish onto the coffee table and rubs hard with the duster.*) I'm polishing – and polishing – and – if I go like this – (*bends down so that her eyes are on a level with the surface of the table*) there's nothing but dust again. A whole layer of dust across the surface of the table and I've only just finished polishing it. You saw me – just now. (*Insistent.*) You saw me –

Tony (*quiet*)   I saw you.

Angela (*polishing vigorously*)   You can't take your eyes off anything for a second or – (*she stops polishing suddenly*) I can't cry. Why can't I cry? Why aren't I crying? I just need to cry then – You heard Mark today. If he carries on crying like that I'm going to, I don't know, rip his throat out or something, just rip it out.

Tony   Come and sit down.

Angela   I can't. I've got all this dusting to do –

Tony   So I'll dust.

Angela   I like it done in a certain way.

Tony   Well, you sit there and watch me – then you can tell me where I'm going wrong.

Angela   No – I'm fine. I'm fine. *As she says this, she slowly relinquishes the polish and allows* **Tony** *to help her onto the sofa.*

Tony *starts to polish.*

Angela   To the left a bit. Look – more's been falling.

Tony   I've got it.

Angela   Now to the right – look.

Tony   I'm there.

Angela   Caitlin was pregnant, Tony. (*Beat.*) Not when she – I mean – she got rid of it . . . before. About a month ago. (*Beat.*) You don't look surprised.

Tony   D'you need me to?

Angela   I don't know –

Tony   How pregnant was she?

Angela   Only about six, seven weeks.

Tony   Who was it?

Angela   She wouldn't tell me, but I knew. I knew exactly who it was – I saw him round here with her once. They were laughing about something. I hadn't seen her happy like that since she was like ten or something. Thought she'd forgotten how to be – until I saw her that night. (*Beat.*) She hated me seeing her, catching her out like that, but there was nothing she could do about it. She was stung by it – all swollen with it. Happiness does that to you – stings you so you all swell up. (*Beat.*) It was that boy – Ben.

Tony   Yeah – I know Ben.

Angela   They had some sort of fall out – I think he started making fun of her when she started at college. I knew something was up cause she didn't come out her room for days – I had to keep phoning the college office telling them she was sick. Then I finally got her downstairs to eat something and we were watching some reality shit on TV and Caitlin just started to cry. She cried so much I got scared. That's when she told me she was pregnant – and I knew it had to be Ben. I mean – I know some of them sleep around a bit, but not Caitlin. And she went nuts when I said I was speaking to him about it – nuts. Got the carving knife out the kitchen drawer – said she was going to cut herself up proper if I so much as breathed anything to him. (*Beat.*)

It wasn't her decision – the abortion. I went to work on her day in day out, about her future, finishing her course, waiting, doing it properly with someone she wanted to be with. (*Beat.*) Thing is it was *him* she wanted to be with, and she hated the course she was on anyway.

Tony   I would of said the same things to Lauren you said to Caitlin.

Angela   You would? (*Beat.*) I wanted it done properly, but we've got no cash at the moment. Mark's got that stupid car half the size of the house he won't get rid of and we can barely afford to shop at Lidl. (*Beat.*) I never said anything to Ben, but I saw his mum – met her in the café at Sainsbury's and told her, and she just went for me. Everybody was staring. The stuff she said about me and the stuff she said about Caitlin. She wasn't having it about Ben and Caitlin either until I told her I was telling him myself if she didn't pay for the abortion. Don't look at me like that Tony – I know it wasn't right it's just the money's doing my head in at the moment. We're having trouble finding the mortgage, and – it was horrible, us sat there in that café and the tills going off behind us. If she hadn't said those things – about Caitlin – maybe I would have left it and found the money somehow, but I just lost it with her.

Tony   Why didn't you come to me?

Angela   I didn't think of it.

Tony   You should have just come to me.

Angela   Yeah. Should of. (*Beat.*) Now my head's full to cracking knowing that me making Caitlin go through with that was probably the death of her. And what for? What was I thinking? Was it about Caitlin – really? Or was I just ashamed – scared of what people would say? You're only ever this week's news, aren't you? She gave them something to talk about anyway. What if I'd just told Mark – everyone? Then people would be talking about Caitlin being pregnant and not Caitlin being dead. What if I'd just stood by her? I didn't though, did I? Acted ashamed.

Tony   It wasn't that.

Angela   How d'you know? You don't know. You don't know anything.

Tony   Angela –

Angela   Sorry. (*Beat.*) I should take some of that Benpathol I gave Mark and shut myself up.

Tony   I got prescribed that after Tanya walked out on us.

Angela   Ever take it?

Tony   Once.

Angela   Because of the nightmares?

Tony   Yeah –

Angela   Me too. (*Beat.*) We're neither of us sleepers though, are we?

Tony   It would be nice sometimes though, to just sleep.

Angela   And sleep and sleep.

Tony   Yeah –

Angela   Like we did that time. Remember?

Tony   Yeah.

Angela   Feels like the only time I ever slept properly in my life – that afternoon. D'you ever think about it?

Tony   I think about it.

Angela   Shame it never happened again. (*Beat.*) I felt so guilty afterwards. Not because of Mark – about you, moving in on you like that when you were all messed up about Tanya.

Tony   I never saw it like that. It was just the right thing to happen at the time.

Angela   Still – shame it never happened again. (*Beat.*) D'you really think about it?

Tony   Yeah.

Angela   You're not just saying that?

Tony   No –

Angela   We were good together. You're a good man, Tony. (*Beat.*) Seems like me and Mark have been arguing ever since then.

Tony   What – he knows?

Angela (*impatient*)   No – nothing like that. It was just a turning point for me. Something happened and I couldn't go back. And now (*Beat.*) I saw something in the papers – the other weekend. You know – they're offering courses.

Tony   Courses?

Angela   Survival courses. In the woods. How to make fires without matches. How to forage for food – is that what you say, forage?

Tony   Forage – yeah.

Angela   People are signing up for these courses so that when it all comes crashing down – they'll be able to take to the woods, and survive. Have you heard about these courses?

Tony   I haven't. No.

Angela   Well, you read something like that and you think –
so what about the mortgage? So what about anything? I mean,
if it's the end – If the end's coming – soon – and it must be
soon, mustn't it, if them people are running those courses.
Then – what's the point? (*Breaking off.*) You're leaving?
Tony – don't go. Feels like you might never come back. Tony –

Tony   What?

Angela   You're the magician. Bring her back for me –

Tony   Only thing I ever had a real talent for was Vanishing
Acts – and that was a long time ago. Now it's Spiderman
balloons and making socks appear out of plastic washing
machines at kids parties. (*Beat.*) I even lost Harvey today.

Angela   Harvey?

Tony   My rabbit – Harvey.

Angela (*starts to laugh*)   Your rabbit's called Harvey?

Tony   After the movie – with James Stewart.

Angela   What – the one where he spends the whole time
talking to a giant rabbit?

Tony   Yeah. Harvey's my one upmanship on everybody else
in the Yellow Pages. Harvey gets me my bookings.

Angela   I'm laughing, Tony. That's terrible. Listen to me. I
shouldn't be laughing.

Tony   It's Harvey.

Angela   Stop it.

Tony   What?

Angela   You're making me laugh. (*Beat.*) Never been much
laughter in this house.

Tony   Caitlin knew how to laugh.

Angela   I couldn't have loved her enough, could I? Or she'd
still be here. You've still got Lauren.

Tony   You know how to love, Angela.

Angela   What are you doing?

Tony   Giving you some Benpathol.

Angela   You're drugging me?

Tony   Yeah, I'm drugging you – lie down.

Angela *lies down and takes the tablets.*

Angela   Stay with me.

Tony   I'll stay.

Angela   Stay with me till I'm asleep. Lie down with me – here.

Tony   Well, budge up then lard arse.

They lie together along the sofa.

Lights.

Scene Seven

The forest.

The Pavilion doors are ahead.

Ben   There it is.

They stop and pass a bottle of vodka round.

Ben (*to* **Cass**)   Got any of the Valium left?

Cass (*shaking her head*)   Gone.

Dante *has the vodka bottle raised to his eye, and is trying to pour vodka into it.*

Ben   What the fuck you doing, Dante?

Dante   Eye shots. Best way to drink it – goes straight into the bloodstream.

Tasha   It's going everywhere – you're wasting it. (*Takes bottle from him.*)

Ben (*to* **Cass**)   What you looking for?

Cass (*looking up at the sky*)   Nothing. (*Beat.*) Thought it was starting to snow, but it isn't.

Ben   So – we going in?

Tasha   Why do we have to go in?

Ben   Cause I feel like it. Say our own goodbyes. Make our own tributes. Or maybe change our minds and burn the whole fucking place down.

Tasha   You wouldn't.

Ben   Don't know what I might feel like in five minutes' time. But I do know Frayne's not getting the last word. Did you see the way she tried to make eye contact with us all – one after the other – but her bifocals screwed it up for her and she lost track – eyeballed me about five times.

Tasha   What was she wearing?

Cass   Yeah – on her salary there's no excuse.

Ben   It's like she thinks driving a Ford Fiesta and shopping at Primark – when she doesn't have to – is a sign of humility or something. Like Primark and her Ford Fiesta are her way to God, who might just overlook the fact that she hasn't done a lot over the years about the fact that her husband's probably been fiddling with every kid including their own in like a ten-mile radius or something.

Dante   Man, you go on.

Ben   Cause there's stuff to go on about. OK – we're going in?

Tasha   I'm not. Place feels all wrong.

Cass   Yeah, cause someone died here, Tasha.

Tasha   Yeah, and I have a problem with that. Maybe you don't, but I do –

Ben   So go home.

Tasha *turns away from the group, notes how dark it's become in the forest.*

Tasha   Fuck you, Ben.

Cass   They used to have dances here in the thirties, forties, fifties – right up until the late sixties. (*Beat.*) My grandad used to come here.

The Pavilion is suddenly illuminated from the inside. There's the sound of people dancing and music playing.

Ben, **Cass**, **Lauren**, **Dante**, **Tasha** *move slowly towards the Pavilion.*

The lights go out and the music stops.

They enter the Pavilion.

Ben *turns on a torch and shines it round.*

Ben   How come I'm the only one with a torch?

Dante   Yeah, how come you are the only one with a torch?

Ben   Thought we might come here.

Tasha   Sick.

Cass   What – you actually packed a torch? Before the funeral?

Ben   Even checked the batteries.

Tasha   Sick.

Ben   Yeah, I heard the first time. (*He shines the torch up to the roof.*) There.

Lauren   How d'you know?

Ben   Only place you could manage to get a scarf round the beam from that platform there.

Tasha   Stop it.

Ben *shines the torch briefly into her face then swings it back to the platform.*

Cass   She'd been in the Pavilion two days when they found her.

Dante   How come they took so long to find her?

Ben   Cause she wanted to do it properly.

Cass   A body can swell up to two or three times its normal size in that time because of the methane gas.

Tasha   That's disgusting.

Cass   The accumulation of gas then dislodges the internal organs, which bloom out from the body's lower orifices.

Lauren   I don't want to imagine that.

Cass   I think it's kind of beautiful.

Dante   Yeah and flies lay eggs on the body even before it's dead, which means maggots hatch in like under twenty-four hours. And these maggots – they don't crawl, they jump. I got this crime-scene book about America's most famous serial killers –

Ben   Infamous –

Dante   You're interrupting.

Ben   Serial killers are infamous – not famous.

Dante   What I said.

Ben   No you didn't. You said famous, which is misleading cause it makes me think you think serial killers are something to aspire to.

Dante   Whatever. In my book it says these maggots can jump as high as thirty centimetres into the air, and they attack the corpse in packs. Imagine a pack of maggots.

Ben   Well my dad heard it was maggots that knocked some of her teeth out.

Lauren   What is it with you?

Ben   What?

Lauren   Talking about Caitlin like that – like you're terrified we all might think you actually had feelings for her.

Ben   You're chatting shit, Lauren.

Lauren   You know how she felt about you – couldn't quite believe you were going out with her. She never talked about it cause it was like she thought if she did – her luck would run out. Only it wasn't luck. Caitlin was beautiful.

Ben   I never said she wasn't.

Lauren   And you never told her she was either. I know you never told her. You never told her on purpose cause that would have changed everything wouldn't it, Ben? You would have had to go public and we all know what that means. People everywhere – hands on their phones – ready. Cause it's not right, is it – someone like you seeing someone like Caitlin. It just doesn't happen. People don't like stuff like that happening; people don't want stuff like that happening. We're policing ourselves to death. Look at us. The adults don't need to worry –

Ben   Adults? Listen to yourself, Lauren. Fuck – When did you last see an adult? A real live adult? There are no adults. All I see is grown-up kids with wrinkles wearing bad clothes. (*Beat.*) Me and Caitlin had fun together, but she spent too much of her time airbrushing nails and removing excess body hair from strangers for us to really think about anything long term.

Lauren   You told her you were going to get engaged.

Ben   She told you that? I forgot that.

Lauren   I saw you in the art block that day. I saw you –

Ben   Not the art block story again, Lauren. We've done the art block story.

Cass   She's right.

Ben   About what?

Cass   You and Caitlin. I saw you with her. I saw you here with her. I followed you through the woods, talking and laughing together.

Ben   That's pretty fucking creepy, Cass.

Cass   You put your coats on the floor. You had candles in your pocket. There they are – down there still. You made a fire in that old bucket – even the empty fucking doughnut box is still here.

Ben   Yeah? So? Get it on your phone? Haven't seen it on YouTube yet. Never had you down as a stalker, Cass.

Dante   Stalking can get intense. You're like not in control. When I was in Year Nine I stalked this Italian teacher for like a whole term. I kept a diary of sightings – how many times a day I saw her – the time and place – what she was wearing – whether she looked happy or sad. When she had lunch duty on the playing fields, I'd go up to the cricket hut afterwards and collect the cigarette stubs. I used to grade them according to how much lipstick was round the tip. She was a heavy smoker. When I saw the butts lying in the grass I'd get this like thrill – this deep thrill in my stomach – just before picking them up.

Cass   I'm not a fucking stalker, Dante.

Dante   You followed them through the woods and watched them fuck.

Cass   They didn't fuck.

Dante (*to* **Ben**)   You didn't fuck? Long way to come to eat doughnuts.

Ben   They were good doughnuts. (*Beat. To* **Cass**.) You've got nothing on me.

Cass   All that stuff you put about like *mocking* 'how sentimentality in the media's turning us into emotional émigrés'. You're no émigré, Ben – I saw you.

Ben   Can't believe you did that. I trusted you –

Cass   With what?

Ben   I know what this is about – And I'm sorry I never got round to poking you like I poked Caitlin – truth is I just never really felt like it.

Tasha   Yeah, you always had a thing about Ben. Even when we were at St Joseph's.

Ben   I'd rather poke your mum than you – Last time I was round she tried to get me to do some blow with her – share the hot tub . . .

Cass   She never.

Ben   Did.

Dante   She does blow? I just thought she had like bad dandruff.

Ben   No – that's fallout from her nostrils.

Dante   How come she never asked *me* to share her tub?

Cass   Fuck off, both of you.

Ben   You act like you've got all this stuff inside you and it's tormenting you, but you're empty, Cass. Nothing but a void.

Cass   I'm not empty. I feel stuff.

Ben   There's nothing there, Cass. You're not there.

Cass   I'm here.

Ben   Can't hear you.

Cass (*shouting*)   I'M HERE.

Ben   Can't see you neither.

Cass (*shouting*)   I'M HERE.

Ben   Just can't see you.

Cass   I'm here – aren't I?

Silence.

Aren't I?

Ben   It's like you've gone already.

Lauren   Shut up, Ben. Cass –

Ben (*to* **Cass**)   You've thought about it, haven't you?

Lauren   We've all thought about it, Ben.

Tasha   I think about it. When I get exhausted – like so exhausted I can't be bothered to turn my head on the pillow even though I'm lying in my own drool, but it's more like I just want to stop. Stop completely, but without having to . . . to die or anything. (*Beat.*) It's the hanging I don't get. Why not pills? Something quiet.

Ben   Hanging's quiet.

Tasha   It hurts though.

Ben   That's a myth. It doesn't hurt – I'm telling you. Your neck snaps in like seconds.

Lauren   Don't listen to him –

Tasha   It's weird – it could have been any of us, couldn't it?

Lauren   Only it wasn't. It was Caitlin.

Ben   She made up her mind. (*Beat.*) She wanted to go, Lauren. It was her time to go. It's like she'd accessed all the inbuilt codes in the game and was operating on like a totally different level.

Lauren   I want you to see this.

They all crowd round **Lauren***'s phone.*

Ben   That's Caitlin's phone.

Lauren   Her mum gave it to me. (*Beat.*) She didn't know what else to do with it.

Lights.

Caitlin (*voice off*)   Ben?

Various   Shit – that's Caitlin.

The sound of rain – and someone walking slowly through the forest. An image is projected or can be sent onto audience's mobiles.

A pair of feet, in trainers, walking. Trees, sky, then the feet walking again.

Caitlin (*voice off*)   Rain. (*Beat.*) All it ever does.

The Pavilion doors come up.

Recognise it?

The camera goes into the Pavilion. Jerky shots of interior. The candles on the floor, etc. The film blacks out for a while. When the image is restored, the candles are lit. Film focuses on candles for quite a while then **Caitlin***'s face, staring straight ahead – almost expressionless.*

Remember that afternoon we took Valium? Nothing happened – we just sat on my bedroom floor for hours, watching the curtains blow and that rainstorm coming closer. Then it broke and the rain was coming through the window and soaking the curtains and they stopped flapping. Rain soaked the carpet, our feet . . . and the TV was on, busy behind us, but we just carried on sitting there. (*Beat.*) That was the best afternoon I ever had.

Beat.

Best afternoon of my life – even though nothing happened. Better than that time we came here. Why is that? (*Beat.*) Don't know why I'm talking to you like this. I'm not good on my own. Dad says I can't walk down the street alone.

Caitlin *smiles suddenly.*

Yeah, well, life's a can of worms. (*Beat.*) Sleep tight. (*Beat.*) Ta-ta.

Film cuts out.

Scene Eight

Tony *is sitting on the sofa, talking on the phone. There's a box of pizza on the coffee table.*

Enter **Lauren***, snow on her coat and in her hair.*

Tony   I'll phone tomorrow – yeah.

Lauren   Who was that?

Tony   Angela.

Lauren   How is she?

Tony   Not good. Can't sleep. Where've you been?

Lauren   Out and about.

Tony   I ordered pizza.

Lauren   When?

Tony   About an hour ago.

Lauren   You should of started – it'll be cold.

Tony   I like cold pizza.

Lauren *sits down on the sofa next to him. They stare at the pizza.*

Lauren   What did you order?

Tony   Can't remember.

They continue to stare at the box.

Lauren   What's the time?

Tony   About seven.

Lauren   Not late.

Tony   Feels like midnight.

Lauren   Been a long day. (*Beat.*) You should go.

Tony   Where?

Lauren   See if Angela's OK.

Tony   I should?

Lauren   You're worried about her.

Tony   Yeah –

Lauren   Go on –

He gets up.

Tony   You'll be OK?

Lauren   Dad –

Tony   Love you.

Lauren   I know.

Tony   I'll phone.

Lauren   Yeah –

Tony   There might be something on TV.

Lauren   Yeah –

Lights.

Scene Nine

Doug *is sitting by the window in his wheelchair.*

Enter **Cass**, *covered in snow.*

Doug   It's snowing at last.

Cass   Yeah – it's snowing heavy. Already lying. You should come away from the window, Grandad – it's cold over there.

Doug   I've been waiting for you.

Cass   Well, I'm here now.

Doug   Your hair's wet.

Cass   It'll dry.

Doug   Don't want to catch cold.

Cass (*using her scarf to dry it*)   There.

Doug   Come here. I'll give it a brush through.

Cass *hesitates then goes and kneels by* **Doug**, *who starts brushing her hair.*

Lights.

Scene Ten

*There are three rooms in this scene – the lounge, **Ben**'s bedroom and the Samaritans office. **Paul** and **Alex** are sitting on the sofa, watching TV. **Paul** is asleep. Enter **Michelle**, blowing on a cup of tea. She sits down at a desk in the Samaritans office, yawns, and starts to sort through some papers. Enter **Ruth** who also sits down at a desk in the Samaritans office.*

*Enter **Ben**.*

Alex   Ssh – Dad's asleep.

Ben   What you watching?

Alex   *Dr Who*.

Ben   Thought that was only on Saturdays.

Alex   Repeats. Dad'll be mad when he wakes up. You were meant to be home at six and you weren't.

Ben   So –

Alex   And Mum's been phoning.

Ben   So –

Alex   Ssh – I'm trying to watch this.

Ben   You're the one talking.

*Exit **Ben**, upstairs.*

Ben *lies on his bed then after a while gets up again, puts some music on and takes some Valium. He makes a couple of movements in time to the music then stops, laughing. He notices **Alex**'s cyborg mask.*

Ben (*calling out*)   Alex! Alex – you been in my room again?

He sits on the side of the bed, checks his phone, throws it to the end of the bed then retrieves it, and makes a call – his movements slow and heavy.

The phones in the Samaritans office start to ring.

Ruth   I got it. Hello, this is Samaritans.

Silence.

Is there something you want to talk about?

Ben   No.

Ruth   That's fine. We don't have to talk.

Ben   I don't know why I phoned.

Ruth   You don't need a reason to phone.

Ben   You sound fake. (*Beat.*) What's your name?

Ruth   Ruth.

Ben   Ruth – bet that's not your real name. (*Beat.*) You still there, Ruth?

Ruth   I'm here.

Ben   Well, I don't want to speak to you.

Ruth   D'you want to speak to somebody else here?

Ben   No. (*Beat.*) Ruth?

Ruth   Yes?

Ben   Nothing. (*Beat.*) My legs are shaking. I'm like staring down at them and they're shaking. It's weird – this doesn't normally happen.

Ruth   Have you taken something?

Ben   Valium.

Ruth   Does it hurt?

Ben   Don't think so – they're just shaking.

Ruth   Has it happened before?

Ben (*suddenly angry*)   What are you? Fucking NHS Direct?

Ruth   How much Valium did you take?

Ben   Lost track. Valium's made a real comeback. Did you ever take it first time round when you were, like, an eighties housewife?

Ruth   I didn't – no.

Ben   But you could have done.

Ruth   I could have.

Ben   How old are you?

Ruth   Thirty-one.

Ben   Fuck. That's old. How long have you been doing this for?

Ruth   Twelve years. (*Beat.*) Are you at home?

Ben   Yeah.

Ruth   Is anyone there with you?

Ben   Yes and no. My kid brother – who thinks he's a cyborg. Shit – I feel sick just looking at my legs shaking.

Ruth   D'you want an ambulance?

Ben   No. Think I'll take a walk. Just need to breathe. Is it still snowing?

Ruth   D'you like the snow?

Ben   Used to. When I was a kid. Now it's just cold stuff.

Ruth   Not if you wrap up warm. (*Beat.*) If it lies, it'll be the first white Christmas in ten years.

Ben   Ten years is a long time. Can you hear that? It's the planes coming over like all the time – they must have changed the flight path. Sky's full of them. Hear that? They're beginning to sound like ice-cream vans. Maybe they are ice-cream vans. Maybe – at a certain time of night – all the aeroplanes turn into ice-cream vans. (*Beat.*) So – you been doing this for twenty years?

Ruth   That's right.

Ben   You saved anybody?

Ruth   I hope so.

Ben   Did my friend Caitlin phone you?

Ruth   I don't remember speaking to Caitlin. She might have spoken to somebody else here.

Ben   Well Caitlin died. She did it herself.

Ruth   You were close?

Ben   I never thought about it much till now – but, yeah. I've been going over stuff in my head.

Ruth   What sort of stuff?

Ben   I don't know just stuff. I said so much stupid stuff to her. I'm saying stupid stuff to you as well – maybe that's all I ever do – say stupid stuff. I'm too tired to explain and anyway you sound like maybe you're a bitch in your other life.

Silence.

You still there? (*Beat.*) Mum?

Ruth   I'm still here.

Ben *drops the phone and the line goes dead. Throughout the following exchange,* **Ben** *goes downstairs, puts on his coat, picks up an apple and* **Alex***'s cyborg mask.* **Alex** *has fallen asleep and is lying across* **Paul***'s lap.*

Ruth *rubs her face, exhausted.*

Michelle   You OK?

Ruth   Yeah.

Michelle   Want me to make you a cup of tea before I go?

Ruth   No – you go. (*Beat.*) Young boy I was speaking to just called me Mum. A lot of them do that – don't even know they're doing it. That ever happened to you?

Michelle   Once.

Ruth   Used to happen when I was teaching, as well. Suppose they're so used to saying it –

Michelle   You're sure you're OK?

Ruth   Just tired. See you tomorrow.

Michelle   I'm not in tomorrow. Day after that. Whatever day that is – I've lost track.

Ruth   Drive home carefully. It was snowing earlier.

Michelle   See you –

Ruth   Yeah – see you.

Lights.

Scene Eleven

Ben *is walking around the forest in the snow. He's still wearing the cyborg mask and keeps walking into trees. The Christmas tree has now grown.* **Ben** *circles it a few times, then starts to climb, an old school tie just visible, hanging out of his pocket.*

Lights.

The Pavilion door opens slowly, a faint light coming from inside, which gets gradually brighter.

The sound of a child, laughing.

Enter **Caitlin***, aged eight, in a blue dress with a rabbit on it, barefoot and holding a yellow scarf, laughing.*

Caitlin *runs out into the snow between the trees as though somebody's chasing her. She hesitates, as though she can hear someone speaking to her, quickly ties the yellow scarf round her neck as though she's dressing up then goes over to the tree* **Ben** *climbed, staring up into the branches.*

After a while, **Ben***, also aged eight, dressed in his school uniform and still wearing the cyborg mask, climbs down from the tree. The two children stare cautiously at each other. Then* **Caitlin** *re-ties Ben's tie, which hasn't been done properly, and* **Ben** *re-arranges* **Caitlin***'s yellow scarf. They hold hands and run back towards the Pavilion door, disappearing inside.*

The Pavilion door shuts.

Alice's Adventures in Wonderland

Simon Reade

based on the novel by Lewis Carroll

About the Author

Simon Reade is Associate Producer for Theatre Royal Bath Productions and Producer for Filter Theatre Company. His plays for the theatre include: *Pride & Prejudice* (Theatre Royal Bath, 2009); Salman Rushdie's *Midnight's Children* (2003), Ted Hughes's *Tales from Ovid* (both with Tim Supple, 1999) and *Epitaph for the Official Secrets Act* (with Paul Greengrass, 2009) all for the Royal Shakespeare Company, where he was Literary Manager and Dramaturg; Geraldine McCaughrean's *Not the End of the World* (2007), Jill Tomlinson's *The Owl Who Was Afraid of the Dark* (2003) and Philip Pullman's *Aladdin and the Enchanted Lamp* (with Aletta Collins, 2005) all for Bristol Old Vic, where he was Artistic Director; and Philip Pullman's *The Scarecrow and His Servant* (Poonamallee Productions/Southwark Playhouse, 2008). Simon's adaptations of Michael Morpurgo's *Private Peaceful* (2008), *The Mozart Question* (2008) and *Toro! Toro!* (2010) have been seen on tour throughout the UK, Sweden and North America. His books include a history of the international touring company Cheek by Jowl and *Dear Mr Shakespeare: Letters to a Jobbing Playwright*.

About the Play

Alice Liddell, one of the Dean of Christchurch Oxford's three young daughters, asked Charles Dodgson to make up a story during a picnic taken along the River Cherwell one hot summer's afternoon in 1862: 'I had sent my heroine straight down a rabbit-hole, to begin with, without the least idea what was to happen afterwards,' recalled Dodgson. Its themes had been gestating all his life.

Charles Lutwidge Dodgson grew up in Cheshire where he had a cat. His juvenilia includes cautionary tales satirising the censorious moralising of adults: 'Don't dream'; or 'Never stew your sister'. Boarding at Rugby School, the rules were draconian, but there were some comforts: untreated water in the mid-nineteenth century was disease-carrying, so the powers-that-be gave the adolescent pupils beer instead with their school dinners. The 'Drink Me' effects of alcohol were learnt young.

A mathematician and logician, Charles Lutwidge Dodgson wrote under the pseudonym Lewis Carroll: a Latinisation of his first and second names inverted. With the propriety expected of an Oxford don, Dodgson dodged behind his Carroll persona and thus was able to lambaste the arbitrary codes of behaviour demanded by an institutionalised society hostile to the imaginative, maverick individual. As we mature, we succumb to the immature nonsense of decorum and manners and respect for authority. Yet the raw, gleeful spark of our childhood self is something we seek to re-ignite. The story transcends the Victorian Age in which it was written because of the intrepid childlike imagination of Alice and the vivid childishness of the adult creatures. Her attempt to impose order on the adult chaos (the quarrelsome mayhem of rule-abiding games such as croquet or a caucus race) is her rite of passage into an aggressively adult world. And yet it's a world of wonder if we allow our curiosity to keep challenging it.

Producing the Play

When I ran Bristol Old Vic with David Farr part of our policy was to produce innovative family work throughout the year in the Main House and Studio, and spill the energy and inventiveness into our radical, classical repertoire – work that Tom Morris, the current Artistic Director, continues.

The space of the Theatre Royal itself inspires: a dilapidated Georgian auditorium with a disproportionately deep modern stage. Into this space came Melly Still, designer and choreographer turned director, to stage the play in December 2004. She pursued the truth of the story, of the situations, to give psychological perspectives on character. So the Mad Hatter's tea party was a lunatic study in despair. The White Rabbit's omnipresence became sinister. The Queen's predilection for decapitation climaxed with Alice being led to the guillotine and only waking up from that nightmare after the blade had dropped – but had failed to chop off her head.

As a designer, Melly relished the tricks of visual perspective. She knew how to deal with stage directions such as '*Now she is growing enormously tall*'. Alice picks up a tiny matchbox-sized table one moment; the next, she is dwarfed by huge table legs dangling from above, all but drowning in the copious fabric of her dress now that '*she's shrunk*'. We also used puppets: after Alice had grown again by eating the magic mushroom after her conversation with the three-inch-tall, hookah-smoking caterpillar, a puppet butterfly fluttered by, puffing on a miniature hookah.

For expediency, we had a small ensemble playing multiple roles. This could be how the Cheshire Cat came to be a projected film – although one of Carroll's many talents was as a brilliant pioneer of photography, and the Cheshire Cat's appearing smile seems to owe much to early photographic image-developing techniques.

Make of the play what you will. It's a dream. Have fun.

For Rose, Amy, Hazel and Otto

Characters

Alice's Sister
Alice
(*their* **Mother**)
White Rabbit
Cheshire Cat
Mouse
Duck
Dodo
Parrot
Eagle
Caterpillar
Duchess
Baby
Cook
March Hare
Hatter
Dormouse
Three gardener-playing-cards: **Seven**, **Five**, **Two**
Gryphon
King of Hearts
Queen of Hearts
Mock Turtle
(Whiting)
(Snail)
Alice's **Child**
(*Alice's Child's* **Dad**)

Birds, Soldiers, Hedgehogs, Flamingoes, Beasts, Pack of Cards

curiouser

and curiouser

Scene One: Playing

*A bare stage. An attic playroom. A girl, **Alice**, is having a tea party with her toys, such as: a cuddly rabbit; a doll with a crown; a metallic, clock-work mechanical tortoise, etc. She's got a miniature china tea set and some tiny pots and pans. There are also a pack of cards; a globe; a heart cushion; a croquet mallet; a pram; etc. scattered around. She also gives her cat, serenely curled up in its basket and appearing to grin, an affectionate stroke and a saucer of milk. From her pocket, she hands out some tiny sweets to the toys, eats a generous few herself, returns the rest to her pocket.*

*Her **Sister** is there too, playing a musical instrument quite nicely. **Alice** uses the music as accompaniment to her improvised game – to her **Sister**'s increasing irritation. After enough of this:*

Sister   Alice! Please be quiet, Alice!

Alice   Why? You're making a noise too. The louder you play, the louder I have to speak.

Sister   Well, do something else.

Alice   But what should I do?

Sister   Anything, as long as you play without talking.

Alice   You try playing without squeaking!

Sister   Read a book – you can borrow one of mine.

Alice   Your books are all words. What is the point of a book without pictures or conversation in it? It's nonsense.

Sister   Well go outside, or something.

Alice   I can't. It's snowing.

Mother (*off*)   Alice! Alice! Alice!

Alice   What is it?

Mother (*off*)   It's tea-time!

Alice   I'm not hungry!

Mother (*off*)   Stop eating sweets then!

Alice (*flabbergasted*)   But how? . . . Have you been spying on me? . . . It's a secret!

Sister   Alice! Do as you're told!

Mother (*off*)   And tell your sister to come too.

Alice   No!

Sister   You're such a baby.

Alice   I'm not a baby. I'm a grown-up girl. I'm Alice.

Sister   You're spoilt.

Alice   Right. That's – it!

Alice *chucks the rabbit off and lies down – flat out, a little girl fed up and barely avoiding a tantrum.*

Sister (*sotto voce*)   Pig.

Alice   What did you say?

Sister   I said fig.

The **White Rabbit** *reappears, human-size now, and* **Alice** *notices:*

Alice   Curiouser. And curiouser.

The **Sister** *doesn't notice the* **White Rabbit** *and continues to play her musical instrument.* **Alice** *starts to leave the attic.*

Sister   Where are you going?

Alice   Out.

Sister   Wrap up warm.

The music develops into a musical transformation transporting us into Wonderland . . .

Scene Two: Down the Rabbit-hole

The **White Rabbit** *takes its fob-watch out of its waist-coat pocket.*

White Rabbit   Oh dear, oh dear. I shall be too late.

Alice, *burning with curiosity, runs after the* **White Rabbit** *who disappears down a rabbit-hole.* **Alice** *follows it down . . .*

Alice *is falling down a rabbit-hole.*

Alice   I wonder what's going to happen next?

'Down' song.

Maps and pictures, cupboards and shelves rush by. **Alice** *grabs a jar of orange marmalade from a shelf.*

(*sung*)
   Down, down, down.

(*spoken*)   Marmalade – oh, it's empty. I'd better not drop it: it might kill somebody.

She puts the jar back.

(*sung*)
   Down, down, down.
   I wonder: how many miles have I fallen?
   Four thousand miles down? I must be near the centre of the
   earth.
   I wonder: what latitude or longitude am I at?
   I wonder: will I fall right through the earth?

   I'll come out where
   they walk upside down:
   'if you please,
   would this be Australia
   or New Zealand?'
   Down, down, down.

A grinning **Cat** *appears and disappears.*

Alice (*spoken*)   I hope they'll remember to give my cat a saucer of milk. I wish you were here: there are no mice in the air, but you might catch a bat, and a bat's a kind of flying mouse, after all.

(*sung*)
   I wonder:
   do cats eat bats?

do bats eat cats?
do cats eat bats?
do bats eat cats?

Down down down.

Scene Three: Drinking and Shrinking, Eating and Growing

Alice *lands with a thump, sees the* **White Rabbit** *disappearing.*

White Rabbit   Oh my ears and whiskers, how late it's getting.

Alice *finds herself in a long, low hallway, dimly lit by lamps hanging from the ceiling, with dozens of doors on both sides.*

Alice   Oh. So many doors.

They're all locked.

I wonder how I'll ever get out again? I ought to get back for my tea. Help!

There is a tiny golden key on a three-legged glass table.

I suppose this is the key . . .

. . . it doesn't fit any of the doors . . .

. . . No . . .

– *except for a tiny one behind a curtain.*

It fits!

She kneels down.

Oh look, look, a wonderful garden: what lovely fountains; what bright flower-beds. And it's summer-time! If I could just get my head – but then my shoulders . . . If only I could close up like a telescope – maybe I can? . . . I must get into that garden – maybe it's the way home?

She returns to the glass table – there's a bottle on it with a label: 'Drink Me.'

That certainly wasn't there before. It's all very well saying
'Drink Me' but you won't catch me doing that in a hurry! I
may be thirsty but what if it's poison? I know about children
who get burnt and eaten up by wild beasts, because they don't
remember things like:
a red-hot poker will burn you if you hold it too long;
or:
if you cut your finger with a knife it usually bleeds;
and:
if you drink from a bottle labelled 'poison' it's almost certain
to disagree with you sooner or later. But it doesn't say 'poison'
does it? It says 'Drink Me'.

She drinks it.

That's very nice. It's a sort of cherry-tart-and-custard, pine-
appley-roast-turkey-toffee-hot-buttered-toasty kind of flavour.

She starts to shrink.

What a curious feeling: I *am* closing up like a telescope.

She goes to the door.

Oh no! Now I've forgotten the key!

*She returns to the table, but now can't reach the key on top of it, although
she can see it through the glass. It's too slippery to climb, and she flops
down and cries and cries and cries.*

There's no use crying like that, Alice. I advise you to leave off
this minute –
Yes, I generally give myself good advice. Not that I always
follow it. I remember I once boxed my own ears because I
cheated in a game of croquet – I was playing against myself.
But it's no use now pretending to be two people: there's hardly
enough of me to make *one* person. I've got to get home. I've
got to get into that garden. But what has happened to me?

Alice *spies a glass box beneath the table. She opens it and finds a very
small cake with the words: 'Eat Me.'*

'Eat me.' I will. I'm starving! And if it makes me grow bigger,
I'll be able to reach the key. And if it makes me get any

smaller, well I can creep under the door. Either way, I'll be able to get into the garden and find my way home.

She nibbles a bit of cake and holds the top of her head in anticipation. Nothing happens. She nibbles a bit more. Still nothing. She finishes off the cake.

Curiouser and curiouser.

Now she is growing enormously tall.

Now I'm opening up like the largest telescope ever.

Her head hits the ceiling.

Ow!

She grabs the key from off the table, unlocks the door –

Hurray! The garden.

– but now she's so large, she can barely even look through the little door. She starts crying again.

Please. I want to go home!

You ought to be ashamed of yourself, a great girl like you. Stop this moment I tell you!

*She has shed gallons of tears. A pool spreads around her, along the hallway – from where the **White Rabbit** reappears, splendidly dressed, carrying a pair of white kid gloves in one hand and a fan in the other. **Alice** dries her eyes.*

Alice   Please, Sir –

*The **White Rabbit** takes fright, drops the tiny gloves and tiny fan, and scurries away into the darkness.*

Alice   Your fan!

She picks up the gloves and fan, with which she starts cooling herself.

How strange everything is today. Yesterday things went on just as usual. I wonder if I've been changed for one of my friends in the night? Let me think: was I the same when I got up this morning? I almost think I can remember feeling a little different. But if I'm not the same, then the next question is: Who in the world am I?

(*despairing:*)   Who in the world am I?
That's the great puzzle.

Pause.

I'm tired of being here all alone. I'm dying of hunger. I think I'm a bit scared.

She cries some more. She's shrunk. She's waving the fan.

I've shrunk! How?

She notices the now huge fan, stops fanning, and drops it hastily.

Scene Four: The Pool of Tears

Alice *rushes to the glass table with the gold key on it, but again she cannot reach it.*

Alice   I've never been as small as this before. Never!

Her foot slips. Splash! She's up to her chin in water.

Help!

Salty? That's funny. This tastes like the sea – but I like the seaside. Oh. This is what comes of crying so much. I'll be punished now, I suppose, by drowning in my own tears!

She hears something splashing and swims towards . . . a **Mouse**.

Alice   O Mouse, I'm trying to find the garden.
I am very tired of swimming – do you know the way out of this pool?
O Mouse.

The **Mouse** *doesn't respond.*

Alice   Perhaps it doesn't speak English? Maybe it's a French mouse, come over with William the Conqueror?
Excusez-moi, madame mouse, où est ma chatte?

The **Mouse** *almost leaps out of the water.*

Alice   Oh I do beg your pardon. How thoughtless – a *chatte*'s a cat. You probably don't like cats.

Mouse Not like cats! Would you like cats if you were me?

Alice   Probably not, but please don't get angry. Sorry. We won't talk about cats any more.

Mouse   *We?* *I* wasn't. My family's always hated cats – nasty, low, vulgar things.

The **Mouse** *swims back.*

Swim to the shore, and I'll tell you my story: then you'll know why I hate cats. And dogs.

They both swim to the shore, followed by a flock of birds: a **Duck**, **Dodo**, **Parrot**, **Eagle**, *etc. They all step out of the pool, soaked through.*

Scene Five: A Dry History, a Caucus Race and a Long Tale

Stillness.

Alice   Where did all these birds come from?

Eagle   So how are we going to get dry then?

Parrot   Dry?

Eagle   I'm dripping wet.

Duck   I like the wet.

Eagle   But how are we going to get dry?

Parrot   Dry?

Alice   Let's think.

Parrot   Let's think.

Alice   That's what I said.

Parrot   That's what I said.

Alice   Are you copying me?

Parrot   Are you copying me?

Alice   How old are you?

Parrot   How old are you?

Alice   How old am I?

Parrot   How old am I? I'm older than you, so I know best.

Silence.

Eagle   I'm still wet.

Parrot   You are wet.

Mouse   Listen to me. I'll soon make you dry.

Alice   Thank you.

They all sit in a large ring with the **Mouse** *in the middle.*

Mouse   This is the driest thing I know:
(*the* **Mouse** *clears its throat:*)
'William the Conqueror –'

Parrot (*shivers*)   Ugh!

Mouse   Did you speak?

Parrot   Speak?

Mouse   Now stop that, I'm trying –

Parrot   Drying?

Pause.

Mouse   'William the Conqueror, whose cause was favoured by the Archbishop of Canterbury, who found it advisable –'

Duck   Found what?

Mouse   Found *it*. You know what 'it' means?

Duck   Yes I know what 'it' means. When I find a thing, *it*'s generally a frog or a worm. The question is: what did the Archbishop find?

Mouse   'He found it advisable to go with Edgar Atheling to meet William and offer him the crown.' (*To* **Alice**.) How are you getting on now my dear?

Alice   As wet as ever. This story doesn't seem to dry me at all.

Dodo   In that case, I move that the meeting adjourn, for the immediate adoption of more energetic remedies.

Eagle   Speak English! I've no idea what you mean and, what's more, I don't believe you do either.

Dodo   The best thing to get us dry would be a Caucus-race.

Pause.

Alice   What's a Caucus race?

Dodo   Why, the best way to explain it is to do it.

He demonstrates:

First: I mark out the race course.

It's a sort of circle.

Now, you stand here, and you there – there and here, here and there. The exact shape doesn't matter.

They all stand about randomly.

So: run when you feel like it.

They do – a musical interlude.

When everyone seems to be dry the **Dodo** *suddenly calls out:*

The race is over!

Eagle   But who's won?

Parrot   Who's won? Who's won?

Dodo   Everybody has won and all must have prizes.

Parrot   Pri-zes! Pri-zes! Pri-zes!

Eagle   But who's to give out the prizes?

Dodo (*pointing to* **Alice**)   Her, of course.

Alice   Me?

Dodo   What have you got?

Alice   Well, nothing. (*She feels in her pocket.*) Only these sweets.

Parrot   Sweets!

All   Sweets!

Alice   But I was saving them for later, just in case.

Parrot   Pardon?

Alice   I suppose I could share them . . .

They all snatch and guzzle them greedily.

Alice   Hey! That's not fair!

Duck (*to the* **Mouse**)   So, tell us some more.

Mouse   I'd love to, Ducky: 'William the Conqueror, whose conduct was, at first, moderate −'

Alice   You promised to tell me *your* story, and why it is that you hate cats − and dogs . . .

Mouse   Mine is a long and a sad tale . . .

Alice (*looking at its tail*)   It is a long tail, certainly, but why do you call it sad?

They all look at **Alice**.

The **Mouse** *leads them a song-and-dance which snakes around the stage.*

'Cat' song.

Mouse (*sung*)
We lived beneath the mat
warm and snug and fat
but one woe, and that
was the cat!

When the cat's away,
then the mice will play,
but, alas! one day
(so they say)

came the dog, and cat,
hunting for a rat,
crushed the mice all flat,
each one as he sat
underneath the mat,
warm and snug, and fat –
think of that!

Alice *has got increasingly excited by the song, playing a game of cat-and-mouse chase; but by the climax, they've all gone, leaving* **Alice** *alone.*

She hears the pattering of rabbit paws.

White Rabbit   Oh my fur and whiskers, oh my dear paws. She's sure to see to it that I'm executed, as sure as ferrets are ferrets. Where can I have dropped it, I wonder?

Alice   Are you looking for your fan?

White Rabbit   Why! Mary Ann! Where have you been?

Alice (*aside*)   Mary Ann?

White Rabbit   Run home this instant and fetch my fan. Quick now. I shall be too late!

Alice *runs off, obediently. The* **White Rabbit**, *calmly now, with a steely glint in its eye, retreats.* **Alice** *reappears, empty-handed.*

Alice   Wait! How do I get into the garden? 'Mary Ann' – I know I'm not her, whoever she is . . . I wonder what will become of me?

Now, the first thing I must do is grow back to my right size. Then the second thing I must do is find my way into the garden. Yes. That's the plan. I suppose I really need to eat or drink something or other? But the great question is: what?

'What' song.

(*sung*)
What? What?
What will hit the spot?
That flower perhaps –
or not?

What? What?
A forgetmenot?
Is this grass greener?
What rot!

What? What?
Do I know what's what?
Not what but whatnot.
What? What? What?

What's the great question?
What!

Scene Six: Advice from a Caterpillar

There is a mushroom a tiny bit taller than **Alice***. Stretching up to see what's on top, she comes face to face with a languid, blue* **Caterpillar***, smoking a hookah.*

Caterpillar   Who are you?

Alice   Good question. I hardly know, just at present. At least I know who I was when I got up this morning, but I think I must have changed several times since then.

Caterpillar   What do you mean? Explain yourself.

Alice   I can't explain myself, I'm afraid, because I'm not myself, you see.

Caterpillar   I don't see.

Alice   I'm afraid I can't put it more clearly because I don't understand it myself really. Being so many different sizes in one day is very confusing.

Caterpillar   It isn't.

Alice   Well perhaps you haven't found it confusing yet, but when you turn into a chrysalis, and then after that into a butterfly, I think you will find it a little strange, won't you?

Caterpillar   Not a bit.

Alice   Well, perhaps you're different. I know I'd feel strange. I do feel strange.

Caterpillar   You? Who *are* you?

Alice   I think you ought to tell me who you are first.

Caterpillar (*unpleasantly*)   Why?

Puzzled, exasperated, **Alice** *turns away.*

Caterpillar   Come back! I've got something important to say.

Alice *turns back.*

Caterpillar   Keep your temper.

Alice   Is that all?

Caterpillar   No.

Alice *waits. The* **Caterpillar** *puffs away. Silence.*

Caterpillar   So, you think you're changed, do you?

Alice   I'm afraid I am. I can't remember the things I used to know – and I can't stay the same size for more than ten minutes at a time.

Caterpillar   Can't remember what things?

Alice   Well, I can't remember where I'm trying to get to all of a sudden. And I can't even remember the simplest of rhymes: 'How doth the little busy bee . . . ' – See. I've forgotten.

Caterpillar   Try 'You are old, Father William'.

Alice *folds her arms and concentrates.*

Alice   'You are old, Father William,' –

Caterpillar (*encouraging her to remember*)   – the young man said,

Alice
'You are old, Father William,' the young man said,
'And your hair has become very white;
And yet you incessantly stand on your head –
Do you think, at your age, that is right?'

'You are old,' –

Caterpillar   – said the youth, as I mentioned before –

Alice
'You are old,' said the youth, 'as I mentioned before,
And have grown most uncommonly fat;
Yet you turned a back-somersault in at the door –
Pray, what is the reason for that?'

'You are old,' –

Caterpillar   – said the youth, –

Alice   – 'Now, that is enough!' –

Caterpillar   – Said his father; –

Alice
– 'don't give yourself airs!
Do you think I can listen all day to such stuff?
Be off, or I'll kick you down stairs!'

Pause.

Caterpillar   That is not said right.

Alice (*timidly*)   Not quite right, I'm afraid. Some of the words
have got altered.

Caterpillar   It is wrong from beginning to end.

Pause.

What size do you want to be?

Alice   Now I remember! Big enough to reach a key on top of
a table; small enough to get into the garden through the door.

But the same size. All the time. I don't like changing so often, you know.

Caterpillar   No, I don't know.

Pause.

Are you happy with your size now?

Alice   No. I need to be a little larger. Three inches is such a wretched height to be.

The **Caterpillar** *rears itself up to its full three inches.*

Caterpillar   It is a very good height!

Alice   But I'm not used to it – (*aside*)   I wish these creatures wouldn't take offence so easily.

Caterpillar   You'll get used to it in time.

The **Caterpillar** *puffs away for some moments, yawns, then descends from the mushroom and crawls away.*

One side will make you grow taller. The other side will make you grow shorter. Good-bye.

Alice   One side of *what*? The other side of *what*?

Caterpillar   Of the mushroom.

The **Caterpillar** *has gone.*

The mushroom is perfectly round.

Alice *breaks a bit off with each hand.*

Alice   But the mushroom doesn't have any sides – it's round.

She nibbles a bit from her right hand and shrinks rapidly. So she eats some from her left hand and swiftly grows.

Which is which? What is what?

A small butterfly now flutters by – puffing on a miniature hookah.

How puzzling all these changes are. You can never be sure what you're going to be from one moment to the next.

Scene Seven: The Duchess's House

A small house. **Alice** *approaches and knocks on the door.*

Howling and sneezing is heard from within. And then the great crash of a dish breaking.

Alice   How am I to get in?

The door opens suddenly and a large plate flies out, just missing **Alice***'s nose. The door slams again.*

Alice *knocks again. More sneezing, crashing, a* **Baby** *wails. And then* **Alice** *opens the door herself and enters the house.*

The door opens straight into a kitchen, full of smoke. The **Duchess** *is sitting on a three-legged stool nursing a* **Baby** *in a pram. A* **Cook** *is stirring a large cauldron. The* **Cook** *has a pepper-pot.* **Alice** *sneezes.*

Alice   There's too much pepper in that soup.

The **Duchess** *sneezes occasionally. The* **Baby** *sneezes and howls unremittingly. The* **Cook** *doesn't sneeze. Nor does a large* **Cat** *sitting on the hearth, grinning form ear to ear.*

Alice *sees the* **Cat**.

(*to* **Duchess**)   Please will you tell me why your cat grins like that?

Duchess   It's a Cheshire Cat and that's why. Pig!

Alice   I'm not a pig. (*Aside.*) How rude.

Duchess   Not you – the baby – Pig!

Alice (*aside*)   Pig? (*To the* **Duchess**.) Well, I didn't know that Cheshire cats could grin. In fact, I didn't know that cats could grin at all.

Duchess   They all can, and most of 'em do.

Alice   I don't know any that do.

Duchess   You don't know much, and that's a fact.

The **Cook** *starts throwing saucepans, plates, dishes, etc. at the* **Duchess** *and the* **Baby***. The* **Duchess** *takes no notice. The* **Baby** *is howling anyway.*

Alice   Mind what you're doing!

Duchess   If everybody minded their own business, the world would go round a great deal faster than it does.

Alice   Which would not be an advantage. Just think what would happen to day and night. You see, the earth takes twenty-four hours to turn around –

Duchess   Oh, don't bother me. I could never abide figures. (*To* **Baby**.) Shush, shush, (*suddenly screaming*) Shush!

The **Duchess** *sings a sort of lullaby. At the end of the first verse, in the 'Wow! wow! wow!' chorus, she gives the* **Baby** *in the pram a violent shake.*

'Speak Roughly' song.

Duchess (*sung*)
    Speak roughly to your little boy
    and beat him when he sneezes.
    He only does it to annoy
    because he knows it teases.

Cook/Baby/Cat (*sung*)
    Wow! wow! wow!

During the second verse, the **Duchess** *attacks the* **Baby** *even more violently.*

Duchess (*sung*)
    I speak severely to my boy.
    I beat him when he sneezes
    for he can thoroughly enjoy
    the pepper when he pleases.

Cook/Baby/Cat (*sung*)
    Wow! wow! wow!

The **Duchess** *thrusts the* **Baby** *in the pram at* **Alice**.

Duchess   Here, you may nurse it, if you like. I must go and get ready to play croquet with the Queen.

As the **Duchess** *hurries out, the* **Cook** *throws a frying-pan after her, which narrowly misses. The* **Baby** *snorts;* **Alice** *wheels the* **Baby** *in the pram outside.*

Alice   If I don't take this child with me, they're sure to kill it in a day or two. And maybe cook it. And eat it. It would be murder to leave it behind.

The **Baby** *grunts.*

Alice   Don't grunt – it's not polite.

The **Baby** *grunts again.*

Alice   Although what am I going to do with this creature when I get home? What will people think of *me*, having a *baby*?

The **Baby** *escapes from the pram and transforms into a pig.*

Alice   What are you doing? Get back in the pram, baby. Stop it! Where are you going? Stop it I say. You're a very naughty baby. Come back.

The **Pig-Baby** *grunts again.*

Alice   Pig.

The **Pig-Baby** *trots off.*

Alice   How absurd.

Scene Eight: The Cheshire Cat

Alice *is startled to see the* **Cheshire Cat** *sitting on the bough of a tree in front of her. The* **Cheshire Cat** *grins.*

Alice   Maybe the cat will know how to get into the garden?

Cheshire puss – would you tell me, please, which way I ought to go from here . . . ?

Cheshire Cat   That depends a good deal on where you want to get to.

Alice   I don't much care where, as long as . . . –

Cheshire Cat   Then it doesn't matter which way you go –

Alice   So long as I get somewhere that will take me to . . .

Cheshire Cat   Oh, you're certain to do that if you walk for long enough.

Alice   True. (*Aside.*) This isn't helping. (*To the* **Cat**.) What sort of people live round here?

Cheshire Cat   In that direction lives a Hatter. In that direction lives a March Hare. Visit either. They're both mad.

Alice   But I don't want to mix with mad people.

Cheshire Cat   You can't help it. We're all mad here. I'm mad. You're mad.

Alice   Excuse me, but how do you know I'm mad?

Cheshire Cat   You must be, or you wouldn't have come here.

Alice (*aside*)   I don't think that proves it at all – although . . . (*to* **Cat**) How do you know that you're mad?

Cheshire Cat   Well, to begin with, a dog's not mad. Agreed?

Alice   I suppose so.

Cheshire Cat   Well then, you see. A dog growls when it's angry, and wags its tail when it's pleased. Now, I growl when I'm pleased, and wag my tail when I'm angry. Ergo: I'm mad.

Alice   I call it purring, not growling.

Cheshire Cat   Call it what you like.
Are you playing croquet with the Queen today?

Alice   Croquet? The Queen? I suppose . . . I mean, I'd like to; but I haven't been invited.

Cheshire Cat   You'll see me there.

The **Cheshire Cat** *vanishes – and then appears again somewhere else.*

By-the-bye, what became of the baby? I forgot to ask.

Alice   It turned into a pig.

Cheshire Cat   I thought it would.

The **Cheshire Cat** *vanishes again.*

Pause.

Alice   Well.

Pause.

Alice *turns to go. The* **Cheshire Cat** *appears again on the branch of a tree.*

Cheshire Cat   Did you say pig, or fig?

Alice   I said pig.

Cheshire Cat   Well, you saved its bacon.

Alice   I do wish you wouldn't keep suddenly appearing and then vanishing just as quickly. You're making me feel quite giddy.

Cheshire Cat   All right then.

The **Cheshire Cat** *vanishes slowly this time – beginning with its tail and ending with its grin, which lingers.*

Alice   Well! I've often seen a cat without a grin, but a grin without a cat! It's the most curious thing I've ever seen in my life!

Scene Nine: A Mad Tea Party

Alice *arrives at the* **March Hare**'s *house.*

Alice   This must be the March Hare's house. I hope it knows the way into the garden. Suppose the March Hare is raving mad? Maybe I should have gone to see the Hatter? . . . Hello . . .

In front of the house is a large table set for tea. In one corner the **March Hare** *and the* **Hatter** *sit either side of a sleeping* **Dormouse**. **Alice** *approaches.*

Alice   Oh, wonderful! Tea!

March Hare/Hatter   No room! No room!

Alice   There's plenty of room.

March Hare   Have some wine.

Alice   Some wine? Thank you! (*Pause.*) I don't see any wine.

March Hare   There isn't any.

Alice   Then it wasn't very polite of you to offer it.

March Hare   It wasn't very polite of you to sit down without being asked.

Alice   I didn't know it was your table. And your tea is laid for a lot more than just three.

Hatter   Your hair wants cutting.

Alice   Don't make personal remarks. It's rude.

Hatter   Why is a raven like a writing desk?

Alice   A riddle. What fun! I believe I can guess –

March Hare   Do you mean that you think you can find out the answer?

Alice   Exactly.

March Hare   Then you should say what you mean.

Alice   I do. At least I mean what I say, and that's the same thing.

Hatter   Not the same thing a bit! You might just as well say that 'I see what I eat' is the same thing as 'I eat what I see'.

March Hare   You might just as well say that 'I like what I get' is the same thing as 'I get what I like'.

Dormouse   You might just as well say that 'I breathe when I sleep' is the same thing as 'I sleep when I breathe'.

Hatter (*to* **Dormouse**)   It is the same thing with you.

Silence.

March Hare   Tea!

Hatter   What day of the month is it?

The **Hatter** *consults his fob-watch, shakes it, holds it to his ear.*

Alice   The fourth.

Hatter (*to himself*)   Two days wrong. (*To* **March Hare**.)
I told you butter wouldn't suit the works.

March Hare   It was the best butter.

Hatter   Yes, but some crumbs must have got in as well.
You shouldn't have put it in with the bread-knife.

The **March Hare** *takes the watch, dips it into his tea, looks at it.*

March Hare   It was the best butter.

Hatter (*to* **Alice**)   Have you guessed the riddle yet?

Alice   Why is a raven like a writing desk? . . . No. I give up.
What's the answer?

Hatter   I haven't the slightest idea.

March Hare   Nor have I.

Alice   I think you should do something better with your time
than waste it by asking riddles which have no answer.

Hatter   If you knew Time as well as I do, you wouldn't talk
about wasting *it*. It's a him.

Alice   I don't know what you mean.

Hatter   Of course you don't. I dare say you've never even
spoken to Time.

Alice   Perhaps not – but I know I have to beat time when
I'm learning music. (*She beats 4/4 time as she sings.*)

(*sung*)
    Twinkle, twinkle, little star –

Hatter   Well that explains it.

Alice   What?

Hatter   Time won't stand a beating. Now, if only you kept on good terms with him, he'd do almost anything you liked with the clock. As for me, I quarrelled with Time last March (*pointing to the* **march hare**) – just before he went mad – it was at the great concert given by the Queen of Hearts, and I had to sing:

(*sings*)
   'Twinkle, twinkle . . .'

(*spoken*)   – perhaps you know the song?

Alice   I think I've heard it before . . .

Hatter   It goes like this:

'Twinkle' aria.

(*sung*)
   Twinkle, twinkle little bat
   how I wonder what you're at.
   Up above the world you fly
   like a tea-tray in the sky.
   Twinkle, twinkle –

Dormouse   Twinkle twinkle twinkle twinkle.

The **March Hare** *and* **Hatter** *pinch the* **Dormouse** *to make it stop.*

Hatter   Well, anyway, I'd hardly finished the first verse, when the Queen jumped out and bellowed: 'He's not killing Time, he's murdering him! Off with his head!'

Alice   How savage!

Hatter   And ever since that, he won't do a thing I ask. It's always six o'clock now.

Alice   Is that the reason there are so many tea things?

Hatter   Yes. It's always tea-time, and we've no time to do the washing-up in-between.

Alice   So you keep moving around the table?

Hatter   Exactly – as the things get used up.

Alice   But what happens when you get back to the beginning again?

March Hare   Suppose we change the subject? I'm getting tired of this. I vote the young lady tells us a story.

Alice   A story?

March Hare/Hatter   Or the Dormouse shall! Wake up, Dormouse!

The **March Hare** *and* **Hatter** *both pinch the* **Dormouse**.

Dormouse   I wasn't asleep. I heard every word.

March Hare   Tell us a story.

Alice   Yes, please do.

Hatter   And quick about it or you'll be asleep again before it's done.

Dormouse   Once upon a time there were three little sisters and their names were Maisy, Daisy and Lazy and they lived at the bottom of a well –

Alice   What did they live on?

The **Dormouse** *thinks for a moment.*

Dormouse   They lived on treacle.

Alice   They couldn't have done that – they'd have been ill.

Dormouse   So they were – very ill.

Alice   But why did they live at the bottom of a well?

March Hare (*to* **Alice**)   Have some more tea.

Alice   I haven't had any yet, so I can't have more.

Hatter   You mean you can't have less. It's very easy to have more than nothing.

Alice   Nobody asked your opinion.

Hatter   Who's making personal remarks now?

Alice   Why did they live at the bottom of a well?

The **Dormouse** *thinks for a moment.*

Dormouse   It was a treacle-well.

Alice   There's no such thing!

Hatter/March Hare   Sh! Sh!

Dormouse   If you can't be civil, then you'd better finish the story yourself!

Alice   No please go on. I won't interrupt again. I suppose there might be one treacle-well. Somewhere.

Dormouse   One indeed!
And so these three little sisters, they were learning to draw –

Alice   What did they draw?

Dormouse   Treacle.

Hatter   I want a clean cup. Let's all move on one place.

They do, the **March Hare** *spilling the milk jug – he cries over the spilt milk.*

Alice   But I don't understand: how did they draw treacle?

Hatter   You can draw water out of a water-well, so I think you could draw treacle out of a treacle-well. Stupid.

Alice   But they were in the well.

Dormouse   Of course they were: well in.

They were learning to draw, and they drew all manner of things, everything that begins with a M – (*pronounced 'm' as in 'mercy'*)

Alice   Why with a M?

March Hare   Why not?

Silence. The **Dormouse** *is about to nod off but is pinched by the* **Hatter**.

Dormouse   – everything that begins with an M (*pronounced 'em' as in 'Emily'*), such as mouse-traps, and the moon, and memory, and muchness. You know you say things are 'much of a muchness'? Well, did you ever see such a thing as a drawing of a muchness?

Alice   Well, since you ask, I don't think –

Hatter   Then you shouldn't talk.

Alice   Oh! You're all mad!

Alice *gets up in despair. The* **Dormouse** *falls asleep instantly. Neither the* **Hatter** *nor the* **March Hare** *notices* **Alice***'s departure as they try to put the* **Dormouse** *in the teapot.*

Scene Ten: Back to the Hallway

Alice   Well, I'm never going there again! I didn't even get to eat any tea. Or do you drink tea? Oh! It's the stupidest tea party I've ever been to in my whole life!

As **Alice** *makes her way back, she passes a tree which has a door in it.*

That's very curious.

In she goes – but she's back in the hallway.

Oh.

She sees the gold key on the glass table.

I'll do this properly this time.

She takes the gold key and unlocks the door which leads into the garden. Then she nibbles some more mushroom, shrinks, walks through the doorway, down the passage and . . .

The garden!

Interval.

Scene Eleven: The Garden

. . . and **Alice** *enters the garden with its bright flower-beds and cool fountains. The music of paradise. There's a large rose-tree with white roses being painted red by three gardener-playing-cards:* **Seven**, **Five** *and* **Two**.

Alice   The garden!

Seven   Five!

Two   Look out now, Five! Don't go splashing paint over me like that.

Five   I couldn't help it. Seven jogged my elbow.

Seven   Oh that's right, Five. Always blame someone else!

Five   You can't talk. I heard the Queen say only yesterday that you deserved to be beheaded.

Two   What for?

Seven   That's none of your business, Two!

Five   Yes it is her business, so I'll tell her: it was for bringing the cook tulip-roots instead of onions.

Seven *flings down the paintbrush.*

Seven   Well of all the unjust things!

Suddenly they all spot **Alice** *and bow.*

Alice   Why are you painting the roses?

Two   Well, the fact is, Miss, you see, this ought to have been a red rose-tree, but we put a white one in by a mistake. If the Queen found out, she'd have our heads cut off. So you see, Miss, we're doing our utmost, before she comes –

Five   The Queen! The Queen!

Five, **Seven** *and* **Two** *throw themselves down, flat on the ground.* **Alice** *looks round eagerly.*

A grand procession enters (through the auditorium): soldiers, the **White Rabbit***, the* **Gryphon** *leading the* **King of Hearts** *and the* **Queen of Hearts***.*

The procession passes by **Alice***. When the* **Queen** *is opposite* **Alice***, the procession stops.*

Queen (*to the* **Gryphon**)   Who is this?

The **Gryphon** *merely bows.*

Queen   Idiot! (*To* **Alice***.*) What's your name, child?

Alice   My name is Alice, so please your Majesty.

Queen (*pointing to the three gardener-playing-cards*)   And who are these?

Because they are lying face down, only the identical pattern on their backs can be seen.

Alice   How should I know?

The **Queen** *raises an eyebrow.*

Alice   I'd like to go now, please. I need to get back. For tea. They'll be wondering where I am. And I need to go to bed. Soon. Can you tell me how I can get home?

Queen   You can't.

Alice   What?

Queen   Leave.

King (*consoling the* **Queen**)   Consider, my dear, she is only a child.

Queen   Precisely. (*To* **Alice***.*) Now, turn them over!

Alice   Me?

Queen   Yes, you, child.

Alice *turns the gardener-playing-cards over, to whom the* **Queen** *then commands:*

Get up!

The gardener-playing-cards get up and start bowing.

Leave off! You're making me giddy! (*Turning to the rose-tree.*) What have you been doing here?

Two (*going down on one knee*)   May it please your Majesty, we were trying –

Queen   I see! Off with its head!

Two *is manacled – led away by the* **Gryphon** *– and beheaded.*

Queen   Is its head off?

Gryphon   Its head is gone, if it please your Majesty!

Queen   That's right!

A moment of solemn silence.

Queen (*to* **Alice**, *brightly*)   Can you play croquet?

Alice *realises this last question was addressed to her.*

Alice (*covering her terror*)   Yes, as a matter of fact.

Queen   Come on then!

Alice *joins the procession.*

Alice (*aside*)   I don't like this. I need help. (*Seeing* **White Rabbit** *addresses him.*) Isn't the Duchess meant to be here soon?

White Rabbit   Hush! Hush! (*Whispers.*) She's under sentence. Of execution.

Alice   Her too? Why?

White Rabbit   She boxed the Queen's ears – she'd come rather late, and being late is unforgiveable, and . . .

Queen   Get to your places!

Everyone runs about in all directions, and then settles.

The croquet-lawn is all ridges and furrows. The balls are hedgehogs. The mallets are flamingoes. The soldiers' arms and legs are the hoops. The game is quarrelsome mayhem, with everyone playing at once, the flamingoes and hedgehogs and soldiers wandering off ad liberatum.

Alice *(aside)*   I've always thought croquet a difficult game, but this is ridiculous! There aren't any rules.

The grin of the **Cheshire Cat** *appears.*

Cheshire Cat   How are you getting on?

Alice   I'm not getting on terribly well, as a matter of fact . . .

Pause.

(aside)   It's no use speaking to it until its ears have appeared.

The whole head of the **Cheshire Cat** *has now appeared.*

Alice *(to the* **Cheshire Cat***)*   I want to get away. I'm afraid I'm going to be beheaded. And I don't understand the rules.

Cheshire Cat   Oh, they're perfectly fair.

Alice   I don't think they're at all fair, actually; and what's more, they don't seem to have any rules in particular – at least, if there are, nobody seems to follow them; and I can't control my flamingo . . .

Cheshire Cat   How do you like the Queen?

Alice   Not at all, she's so –

Alice *is suddenly aware that the* **Queen** *is listening.*

– likely to win that it's hardly worth finishing the game.

The **Queen** *smiles and walks on. The* **King** *arrives.*

King *(to* **Alice***)*   Who are you talking to?

Alice   A friend of mine, your Majesty. Allow me to introduce the Cheshire Cat.

King   It may kiss my hand if it likes.

Cheshire Cat   I'd rather not.

King   Don't be impertinent! And don't look at me like that! It must be removed. (*To the* **Queen**.) My dear: I wish you to have this cat removed!

Queen   Off with his head!

Gryphon   I can't cut off a head unless there's a body to cut it off from.

King   Don't talk nonsense! Anything that has a head can be beheaded.

Queen   If something isn't done in less than no time –

Alice   This Cat belongs to the Duchess. Perhaps you should ask her about it.

Queen   The Duchess is in prison. Where you'll be, young lady, if you don't mind your manners. You must respect your elders, especially when they're royalty. (*To the* **Gryphon**.) Fetch the Duchess forthwith! Now, back to the game.

Everyone resumes the haphazard game of croquet, except **Alice**. *The* **Cheshire Cat** *fades away.*

The **Gryphon** *returns with the* **Duchess**.

Duchess (*to* **Alice**)   You don't know how glad I am to see you again!

The **Duchess** *takes* **Alice** *by the arm and they walk off together. The croquet continues.*

Alice   Duchess, I need your help. I think it really is a matter of life or death.

Duchess   There's a moral here somewhere. I can't tell you just now what the moral is, but I shall remember it in a bit.

Alice (*timidly*)   Perhaps there isn't one?

Duchess   Tut, tut, child. Everything's got a moral, if only you can find it. And the moral of that is: 'Oh, 'tis love, 'tis love that makes the world go round!'

Alice   If there really is a moral for everything, what is the moral of a game of croquet?

Duchess (*after just a moment's hesitation*)   A flamingo is like mustard: they both bite. And the moral of that is: 'Birds of a feather flock together.'

Alice   Only mustard isn't a bird.

Duchess   Right, as usual. You put things so clearly!

Alice   Mustard's a mineral, I think.

Duchess   Of course it is.

Alice   No, mustard's a vegetable. It doesn't look like one, but it is.

Duchess   I quite agree with you, and the moral of that is: 'Be what you would seem to be.' Or, put more simply: 'Never imagine yourself not to be otherwise than what it might appear to others that what you were or might have been was not otherwise than what you had been would have appeared to them to be otherwise.'

Alice   I think I'd understand that better if I wrote it down.

Duchess   Thinking again?

Alice   I've a right to think.

Duchess   About as much right as pigs have to fly, and the moral –

Queen   I've won!

*Cheers. The **Queen** looms.*

Duchess   A fine day, your Majesty.

Alice   Is it?

Queen (*to* **Alice**)   I heard that. I gave you fair warning.

The **Duchess** *retreats rapidly.*

Alice   Duchess! Wait! (*But she's gone. To the* **Queen**.) This isn't fair!

Alice *is manacled by the* **Gryphon**.

Queen   Now, let's tuck you up in prison like a good little girl . . .

Alice   But I'm not a little girl, I'm a grown-up –

Queen   Silence. You are going to prison.

Scene Twelve: The Mock Turtle's Story

Prison.

Gryphon   Have you seen the Mock Turtle yet?

Alice   No. I don't even know what a mock turtle is.

Gryphon   It's what mock turtle soup is made from. Come on.

They enter a cell where the **Mock Turtle** *sits alone, sighing.*

Alice (*to the* **Gryphon**)   Why is he so full of sorrow?

Gryphon   Him? It's his fancy. He knows no sorrow really. (*To the* **Mock Turtle**.) This young lady wants to know your history.

Mock Turtle   I will tell it to her. Sit down, both of you, and do not utter a word until I have finished.

Alice *and the* **Gryphon** *sit.*

Silence.

Alice (*aside*)   How is he ever to finish if he never begins?

Pause.

Mock Turtle   Once, I was a real turtle.

Silence. The **Mock Turtle** *sobs a bit.*

Pause.

Alice   Thank you, Sir, for your interesting story.

Pause.

Mock Turtle   When we were little, we went to school in the sea. The master was an old turtle: we used to call him Tortoise –

Alice   If he was a turtle, why did you call him Tortoise?

Mock Turtle   Because he taught us. Stupid!

Gryphon   You ought to be ashamed of yourself, asking such a simple question.

Pause.

(*To the* **Mock Turtle**.)   Come on. Don't be all day about it.

Mock Turtle   Yes, we went to school in the sea, though you may not believe it –

Alice   I didn't say I didn't!

Mock Turtle   You did.

Gryphon (*to* **Alice**)   Hold your tongue! You are a prisoner.

Pause.

Mock Turtle   We had the best of educations, in fact we went to school every day –

Alice   I go to school.

Mock Turtle   An ordinary school, or a school with extras?

Alice   Well, we learn French. And Music.

Mock Turtle   I also had all the usual lessons.

Alice   What were they?

Mock Turtle   Reeling and Writhing, to begin with.
And then the different branches of Arithmetic: Ambition,
Distraction, Uglification and Derision.

Alice   I've never heard of 'Uglification'.

Gryphon   Never heard of Uglification! I suppose you'll be
saying next that you don't know what to beautify means?

Alice   No. Yes. It means – it means to make something, well,
prettier.

Gryphon   So if you don't know what to uglify means, then
you really are a simpleton.

Alice (*to* **Mock Turtle**)   What else did you learn?

Mock Turtle   Mystery, ancient and modern, with
Sea-ography. Then Drawling. The Drawling-master was an
old conger-eel who came once a week. He taught us Drawling,
Stretching and Fainting in Coils.

Alice   What was your teacher like?

Mock Turtle   An old crab. He also taught us Classics:
Laughing (*pronounced laffing*) and Grief.

Alice   How many hours a day did you have lessons?

Mock Turtle   Ten hours the first day, nine the next, and so on.

Alice   How curious!

Gryphon   That's why they're called lessons, because they
lessen from day to day.

Mock Turtle   You may not have lived much under the sea –

Alice   I haven't.

Mock Turtle   – and perhaps you were never introduced to
a lobster –

Alice   I once tasted – No, never.

Mock Turtle   – so you will have no idea how delightful a
Lobster Quadrille is!

Alice   No. But I'm sure you're going to tell me.

Mock Turtle   First, you form a line along the sea-shore –

Gryphon   Two lines!

Mock Turtle   Then, when you've cleared all the jelly-fish out of the way –

Gryphon   That generally takes some time –

Mock Turtle   – you advance twice –

Gryphon   Each with a lobster as a partner!

Mock Turtle   Advance twice, set to partners –

Gryphon   – change lobsters, and retire in the same order.

Mock Turtle   Then you throw –

Gryphon   – the lobsters!

Mock Turtle   – as far out to sea as you can –

Gryphon   Swim after them!

Mock Turtle   Turn a somersault in the sea –

Gryphon   Change lobsters again!

Mock Turtle   Back to land again –

Mock Turtle/Gryphon   – and that's the first figure.

Alice   It all sounds very pretty.

Mock Turtle   Would you like to see a little of it?

Alice   Very much.

Mock Turtle (*to the* **Gryphon**)   We'll do without the lobsters.

Gryphon   Aaaw . . .

Mock Turtle   Oh, all right then. Who'll sing?

Gryphon (*to* **Mock Turtle**)   Oh, you sing.

Mock Turtle   I've forgotten the words.

'Lobster Quadrille' song.

(**Whiting**) (*sung*)
  Will you walk a little faster?

Mock Turtle (*sung*)
  said a Whiting to a Snail.

(**Whiting**) (*sung*)
  There's a porpoise close behind us, and he's treading on my tail.
  See how eagerly the lobsters and the turtles all advance!
  They are waiting on the shingle – will you come and join the dance?

(*chorus*) (*sung*)
  Will you, won't you, will you, won't you, will you join the dance?
  Will you, won't you, will you, won't you, won't you join the dance?

(**Whiting**) (*sung*)
  You can really have no notion how delightful it will be
  When they take us up and throw us, with the lobsters, out to sea!

Mock Turtle (*sung*)
  But the snail replied:

(**Snail**) (*sung*)
  Too far, too far!

Mock Turtle (*sung*)
  and gave a look askance –

(**Snail**) (*sung*)
  I thank you, Whiting, kindly, but I will not join the dance.

(*chorus*) (*sung*)
  Would not, could not, would not, could not, would not join the dance.
  Would not, could not, would not, could not, could not join the dance.

(**Whiting**) (*sung*)
  What matters it how far we go?

Mock Turtle (*sung*)
  his scaly friend replied.

(**Whiting**) (*sung*)
  There is another shore, you know, upon the other side.
  The further off from England the nearer is to France –
  Then turn not pale, beloved snail, but come and join the
  dance.

(*chorus*) (*sung*)
  Will you, won't you, will you, won't you, will you join the
  dance?
  Will you, won't you, will you, won't you, won't you join the
  dance?

Alice   Thank you. A very interesting dance. Such a curious
song.

Mock Turtle   You've seen whitings, of course?

Alice   Oh yes. They're covered in breadcrumbs.

Mock Turtle   You're wrong about the crumbs. Crumbs
would all wash off in the sea. And they're called whitings
because they're what you whiten your boots and shoes with.

Alice   Boots and shoes under the sea? They'd have to be
waterproof. What are they made of?

Gryphon   Soles and eels, of course. Any shrimp could have
told you that. Come. Let's hear some of your adventures.

Alice   I could tell you some of my adventures – beginning
from this morning and ending here in prison. But it's no use
going back to yesterday, because I was a different person then,
in a different world.

Mock Turtle   Now, that's very curious, about as curious as
curious can be. I should like to have that explained.

Gryphon   No, no! The adventures first. Explanations take
such a dreadfully long time.

Mock Turtle   But what is the use of saying all this stuff, if you don't explain it as you go along? It's by far the most confusing thing I ever heard.

Gryphon (*to* **Alice**)   Yes, I think you'd better stop.

Alice   But I haven't started yet.

Pause.

Gryphon (*enthusiastically*)   Shall we have a reprise of the Lobster Quadrille?

Pause.

Or would you like the Mock Turtle to sing you a song?

Alice   Oh, yes, I'd love to hear the Mock Turtle sing.

The **Mock Turtle** *is choked with sobs throughout this song.*

'Beautiful Soup' song.

Mock Turtle (*sung*)
　　Beautiful Soup, so rich and green,
　　Waiting in a hot tureen!
　　Who for such dainties would not stoop?
　　Soup of the evening, beautiful Soup!
　　Soup of the evening, beautiful Soup!
　　Beau-ootiful Soo-oop!
　　Beau-ootiful Soo-oop!
　　Soo-oop of the e-e-evening,
　　Beautiful, beautiful Soup!

　　Beautiful Soup! Who cares for fish,
　　Game, or any other dish?
　　Who would not give all else for two p
　　ennyworth only of beautiful Soup?
　　Pennyworth only of beautiful Soup?
　　Beau-ootiful Soo-oop!
　　Beau-ootiful Soo-oop!
　　Soo-oop of the e-e-evening,
　　Beautiful, beauti-FUL SOUP!

Gryphon   Chorus again!

But the **Mock Turtle** *has stirred himself into his soup.*

Voices Off   The trial's beginning!

Alice   Whose trial?

Gryphon (*to* **Alice**)   Your trial. Come on!

The **Gryphon** *grabs* **Alice** *by her manacled hands and off they both run.*

Scene Thirteen: The Trial

A crowd of birds, beasts and a pack of cards assembled all around. **Alice** *is guarded by the* **Gryphon**. *Near the* **King** *stands the* **White Rabbit** *holding a scroll of parchment. Throughout the scene the theatre audience is addressed as the* **Jury**.

Alice (*pointing to the audience*)   Why are you all looking at me like that?

Gryphon   They probably think you look a bit odd.

Alice   Do I look odd?

Gryphon   Although they should take a look at themselves: look at them, all gawping like cod-fish!

Alice   I don't think we should be rude about them. They're the jury. A jury is very important in a trial, I believe. They're the judge. I think.

Gryphon   Stupid things!

White Rabbit   Silence in court! (*To audience.*) Please be upstanding. (*He makes the entire audience stand up.*) All rise!

The **King** *and* **Queen** *enter and take their places on their thrones.*

Queen (*to audience*)   Please be seated.

King   Read the accusation!

The **White Rabbit** *unrolls his scroll and reads the following:*

White Rabbit   The young aforementioned girl, alias Alice, did, on the aforesaid date of the month, enter the Queen's garden without affording due care and attention to the rules and regulations governing royalty, and entered into the pastime of the as yet to be mentioned game of croquet.

King (*to the audience*)   Consider your verdict.

White Rabbit (*to the* **King**)   Not yet, not yet! There's a great deal to come before that!

King   Call the first witness!

White Rabbit   First witness!

The **Hatter** *enters with a tea-cup in one hand, a piece of bread-and-butter in the other – followed by the* **Dormouse***.*

Hatter   I beg pardon, your Majesty, for bringing these with me, but I hadn't quite finished my tea when I was sent for.

King   You ought to have finished. When did you begin?

Hatter   Fourteenth of March – I think.

Dormouse   Fifteenth!

King   Aha! (*To audience.*) Take note of the discrepancy; it may be irrelevant. (*To the* **Hatter***.*) Remove your hat.

Hatter   It isn't mine.

King   Stolen!

Hatter   I sell them. I've none of my own. I'm a hatter.

The **Queen** *glares at the* **Hatter***, who turns pale.*

King   Give your evidence and don't be nervous – or she'll have you executed on the spot.

Hatter   I'm a poor man, your Majesty, and I hadn't begun my tea, not above a week or so, and what with the bread-and-butter getting so thin – and the twinkling of the tea –

King   The twinkling of the what?

Hatter   It begins with a tea.

King   Of course twinkling begins with a T! Do you take me for a dunce? Go on!

Hatter   I'm a poor man, and most things twinkled after that – only the Dormouse said –

Dormouse   I didn't!

Hatter   You did!

Dormouse   I deny it!

King   The Dormouse denies it – Jury: disregard the Hatter's previous remarks.

Hatter   Well, at any rate, the Dormouse said –

The **Hatter** *waits anxiously for the* **Dormouse***'s intervention again, but the* **Dormouse** *has dozed off.*

Hatter   anyway, after that I cut some more bread-and-butter –

King   But what did the Dormouse say?

Hatter   I can't remember.

King   You must remember, or you will be executed.

Hatter   I'm a poor man, your Majesty –

King   You're a very poor speaker! If that's all you know about it, you may stand down.

Hatter   I can't go any lower, I'm on the floor as it is.

King   Then you may sit down.

Hatter   I'd rather finish my tea.

King   You may go.

The **Hatter** *exits in a hurry.*

King   Call the next witness!

White Rabbit   Call the next witness!

*The **Cook** enters, pepper-pot in hand. The whole court starts to sneeze.*

White Rabbit   Give your evidence.

Cook   Shan't!

*The **King** looks to the **White Rabbit** for guidance.*

White Rabbit   Your Majesty must cross-examine this witness.

King   Very well. What are jam tarts made of?

Cook   Pepper, mostly.

King   What?

Dormouse   Treacle.

King   Interesting. You may go.

*The **Cook** exits.*

King (*to the* **Queen**)   You'll have to cross-examine the next witness. I've got a headache.

Queen   Call the next witness!

White Rabbit   I call the defendant: Alice!

Alice   Here!

Queen (*to* **Alice**)   What do you know of this business?

Alice   Nothing.

Queen   Nothing whatever?

Alice   Nothing whatever.

Queen (*to the audience*)   That's very important –

Alice   Unimportant, your Majesty.

Queen   Silence! Knowing nothing is not admissible in a royal court of law. Rule Forty-Two: you can never be innocent in the eyes of the law until proven guilty. It's the oldest rule in the book.

Alice   Then it ought to be Rule Number One.

Queen   Silence! (*To the* **White Rabbit**.) Proceed.

White Rabbit   Alice: you, the accused, the defendant and the guilty party, are charged with the following offences –

Alice   I hope I never caused offence.

Queen   Silence! This is fun.

Alice   No it isn't.

Shock. Pause.

Queen (*to the* **White Rabbit**)   Continue.

White Rabbit   The charges as proven against the witness are as follows: (*reads from a notebook.*) That you entered a rabbit-hole without due care and attention . . .

Alice   Without what?

White Rabbit   Without a packed lunch . . . You stole a jar of marmalade . . .

Alice   I put it back!

White Rabbit   . . . You drank from a bottle that was not yours to drink from and you had your cake and ate it even though it was not yours for the having . . .

Alice   That's not fair!

White Rabbit   . . . You carelessly lost a valuable fan that I expressly put in your charge . . .

Alice   No you didn't!

White Rabbit   Did . . . You attempted to drown a mouse and a flock of birds and then attempted to poison them . . .

Alice   You're making this up as you go along!

White Rabbit   . . . poison them with modern ideas about cats. You harassed a caterpillar, ravaged the countryside of wild mushrooms, and were given custody of a child whom you then called a pig and is now missing, presumed dead . . .

Alice (*contrite*)   Really?

White Rabbit   Yes really. That you argued with a cat . . .

Alice   I didn't argue with the cat.

White Rabbit   Did.

Queen   You're arguing now. That proves it!

Alice   It proves nothing of the sort!

White Rabbit   . . . That you invited yourself to a tea party . . .

Alice   I suppose so . . . Have you been spying on me?

White Rabbit   . . . You trespassed in a royal garden . . .

Alice   Oh dear.

White Rabbit   You did not follow the rules of croquet . . .

Alice   I've never followed the rules of croquet . . .

White Rabbit   . . . You mocked a Mock Turtle, you disobeyed the Queen, and you are in contempt of this court!

Queen   How do you plead?

White Rabbit   She pleads guilty as charged, your Majesty.

Alice   But you've twisted the evidence – if you call that evidence.

Queen   Evidently we do, my dear – In fact, it's the most important piece of evidence we've ever heard! It's all the proof we need.

Alice   But it doesn't prove anything. I don't believe there's an atom of meaning in it.

Queen   If there's no meaning in it, that saves us a world of trouble since we needn't try to find any. Nothing can be clearer than that.

White Rabbit   Let the jury consider its verdict.

Queen   No, no! Sentence first – verdict afterwards.

Alice   Nonsense! The very idea of having the sentence first!

Queen   Hold your tongue!

Alice   I won't!

Queen   What did you say?

Alice   I said I won't.

Queen   Young lady, I am the Queen of Hearts.

The **King** *and* **Queen** *place black cloths on their heads.*

Queen   Off with her head!

The **Gryphon** *takes* **Alice** *and leads her to the guillotine. The* **King** *and* **Queen** *remove the black cloths from their heads and let them fall to the floor. The* **Gryphon** *lets the blade fall.*

Pandemonium.

But **Alice***'s head has not been sliced off.*

Alice   Am I awake? Am I dreaming?

'Dreamchild' song.

(sung)
　　A dream-child moving through a land
　　Seeks wonders wild and new,
　　And finds she chats with birds and beasts –
　　And half believes it's true.

　　Thus grows a tale of Wonderland:
　　So with a gentle hand
　　Lay it where Childhood's dreams are found
　　Dreamt in a far-off land.

Scene Fourteen: The End

A haunting melody from the musical instrument at the beginning of the play. Then the scattered toys from the opening scene are revealed on stage. We are back in the attic playroom with **Alice** *– older, wiser, a grown-up.*

At which point we hear a **Child** *yelling.*

Child (*off*)   Mum! Mum! Mum! It's tea-time. I'm hungry!

Dad (*off*)   I'll do it.

Child (*off*)   No, not you Dad. Mum!

Dad (*off*)   Alice: what are you doing?

Alice   Nothing. I'm coming!

Alice *picks through the toys, looks at the toy white rabbit, puts it down.*

The hungry **Child** *climbs into the attic.*

Child   Mum?

White Rabbit   Oh my ears and whiskers!

The **Child** *stops in its tracks.*

Child   Curiouser and curiouser . . .

Alice *looks up at the* **Child** *– and smiles . . . The* **Child** *follows the* **White Rabbit** *into the moonlight and snow.*

Alice (*to toy white rabbit*)   Be nice.

Blackout.

Lights up.

'How Doth the Little Crocodile' song.

Company (*sung*)
How doth the little crocodile
improve his shining tail,

and pour the waters of the Nile
on every golden scale.

How cheerfully he seems to grin,
how neatly spread his claws
and welcome little fishes in
with gently smiling jaws.

End.

Punk Rock

Simon Stephens

About the Author

Simon Stephens began his theatrical career in the literary department of the Royal Court Theatre where he ran its Young Writers' Programme. His plays for theatre include *Bluebird* (Royal Court Theatre, London, 1998); *Herons* (Royal Court Theatre, London, 2001); *Port* (Royal Exchange Theatre, Manchester, 2002); *One Minute* (Crucible Theatre, Sheffield, 2003, Bush Theatre, London, 2004); *Christmas* (Bush Theatre, London, 2004); *Country Music* (Royal Court Theatre Upstairs, London, 2004); *On the Shore of the Wide World* (Royal Exchange, Manchester and Royal National Theatre, 2005); *Motortown* (Royal Court Theatre Downstairs, London, 2006); *Pornography* (Deutsches Schauspielhaus, Hanover, 2007, Edinburgh Festival/Birmingham Rep, 2008, and Tricycle Theatre, London, 2009); *Harper Regan* (Royal National Theatre, 2008); *Sea Wall* (Bush Theatre, 2008, Traverse Theatre, 2009); *Heaven* (Traverse Theatre, 2009); *Punk Rock* (Lyric Theatre Hammersmith and Royal Exchange, Manchester, 2009); *A Thousand Stars Explode in the Sky* (with David Eldridge and Robert Holman; Lyric Hammersmith, 2010); and *Marine Parade* (Animalink/Brighton International Festival, 2010). His radio plays include *Five Letters Home to Elizabeth* (BBC Radio 4, 2001) and *Digging* (BBC Radio 4, 2003). Awards include the Pearson Award for Best Play, 2001, for *Port*; Olivier Award for Best New Play for *On the Shore of the Wide World*, 2005; and for *Motortown* German Critics in Theater Heute's annual poll voted him Best Foreign Playwright 2007. His screenwriting includes an adaptation of *Motortown* for Film Four; a two-part serial *Dive* (with Dominic Savage) for Granada/BBC (2009) and a short film adaptation of *Pornography* for Channel 4's Coming Up series (2009).

About the Play

I write often about violence. I write often about a consciousness of mortality. I write often about fear. As much as I do that, I think I write love stories. I hope my plays are imbued with a sense of faith and possibility. I write often

about young people because they inspire and energise me and
because they crystallise and experience that fear and faith
alike quite directly. There are a disproportionate number of
key characters in my plays who are seventeen years old and
on the cusp of adulthood. Many of my plays have been about
working-class characters. Often this can lend itself to a schism
between the theatre audience and the world of the plays they
are watching. Such a schism can lead to a sense of distance
from any idea of responsibility in the audience for the
behaviour they're watching. With *Punk Rock* I wanted to
change that. I wanted to write about the kids of the English
upper middle classes; the wealthiest, most educated kids in our
country. I think that the tensions, anxieties and fears that drive
young people to emotional extremes are not class-specific. I
think they affect the children of middle-class theatre-goers
as much as they affect anybody else. I wanted to write a play
about the kinds of young people that regular theatre-goers
might recognise as their own, and dramatise the possibility for
fear and violence in those kids too. The play was inspired by
the massacre at Columbine High School in the USA in 1999
and by further school shootings over the past decades. As a
parent and a teacher the notion that a school can become a
place not only of fear but of murder terrifies me. The play is
born out of that fear.

Producing the Play

There are a number of works of literature and drama that
inspired the play and any potential companies might want to
look at some of these as preparation. They might read Frank
Wedekind's *Spring Awakening* or see Lindsay Anderson's *If* . . . .
or Gus Van Sant's startling *Elephant*. They should certainly
listen to the music in the original soundtrack to *Punk Rock*,
even if they don't use it. In that music is the energy and fear
of the characters. I am happy for issues of setting or casting
to be left to the director's imagination. The first production
(Lyric Hammersmith, September 2009/Royal Exchange,
Manchester, October 2009) had a beautiful, detailed naturalistic
setting of a nineteenth-century library that juxtaposed the

violence of the story rather brilliantly. The German-language premiere was more expressive and energetic in its own way too. Bigger stages might need more trained actors, who might well need to be older, but this is not necessarily the case and I'd love to see this play acted by a cast of seventeen-year-olds. The most important words of advice I could give to any actor in any of my plays revolve around delivery of lines. Every sentence I give an actor has an action behind it – characters speak in order to do something to the people they are speaking to. Discover what that action might be and make sure it charges every utterance. Ask the question as though you don't know the answers. Often the most important words I write are towards the end of my lines so don't allow the energy to fall. Pick up the cues. Think on the lines not between them. And never forget to do that most important and difficult job of any actor: listen to one another on stage.

Characters

William Carlisle
Lilly Cahill
Bennett Francis
Cissy Franks
Nicholas Chatman
Tanya Gleason
Chadwick Meade
Lucy Francis
Dr Richard Harvey

The play is set in the present day.

The first six scenes of the play are set in the library of the Sixth Form of a fee-paying grammar school in Stockport.

The seventh scene is set in Suttons Manor Hospital.

Scene One

'Kerosene' by Big Black.

It's Monday 6 October, 8.31 a.m.

Lilly Cahill *and* **William Carlisle** *are alone in the library.*

William   When did you arrive?

Lilly   Last week.

William   Whereabouts are you living?

Lilly   In Heaton Moor.

William   Whereabouts in Heaton Moor?

Lilly   At the top of Broadstone Road. By the nursery there.

William   That's a nice street.

Lilly   I think so.

William   Which number's your house?

Lilly   23.

William   23. Right. The houses on that street are some of the oldest in Stockport, did you know that?

Lilly   No.

William   They're old nineteenth-century industrialist houses. Some of the shops on Heaton Moor Road are even older. Practically medieval. Is it very different here?

Lilly   It is a bit.

William   Have you settled in yet?

Lilly   I don't know.

William   It must be slightly disorientating having to adjust to a new town in such a short space of time, is it?

Lilly   It's not too bad. I'm used to moving about.

William   Why?

Lilly　My dad's worked in four different universities in the past twelve years. I've grown immune to it.

William　Was Cambridge the best?

Lilly　Not really.

William　Were the people there unthinkably intelligent?

Lilly　No. They were rude, horrible pigs.

William　Did they have enormous foreheads and big bulging brains?

Lilly　No. They were really rich and stupid.

William　I want to go to Cambridge.

Lilly　Do you?

William　That or Oxford. It's my life's ambition. How did you get here?

Lilly　What?

William　What mode of transport did you use? To get to Stockport, I mean. Not to school. Although you can tell me what mode of transport you used to get to school if you'd prefer.

Lilly　We drove.

William　With everything packed in the car or did you hire a removal company?

Lilly　We hired a removal company. We had some things packed in the car.

William　I like your haircut.

Lilly　Thanks.

William　Is that coat real fur?

Lilly　No.

William　It's *faux*?

Lilly　That's right.

William   That's a relief.

Lilly   Yeah.

William   It'd be terrible if you were some kind of animal killer. Imagine my embarrassment.

Lilly   I'm not.

William   The fur trade's abominable. People who wear fur coats should be skinned alive in my opinion.

Lilly   Mine too.

William   Good. I'm glad. I'm William.

Lilly   Hi William.

William   I've been coming here for five years. I know the place completely inside out. I know every nook and cranny and everything so, if you want any help . . .

Lilly   Great.

William   I know parts of this school that other people don't even know exist. There are secret corridors. Deserted book cupboards. Cellars. Attics. All kinds of things. You want to know about them? Just ask me. This is the Upper School library. Don't you love it?

Lilly   It's –

William   It's completely hermetically sealed from the rest of the school. They tell us it's to keep the Lower School away. I think it's to keep us contained. Look outside.

Lilly   Where?

William   That track leads up to Manchester in that direction and all the way down to London in that direction. The trains come past here all the time. They need to keep us locked in in case we escape.

Most of the Sixth Form can't be bothered to come up here any more. They go to the common room. Or to the main library. They spend hour after hour after hour on the internet there. Or rifling through the DVD section. I prefer it here. It's intimate. People don't like books any more. I do. There's a second edition of Walter Scott's *Waverley* from 1817 on the higher stack. You need permission to see it. I could sort that out for you easily by the way, if you'd like me to. Have you got a locker yet?

Lilly   No.

William   You'll need to speak to Edwards. Edwards is all right. His nose is a slightly odd shape, which I've never trusted. I can speak to him for you if you'd like me to. Do you know where to go to eat?

Lilly   I was going to go to the canteen.

William   Don't. You mustn't. Nobody goes there. You'll die very quickly if you start eating your lunches there.

She breaks into a smile.

I'm being serious.

Bennett Francis *and* **Cissy Franks** *enter.*

Bennett   And this monkey is stood on the bus yelling at all the little Year-Seven babies about how he'd stopped smoking and so anybody who smoked that day was getting glassed before they got off the bus. I looked at him. Pulled three cigarettes out. Lit them all at once. Smoked them.

Cissy   All in one go?

Bennett   Oh yes.

Cissy   Didn't that hurt?

Bennett   Viciously.

Cissy   It doesn't look as though he glassed you.

Bennett   Of course he didn't glass me. He likes my arse too much. How was the rest of your evening?

Cissy   It passed.

Bennett   How was your dad?

Cissy   You know. The same. I wish you'd stayed.

Bennett   Yes.

He notices **Lilly**.

Bennett   Who the fuck are you?

William   Bennett, this is Lilly Cahill.

Bennett   Is it?

William   She's new.

Bennett   Are you?

William   This morning.

Cissy   Is she?

Pause. They look at her. **William** *awaits their verdict.*

Bennett   Did we hear about you?

Lilly   I've no idea.

William   There was a letter.

Bennett   I bet there was. There's always a letter. I'm Bennett.

Lilly   Hello, Bennett.

Bennett   Cahill's a very good name.

Lilly   Is it?

Bennett   It's Irish. From County Galway. It's ancient.

Lilly   Right.

Cissy   I'm Cissy.

Lilly   Hello.

William   Cissy's Bennett's girlfriend.

Lilly   Great.

Cissy   You're not from round here are you?

William   She's from Cambridge.

Cissy   I can tell. From your accent.

Bennett   She's shatteringly astute like that.

William   Yeah. You have to get up really fucking early in the morning to catch her out.

Beat.

Bennett   How long are you here for?

Lilly   I don't know. Until the exams, I think.

Bennett   Brilliant.

Cissy   What are you taking?

Lilly   Geography, History, French and English.

Bennett   Four A levels?

William   She's incredibly clever.

Cissy   Clearly.

Lilly   And General Studies.

Bennett   Yes. Everybody takes General Studies. Nobody goes. Ever.

William   I do.

Bennett   What's Cambridge like?

William   You should too. It's Mr Lloyd. He's great.

Lilly   I hated it.

Cissy   That's good.

Lilly   Why?

Cissy   I only really trust people who hate their home towns.

William   Me too.

Cissy   How are you this morning, William Carlisle?

William   I'm fantastically fucking brilliant, thank you very much for asking. How are you, Cissy?

Cissy   Great. Happy to be here. Happy as a song lark.

William   Good weekend?

Cissy   Thrilling. We had a dinner party on Saturday night. Bennett cooked a salmon. My mother swooned. How was yours?

William   Terrible. Far, far better here.

Nicholas Chatman *enters. He is drinking a protein drink.*

Lilly   Why was it terrible?

Bennett   Shit. I've forgotten everything.

William   What?

Nicholas   You'll never believe what I saw on Sunday.

Lilly   Why was your weekend terrible?

Cissy   What do you mean, you've forgotten everything?

William   You're better off not knowing. Seriously.

Bennett   My English books, my French books, my History books. The works. What did you see?

Nicholas   *One Night in Paris.*

Bennett   Bless.

Cissy   What are you going to do without your books?

Bennett   Lie. Busk it. Copy yours. Steal theirs. I've not seen that film in years and years and years.

Cissy   I've never seen it.

Nicholas   You should do. It's extraordinary.

Lilly   Why?

Nicholas   What?

Lilly   Why's it extraordinary?

William   Lilly, this is Nicholas Chatman. He plays lacrosse. Nicholas, this is Lilly. She's from Cambridge. She's new.

Nicholas *assesses her before he answers her question.*

Nicholas   Right.

Bennett *interrupts him before he's able to.*

Bennett   I like your jacket, Mr Chatman.

Nicholas   Thank you very much, Mr Francis.

Cissy   Can I try it on?

Nicholas   What?

Cissy   Your jacket. Can I? Please.

Bennett   Is it Paul Smith?

Nicholas   Moschino.

Cissy   It's lovely.

Bennett   It looks better on Nicholas.

William   What's your first lesson?

Lilly   Geography. Period 2.

Cissy   Can I keep it?

Nicholas   No. Don't be ridiculous.

William   Who with?

Lilly   Harrison.

William   I've got him, then.

Lilly   What's he like?

Cissy   It smells lovely. It smells all manly.

Tanya Gleason *enters.*

William   He's a little unsettling. He's generally fine.

Tanya *stops and looks at* **Lilly**.

Tanya   Are you Lilly?

Lilly   That's right.

Tanya I'm Tanya.

Lilly Hello.

Tanya Tanya Gleason? MacFarlane asked me to meet you. Did she not say?

Lilly I'm not sure.

Tanya I thought you were going to be in the common room. How did you get up here?

Lilly I just walked.

Tanya She wanted me to look after you today.

Lilly To look after me?

Tanya I've been looking for you for a while.

Lilly I'm sorry.

Tanya We had a letter about you.

Lilly Did you?

Tanya Last Friday. It said you were starting today. That you were coming from Cambridge. That your father was working in the university. That we should be especially nice to you.

Lilly Why did it say that?

Tanya I have no idea. They send us these things. I think they're all a bit dysfunctional. I like your hair.

She smiles. Comes properly into the room.

Lilly My hair?

Tanya It's quite Lily Allen. I noticed something about Year-Seven kids.

Cissy You noticed something about what?

Tanya About the children in Year Seven.

Cissy When?

Tanya This morning.

Cissy   You're very random sometimes Tanya, sweetheart, I have to say.

Tanya   When they line up. If you push them. They all fall on top of one another. Like little toys.

Cissy   That's really mean. They could break their little bones.

Tanya   We were never as rude as they are. I was terrified of Sixth Formers. I was quite literally frozen with fear. I used to think they threw bricks at you. Flushed your head down the toilet. Set fire to your tie.

Nicholas   Can I ask you a question?

Bennett   I've a feeling you're going to, aren't you?

Nicholas   Have you started revising yet?

Bennett   Are you being serious?

Nicholas   I kind of am, actually.

Bennett   Oh my Lord alive!

Tanya   They're only mocks. You don't need to revise for mocks.

Cissy   I never need to. I never need to revise for anything. I just do the exams.

Bennett   And get 'A's. You tart.

William   It defeats the points of mocks if you revise for them. They're a dipstick of what stage you're at, educationally, at this particular moment intended to help you get a handle on how much revision you need to do from this point onwards as you move towards the final exams.

They look at him for a beat.

Nicholas   Cos I've started.

Bennett   You would have done. Swot.

Nicholas   It's not about being a swot.

Bennett   Yeah it is.

Nicholas   It isn't. It's about wanting to do my best.

Cissy   My mum would kill me if I got less than an 'A' in any subject.

William   Would she literally kill you?

Cissy   Yes. Literally. She'd burn me alive.

Bennett   When do they start, exactly?

Beat.

Cissy   Are you serious?

Bennett   Don't I look it?

Cissy   You don't know when the mocks start?

Bennett   You never believe me about these kinds of things.

Cissy   November 3rd, 8.50 a.m., Main Hall. French. 11.55, Main Hall, Geography. 2.05 p.m., Back Pitch, PE. Finishing Monday 10th, 2.05 p.m., Main Hall, History.

Tanya   You don't do PE.

Bennett   Does anybody?

Tanya   How do you know when the PE exam is when you don't even do PE?

Cissy   I memorised it. I've got a photographic memory.

Nicholas   I like your badge.

A pause.

Lilly   Thank you.

Nicholas   I like the White Stripes . I think they're getting better. Some bands go shit the more they keep going. White Stripes don't. They're fucking great.

Lilly   I think so too.

William   He's only got the last two albums.

Lilly   What?

William   Nicholas. He's only got two White Stripes albums. He only got *Elephant* last term. He's never even heard *White Blood Cells*. Have you?

Nicholas   What?

William   Have you ever even heard *White Blood Cells*?

Nicholas   What are you talking about?

William   See.

Chadwick Meade *enters. He's wearing a new coat.*

Bennett   Holy fucking moly on a horse, it's Kanye West!

Chadwick   Who?

Bennett   Have you ever set fire to a tie, Chadwick?

Chadwick   No.

Bennett   I should think not. With a coat like that who fucking knows what might happen?

William   Chadwick, this is Lilly.

Chadwick   Lilly?

William   Lilly Cahill. She's joining our school. She came from Cambridge. Lilly, this is Chadwick Meade.

Lilly   Hello.

Chadwick   Hello, Lilly. I'm sorry. I wasn't expecting a new girl. It's terribly nice to meet you. Welcome to the school. I hope you are very happy here.

Lilly   Thank you, Chadwick.

Chadwick   Whereabouts in Cambridge are you from?

Lilly   Burwell.

Chadwick   With the castle.

Lilly   That's right.

Chadwick   Built under King Stephen. During the anarchy. I like Cambridge.

Lilly   Do you?

Chadwick   I prefer it to Oxford. Not only for its beauty, but I think the university is better. Certainly in its Applied Mathematics Department. Which is my specialism. My hero worked at St John's in the twenties. Paul Dirac. Did you ever hear of him?

Lilly   I didn't I'm afraid.

Bennett   Chadwick, who the fuck ever heard of Paul Dirac?

Chadwick   He predicted the existence of antimatter. He developed the Dirac Equation which described the behaviour of electrons. He won the Nobel Prize in 1933. He said, 'The laws of nature should be expressed in beautiful equations.' He's fundamental to the way we perceive the world. He was at Cambridge.

Lilly   I don't know him.

Chadwick   He died in 1984.

William   Nearly ten years before she was born, Chadwick, you could hardly blame her, pal.

Lilly   Is that really your name, Chadwick?

Chadwick   Yes it is, I'm afraid. It's American in origin.

Tanya   I didn't believe him either, if that's any consolation. I thought he made it up.

Bennett   I think he made his head up. Who christened you Chadwick, Chadwick? Which parent?

Chadwick   I wasn't christened. My parents are atheists.

Bennett   I *bet* they're atheists. You'd have to be with a son like that.

Cissy   With a face like that.

Bennett   Quite. (*He turns to* **Chadwick**.) Stun me.

Chadwick   What?

Bennett   Stun me, Chadwick. Tell me something stunning.
Tell me something the like of which I've never even thought
possible before.

The others look at **Chadwick**.

Chadwick   Do you know how many galaxies there are in
the universe? About a hundred billion. And there are about
a hundred billion stars in most given galaxies. That's ten
thousand billion, billion stars in the universe. Which works out
as about ten million billion planets.

The others look at **Bennett**.

Bennett   It's like having an absurdly clever puppy.

Here. Chadwick.

Chadwick   What?

Bennett   Have a wine gum.

He pulls out a wine gum and pops it in **Chadwick**'s *mouth. He laughs
hysterically.* **Chadwick** *takes it out of his mouth. Looks at it. Puts it
back in again. Leaves.*

Nicholas   Has anybody seen Copley, by the way?

Cissy   The new teacher?

Nicholas   She's not a teacher.

Bennett   Course she's a fucking teacher. What is she if she's
not a teacher? The traffic lady?

Nicholas   She's a student.

Bennett   Yes.

Nicholas   Students don't count. I'm going to ask her out.

Bennett   You should put that on your Personal Statement.
'I am Nicholas Chatman. I am the boy with the biggest horn
in the world.'

Tanya   Are you really going to ask a teacher out?

Nicholas   Why not? She's only about six months older than me, I reckon. She came with us to *Macbeth*. She sat next to me. She's having a tortuous time with Year Nine. She kept asking my advice.

Bennett   Nicholas. You're gorgeous. Did you know that? Gorgeous!

William   Are you incredibly nervous about coming to our school?

Lilly   No.

William   You shouldn't be.

Lilly   I'm not.

Cissy   Unless you get frightened of being bored.

Tanya   Yeah.

Cissy   Because it is quite fucking stupefyingly boring.

William   It's not that bad. Don't listen to her. Sometimes it is.

The bell goes.

Cissy   That's my curtain call, suckers.

Bennett   What have you got?

Cissy   Double Maths.

Bennett   You've always got double Maths. I'm not entirely sure it can be good for you.

Cissy *kisses him. He doesn't kiss her back.*

Tanya *stands to leave.*

Cissy   Where are you going?

Tanya   English.

Cissy   A bit early, aren't you?

Tanya   I'm going to see Mr Anderson.

Bennett   Are you going to ask him to impregnate you?

Tanya   What?

Bennett   Cissy told me about your fantasy. Did you hear this, Nicholas? Tanya's biggest dream is to live with Anderson. To be his secret lover. To have his baby. To waddle about his flat barefoot and pregnant. She's absolutely serious about it, by the way.

Tanya   Fuck off.

Bennett   Aren't you?

Tanya   Did you say that to him?

Cissy   I don't believe you, Bennett.

Bennett   It's true. Am I lying? Are you calling me a liar?

Tanya   Cissy. How could –?

Tanya *goes to say something. Nearly starts crying. Says nothing. Leaves.*

Cissy   Tanya! Tanya, wait!

She follows after her. The rest listen to her calling down the corridor.

Lilly   I need to go and see Mr Eldridge.

William   Do you know where he is?

Lilly   He's in his office. I was there earlier. It's just down the corridor, isn't it?

William   Second left after the common room.

Lilly   That's right.

William   Right then.

Lilly   Good.

William   I'll see you in Geography then, probably.

Lilly   Yes. Probably. Where is that again?

William   J3. Do you know how to get there?

Lilly   I haven't got a clue. If I come back here can I go with you?

William   Of course you can.

Lilly   Are you sure?

William   It would be a pleasure. I don't mind at all.

Lilly   Thanks. Thank you, William. I'll be here at about half past.

William   Perfect. I'll take you the scenic route.

Lilly   Is it always this cold in here?

William   Always. Until they put the heating on. Then it's insufferably hot.

Lilly   I look forward to that.

William   Have fun with Eldridge.

Lilly   I will do. I'll see you in a bit.

William   Yeah. See you in a bit.

Lilly   See you in a bit, Bennett. Nicholas.

Bennett   See you, Lily Allen.

William   Fuck off, Bennett. Leave her alone.

Lilly *smiles at* **William** *then turns to* **Nicholas**.

Lilly   See you.

Nicholas   Bye.

She leaves.

Some time.

Bennett   'I'll take you the scenic route.'

He and **Nicholas** *giggle at* **William**.

Bennett   Can I ask you something, Mr William Carlisle?

William   Go on.

Bennett Have you ever actually had a girlfriend before?

William What are you talking about?

Bennett Have you?

William What do you want to know that for?

Bennett You haven't, have you? I find that quite touching.

William Piss off, Bennett.

Bennett You're a bit besotted, mate, aren't you?

She'll break your heart William.

William I don't know what you're wittering on about.

Bennett *looks at him. Smiles.*

Bennett No.

Scene Two

'Eric's Trip' by Sonic Youth.

It's Tuesday 14 October, 3.30 p.m.

Lilly *and* **William** *are in the common room.*

Lilly Do you know what I've noticed about you? You're very still. You stand very still most of the time. You move your head quite slowly. I really like it. I like your hair too.

William Thanks.

Lilly I like the way it hides your eyes. It looks shy. You've got shy hair.

William *smiles. Looks away slightly.*

Lilly How was History?

William It was unusually dramatic.

We had Lloyd. He was in a peculiar mood.

He came in. We were sitting down. He looked at us for about three seconds. He sat down. We were all chatting. He looked at us. We kept chatting. He looked some more. We chatted some more. He sat still. We chatted. He waited until we stopped. And then he waited until we were silent. This took about a minute. And then he just waited. He waited five more minutes. Said he had decided not to teach us today. He didn't think we deserved it. Until we said sorry to him. And we did. One by one. Went round the class. 'Sorry, sir.'

Lilly   Is he your favourite?

William   I think so. I find his classroom-management skills rather bracing.

Lilly   Have you finished your UCAS form?

William *nods.*

Lilly   Have you sent it off?

William   This morning. Have you?

Lilly   I'm doing it tonight.

William   You better had.

Lilly   Are you applying for a year off?

William   Christ no.

Lilly   Every other fucker is.

William   I can't wait. Just to get out.

Lilly   No. Me neither.

She looks at him. Her gaze unnerves him a little.

William   How was French?

Lilly   *Un cauchemar sociologique.*

William   Un whatty-what-what?

Lilly   Do you ever worry about Chadwick Meade?

William   You're losing me.

Lilly   He's in our French lesson. He's a brilliant linguist. He never says a word. He was rocking for most of the lesson. Ever so slightly. I was sitting next to him. It really unsettled me.

William   Rocking?

Lilly   To and fro.

William   That sounds rather comforting.

Lilly   It was weird. I'm not entirely sure I trust him. I'm not sure I like him.

William   What's not to like? He's the cleverest man in the universe.

Lilly   He's not normal.

William   I hate normal people. Normal people should be eviscerated. He has a monster of a time. He's on a rather considerable scholarship. His home life is rather ghastly, I think. He has a very difficult time here. You should be nice to him.

Lilly   I hate the word 'should'.

William   The pressure he gets. The thoughts he has. People should be careful around him.

Lilly   That was kind of my point.

William   One day he's going to snap, I think.

Lilly   What do you mean?

William   He's too timid half the time. He should stand up to it. Stick his chin out. I wish he would. I've seen it happen.

Lilly   Seen what happen?

William   People like him who get so much abuse and then one day. Pop.

Lilly   Pop?

William   I like him.

Lilly   I'm glad somebody does.

William   We went to Cambridge University together in the summer holidays. On a visit. He's a lot funnier when you get him on his own. I think he gets nervous of speaking too much in front of people like Bennett. People notice him because of his scholarship tie. He said that it's a constant reminder. He took me to where Isaac Newton studied. He took me to the Botanic Gardens there. Showed me a tree which is apparently a descendant of the apple tree that Newton sat under.

It was unlike anything I've ever seen. Nobody from my family's ever even been to university before. We're not a family where that kind of thing happens.

We went to King's. Which is the college I've applied for. Asked somebody where we should go and look. There was a doctor in there. A scientist. Somebody with, he had a white coat on. He told me we should go and look at the chapel there. He said it was rather beautiful. I'd never heard a man use the word beautiful like that before.

It was beautiful, by the way. Parts of it date from the middle of the fifteenth century. The ceiling is spectacular. It has rather breathtaking fan vaulting. It was designed by Wastell. And built by him, actually.

If my application's accepted I'll have my interview next month. I hope I get one, an interview. They do the mock interviews in here. Lloyd does them. It'd be great. Just me and Lloyd. In here. Having an interview!

It's half three. We should be going home.

Lilly   Yeah.

William   It's amazing how quickly this whole place empties. I love it. I love being here when it does. You walk down the whole corridor and you're the only one there.

This room becomes like a kind of cocoon.

It's cold today. It feels like it's turning into autumn. I always think you can feel the exact day when that happens in this country.

Can I ask you: how are you getting on?

Lilly   What do you mean?

William   Here. How was your first week?

Lilly   It was all right. It was a bit odd. Some of the teachers are a bit strange. It's strange that there are so few of us. It can feel a bit claustrophobic. Bennett does my head in occasionally.

William   What I meant was: what do you think of Stockport?

She thinks.

Lilly   Honestly?

William   Honestly.

Lilly   I've been to worse places. I've lived in worse places. It's not as bad as Plymouth. It's not as bad as Hull. Heaton Moor's nice. We went to Lyme Park at the weekend. It was gorgeous.

William   The deer park there's medieval. If you move slowly enough there are fallow deer there that let you stroke them.

Lilly   The shopping centre in town makes me want to gouge my eyes out, though.

William   Ha!

Lilly   And I hate all the people.

Pause.

William   All of them?

Lilly   Apart from you lot, here.

William   You hate all of the people you've met in Stockport?

Lilly   Yeah.

He looks at her.

William   With their tied-back hair. And their stupid ugly make-up and their burgers?

Lilly   And their faces.

They smile at each other.

William   'What the fuck are you looking at?'

Lilly   'I'm looking at you, you Chav shit.'

William   I know what you mean.

Lilly   Poundstretcher store-card holders, the lot of them.

William   And all the boys are fathers at seventeen and banned from being within a square mile of their children at nineteen and jailed at twenty-one.

Lilly   They deserve it.

William   Because they're thick and they're vicious.

Lilly   And they're fat and they're ugly.

William   And frightened of anything that's different from what they're like.

Lilly   And terrified of intelligence or thought.

William   They're nervous about thinking because if they think too much they might just realise that the way they live their lives with their shell suits and their vicious little ugly little dogs is not necessarily the only way to lead a life.

Lilly   And they can't fucking wait till Christmas. And the furthest they've ever been to is Spain.

William   And even then they hated it.

Lilly   And wanted to eat more egg and chips.

William   Do you know something?

Lilly   What?

William   I always thought I was the only person who thought those kind of thoughts.

Can I tell you: I sometimes think I'm the best person in this town. Is that terrible?

Lilly   No.

William   I'm definitely the cleverest. And the funniest. Don't you think?

She thinks.

Lilly   Yeah.

William   Do you?

Lilly   Yeah.

William   I do too. I think I'm hilarious. Do you ever think about the person you wished you were?

Lilly   Sometimes.

William   When I think of that person, do you know what I realise?

Lilly   What?

William   I realise I *am* him.

Can I ask you? Do Bennett and Nicholas and Cissy ever say anything about me?

Lilly   No.

William   Never?

Lilly   No.

William   Do they never talk about my family?

Lilly   No.

William   Or my job?

Have they told you about my job?

Lilly   What job's that?

Pause. He has to stop himself from chuckling a little, which makes her chuckle a little too.

William   If I told you, you wouldn't believe me.

Lilly   Go on.

William   Nobody believes me.

Lilly   I would.

William   Why?

Lilly   What do you mean?

William   Why would you believe me when nobody else in their right mind would?

Lilly   I'm very trusting.

William   I bet you are.

Lilly   What?

William   I said I bet you are.

He stops chuckling and becomes suddenly serious. She can't stop so quickly.

I work for the government.

Lilly   Do you?

William   See?

Lilly   What?

William   You don't believe me.

Lilly   I never said that. Of course I believe you.

William   Then you're mad.

Lilly   Why?

William   As if a seventeen-year-old would work for the government!

Lilly   You told me you did. I believe you. Even if you try and deny it now, I'll still believe you.

Pause.

William   It's covert.

Lilly I'm sure.

William They don't tell anybody about it. People would get freaked out. They'd think I was a bit young.

Lilly I can imagine. What do you do for them?

William I observe Muslim teenagers for them. They want to target Muslim teenagers. So obviously they employ a teenager to do it. It would be stupid to employ an adult. So actually they employed me.

Lilly That sounds exciting.

William It isn't. Mostly Muslim teenagers are very boring. I have to fill in a brief form every fortnight.

Lilly Have you cracked any terrorist rings?

William No. Mainly they play football and snog each other behind their parents' backs.

The two giggle together.

Can I ask you something?

Lilly Anything.

William How many hours do you normally sleep?

Lilly Sorry?

William On average? Every night?

Lilly Nine.

William Nine?

Lilly Ten sometimes. Eleven if I get an early night.

William Right.

Lilly Twelve on a weekend.

William I sleep four. Can I ask you something else?

Lilly Of course you can.

William Don't you ever get frightened?

She looks at him, thinks before she answers.

Lilly Yes, I do.

He thinks before he presses her.

William Tell me what kind of things you get frightened of?

She thinks.

Lilly Nuclear war.

Black people.

Dogs. Most dogs. Some birds. Farm animals.

Sexual assault.

I get frightened of waking up in my house and there's somebody there in my room.

Sometimes in the middle of the night when my parents go out my mum storms off. She walks home, comes home early. Really drunk. My bedroom's downstairs. It always is. For the last three houses. I prefer it. She normally forgets her keys so she normally taps on my window to get me to let her in. I sometimes think it's dead people outside. That terrifies me.

William What does she storm off for?

Lilly She gets pissed off at my dad. She drinks two bottles of wine.

William My mum died when I was about four.

I don't really remember her. I never knew my dad. My dad died before I was born.

I don't tell anybody that. That's a secret. Can I trust you to keep that to yourself?

Lilly Of course you can.

William Thanks.

Lilly Do you remember her dying?

William A little bit.

Lilly   What do you remember about it?

William   I remember the police in our living room drinking tea. The police came round for some reason. I remember one of them had four sugars. I remember her funeral. Everybody patted me a lot.

Lilly   So you're a little orphan boy.

William   That's right.

Lilly   Are you in care?

William   No. I live with my auntie.

Lilly   What's she like?

He smiles. He doesn't answer.

I wouldn't feel too sorry for yourself, by the way.

William   I don't.

Lilly   Parents can be complete shits.

William   I'm sure.

What are those scars? On your arm?

She looks at him before she answers.

Lilly   What do you think they are?

William   Do you cut yourself?

Lilly   You're cute.

William   Do you, Lilly?

Lilly   Watch this.

She pulls out a Bic lighter. She lights it. She keeps it lit for ages until the metal on it is roasting hot. She turns it off. She burns a smiley into her arm with the metal on the top of the lighter.

William   Docs that hurt?

Lilly   No. It feels really nice.

He watches her finish it off. She shows it to him.

William   Can I touch it?

She looks at him for a beat. Then she nods.

He does. She winces a bit.

Have you felt how hot I am? Feel my forehead.

She does.

Do you know what I think?

Lilly   What do you think, William Carlisle?

William   I think our bodies are machines.

He moves away from her. Breaking her touch.

You know where the heat from our body comes from. It comes from the energy it burns up carrying out all of its different activities. That's why corpses are so cold. Because the machine has stopped.

Lilly   I'm not a machine. I'm an animal.

William   What kind of animal are you?

Lilly   A wolf. A leopard. A rhinoceros. A gazelle. A cheetah. An eagle. A snake.

William   I feel like I've known you for years.

Lilly   You haven't.

William   When we were little did we go on holiday together or something like that?

Lilly   I don't think so, William.

William   I think we did. Did we go camping together?

Lilly   No.

William   What school did you go to when you were little?

Lilly   St Michael's in Tunbridge Wells.

William   It can't have been that then.

Would you like to go out with me?

Lilly   Go out with you?

William   On a date. We could go to the theatre. Or I could take you out for a meal.

Lilly   A meal?

William   Even though I hate restaurants.

Lilly   You hate them?

William   They scare the life out of me.

Lilly   Why?

William   All those people watching you eat.

Lilly   Why would you take me there then?

William   We could go to the cinema then. Or bowling. Swimming.

Lilly   Swimming?

William   Have you ever been to Chapel?

Lilly   To where?

William   Chapel-en-le-Frith? It's a village. In Derbyshire. It's somewhere else that's beautiful. We could go next week. In the half term, if you'd like to. We can get a train.

Would you like to?

Would you like to go out with me at all?

Lilly   I don't think so.

A beat.

William   Right.

Lilly   I don't really want to go out with anybody at the moment.

William   Right.

Lilly   It's absolutely not you so don't think that. I just can't be doing with a fucking boyfriend.

William   No.

Lilly   I'm sorry.

Pause.

William   I've never done that before.

Lilly   What?

William   Asked anybody out.

It didn't really go very well, did it?

Lilly   It wasn't –

William   I really fucked it up.

Lilly   No. You did all right.

William   Disappointing outcome though, I have to say. A complete embarrassment, if the truth be told.

Lilly   I don't think it was. I think it was romantic.

Scene Three

'Loose' by The Stooges.

It's Thursday 30 October, 12.46 p.m.

Lilly *and* **Nicholas** *are in the common room.*

Lilly   Hi.

Nicholas   Hi.

Lilly   How's it going in there?

Nicholas   It's going OK. How are you getting on?

Lilly *nods her head at him for a while. Smiles. Says nothing.*

Lilly How's the revision?

Nicholas You know.

Lilly You ready yet?

Nicholas Oh. I think so.

Lilly Have you seen William?

Nicholas Not this morning. Not all day.

Lilly He's not been in since the break.

Nicholas I didn't notice.

Lilly Are you coming out for lunch?

Nicholas I'm going to the gym.

She looks at him.

Lilly Come here.

He does.

Take your blazer off.

He does.

Flex your muscles.

He does. She strokes them.

Thank you.

She takes an apple out of her bag. Eats it.

Do you want an apple? I've got a spare one.

Nicholas I'm all right.

Lilly He asked me out. William.

Nicholas When?

Lilly Before half term.

Nicholas What did you say?

Lilly What do you think?

Nicholas   I don't know. Hence me asking.

Lilly   He was really funny. His face went all stupid. I did feel a bit sorry for him.

Nicholas   Why?

Lilly   Have you ever noticed that?

Nicholas   Noticed what?

Lilly   When you think somebody's a complete dick you find out something about them and you can't help feeling sorry for them even if you really don't want to.

Nicholas   What did you find out about William?

Lilly   He told me about his mum.

Has he ever talked to you about her?

Nicholas   Not really. Not much. We're not that close. What did he say about her?

Lilly   She's dead. Did you know that?

His dad died before he was born.

She died when he was little.

He was four. Imagine that.

Nicholas   Did he tell you that, did he?

Lilly   Imagine being four years old and watching your mum die. You have to admit it's a bit heartbreaking.

Nicholas   Is that what he said to you? That his parents were dead?

Pause.

Lilly   Aren't they?

Nicholas   When did he say that?

Lilly   Two weeks ago. When he asked me –

They're not, are they?

Nicholas   His dad's an accountant. His mum's a nursery school teacher in Cheadle. She's lovely. She looks really young for a mum. She's quite attractive as it goes.

Lilly   Fuck.

Nicholas   Yeah.

Lilly   That's quite unsettling.

Nicholas   I know.

Lilly   I'm quite unsettled now.

You've unsettled me.

Nicholas   I didn't intend to.

Lilly   Why would he lie about something like that?

Nicholas   I've no idea.

He had a brother. I think this is true. I think he had a brother who died. When he was just a little kid.

Maybe he was –

Lilly   What?

Nicholas   I don't know.

Lilly   Confused? You can't get confused about something like that. You can't mistake one for the other.

He was doing it for attention.

How selfish can you get? I'm tempted to find where he lives and go round and tell them.

Nicholas   Don't.

Lilly   No.

Hey.

Nicholas   Hey.

Lilly   I've been thinking about you all morning. Did you know that?

Nicholas No.

Lilly Well, it's true. And I have to say that some of the things I've been thinking are a bit filthy.

He goes to her. Kisses her on the lips.

Nicholas I've been thinking about you, too.

Lilly Liar.

Nicholas Last night.

Lilly Yeah? What about it?

Some time.

Nicholas Can I confess something?

Lilly Go on.

Nicholas I'd never had sex before.

Lilly Right.

Nicholas Could you tell?

What?

What are you laughing at?

Lilly Men. Boys. They're so . . .

Nicholas What?

Lilly Nothing. No. I couldn't tell. I didn't care.

Nicholas It was fucking amazing.

Lilly It *was* a bit, wasn't it?

Nicholas You were fucking amazing.

Lilly Chump.

Nicholas Well. It's true.

Lilly.

Lilly Nicholas.

Nicholas   I don't think we should tell anybody.

Lilly   What?

Nicholas   I think we should keep it to ourselves. That we're going out with one another. I think it'd probably be best if people didn't know.

Lilly   Why?

Nicholas   Don't you think?

Lilly   I don't know.

Nicholas   People here are so –

Lilly   What?

Nicholas   They just go on and on.

Lilly   Are you ashamed of me?

Nicholas   No. Don't be stupid.

Lilly   I'm not being stupid in the least.

Nicholas   I'm not saying that.

Lilly   You just want to keep me as your little secret?

Nicholas   Kind of.

Lilly   Prick.

Nicholas   What?

Lilly   You. You're a prick.

How are things going with Miss Copley?

Nicholas   Are you cross with me?

Lilly   Has she fallen for your overwhelming sexual aura yet, Nicholas?

Nicholas   Have you got the slightest idea what people would say about you?

Lilly   Nicholas Chatman, the Casanova of Nurishment. A million pheromones in every muscle.

Nicholas   Shut up.

Lilly   Honestly, one fuck and he wishes he'd never met me.

Your face!

Nicholas   I'm going.

Lilly   Go and do your work-out. Press those benches, baby. Give them a squeeze from me.

Nicholas   Are you around later?

Lilly   Might be.

Nicholas   Lilly.

Lilly   I'm teasing. I'm sorry. Yes. I'm here later. I'll wait for you.

And OK.

I won't tell anybody.

Nicholas   Thanks. I'm really sorry. I just think. Here.

He kisses her.

I'll see you later.

Lilly   See you later. Arnold Schwarzenegger.

He leaves.

She sits. She looks at her apple. She picks a chunk out of it with her fingers. She eats it. She spits it out after a while.

A train passes outside the window. She looks up to watch it.

Cissy *and* **Tanya** *enter.*

Cissy *is eating a large chip sandwich.*

Cissy   The amount of flour in this bread is fucking ridiculous.

Hi.

Lilly   Hi.

Tanya   Hi.

Lilly   Hi.

Cissy   What do you think these chips are made of?

Tanya   Dough, mainly.

Cissy   I shouldn't be having these. I don't even normally have lunch any more. I just have Skittles. Have you ever had four packets of Skittles in one go? Your brain feels amazing.

The girls smile at this idea. Some time.

Tanya   I think that's really dangerous. Human beings have to eat. It's one of the things that we do. Five pieces of fruit and veg a day. Regulated food groups. Thirty minutes' exercise three times a week.

I blame the parents.

The three girls burst out laughing. It takes them a while to recover.

Lilly   Do you ever think about that?

Tanya   Think about what?

Lilly   Being a parent.

Tanya   All the time.

Cissy   She doesn't just mean about having Anderson's children. She means about actually properly being a parent.

Tanya   Yeah.

Lilly   Seriously?

Tanya   Seriously.

A beat.

Lilly   Me too.

Cissy   God.

Lilly   I think I'd be a terrible mother.

Tanya   Don't be silly.

Lilly   My babies would probably all die. Really quickly.
I wouldn't know how to feed them. I wouldn't know what to
do with them. I'd end up putting them in a cupboard.

Tanya   You wouldn't.

Lilly   I would though.

Cissy   They can't remember anything until they're about
five, anyway. You may as well put them in a cupboard. They
wouldn't remember you doing it.

Tanya   I'm going to have four.

Cissy   Four?

Tanya   Yep. I'm going to be brilliant. Home educate them.
Take them to lots of sports meetings. In my big car.

Cissy   In Anderson's big car.

Tanya   In Anderson's big car.

Lilly   He hasn't got a big car. He comes to school on a bike.

Tanya   Tennis lessons. Football lessons. Ballet lessons.
Anything they want. Teach them languages.

Cissy   You don't know any languages.

Tanya   I'd learn. Loads of languages and teach them all to
our children.

You've got to admit he's fucking lovely.

Of course he's got a car. He just uses his bike to keep fit. And
save the world.

Pause. **Cissy** *eats.* **Lilly** *takes a carrot from her bag and eats that.*

Lilly   Would you have Bennett's children?

Cissy   Fuck. Off.

Lilly   Why not?

Cissy   Can you imagine? They'd be impossible.

They eat for a while.

Lilly   Have you never even talked about it?

Cissy   I think it would scare the shit out of him to even think about mentioning it. He'd pick up on my thoughts.

Lilly *looks at her.*

Lilly   What's he like?

Cissy   What do you mean?

Lilly   Bennett.

Cissy   What do you mean, what's he like?

Lilly   You know.

Cissy   No.

Lilly   In bed.

Cissy   Oh Christ.

Lilly   What?

Cissy   I'd rather not go into that while I'm having my lunch.

The girls chuckle together. **Lilly** *watches* **Cissy**.

Cissy   I'm not going to have children until I'm about forty-two. I'm going to wait until I can afford to pay for somebody else to look after them. I've got too many things I want to do. Too many places I want to go. I can't wait to leave England is one thing. Go and live abroad.

I'm going to. As soon as I finish here.

Lilly   Where are you going to go?

Cissy   Edinburgh. Glasgow. Dublin. Paris. Anywhere apart from here.

Pause.

She wraps up her sandwich and puts it away. The other girls watch her.

I'm so fat.

Lilly   You're not fat.

Cissy   Look at me.

Lilly   You're not fat. Don't say it because it's not true and it makes it look as if you're really showing off.

Cissy looks at her. A beat.

Cissy   Yeah.

Another beat. She grins.

What are you girls getting for Christmas?

Bennett *enters.*

Bennett   I'm getting really bored of Mahon telling me about gay heroes of literary history. She finds me every day. It's like she waits around corners for me and leaps out.

She makes me summarise articles from the *Guardian* for her.

Cissy   It's only because she's too thick to read them herself.

Bennett   She keeps telling me that I could be a lawyer if I wanted to. I don't want to be a lawyer. Who wants to be a fucking lawyer for fucksake?

Tanya   Have you ever thought that there might be a reason?

Bennett   What?

Tanya   That she singles you out for those kinds of suggestions?

Bennett   What the fuck are you implying, Miss Gleason?

Tanya   I'm not implying anything, Mr Francis. I'm just asking a question.

Bennett   Have they put the heating on?

This fucking room.

I need to get outside. I need to go and run around a bit. I need to do PE. I really miss PE. I never thought I'd say that, ever.

Tanya   I don't miss PE teachers.

Bennett   That's because they're fucking retards.

Cissy   Apart from Cheetham.

Bennett   He's a retard. He's a retardus primus.

Cissy   He was very sweet to me.

Bennett   That's because he wanted to finger you.

Cissy   He told me he was really impressed with my GCSE results.

Bennett   Yes, because he wanted to fucking finger you. I told you.

Cissy   Bennett.

Bennett   Would you have let him?

Cissy   Don't.

Bennett   I bet you would. Mind you, I can't say I blame him. People get so het up about inter-generational sexual activity nowadays. It's ridiculous. We should just all jolly well calm down, I think. What's the youngest person you'd fuck, Tanya?

She looks at him. Glances at **Cissy**. *Looks back at him.*

Bennett   Sorry, you go in for the older man, do you not?

Tanya   Are you asking me about *my* sexual experiences, Bennett? That's quite bold coming from you.

Bennett   What does that mean?

She smiles. Says nothing.

I'd finger a Year-Eight girl. If she was up for it. And if she wasn't, I'd definitely have a bit of a posh wank thinking about her.

Cissy   Teachers shouldn't have sex. They're too old. I find it really unnerving. The idea of it. All that old skin. Wobbling about.

Chadwick *enters.*

Bennett   You always used to look forward to PE lessons, didn't you, Chadwick?

Chadwick   What?

Cissy   Do you remember in swimming when he went diving for the brick? You nearly drowned didn't you, sweetheart?

Bennett   Missed opportunity that one, folks.

I remember you in the changing rooms. I remember your little tiny needle dick.

Chadwick.

Tanya   Here we go.

Bennett   Is it true you squeeze lemon juice onto your hair? To make it go blonder?

Chadwick   Sometimes.

Bennett   Does it work?

Chadwick   Yes.

Tanya   Does it?

Chadwick   Yes.

Bennett   You're a genius, Chadwick, I think, aren't you? But you've got to admit –

Chadwick   What?

Bennett   You look pretty fucking stupid in that coat.

Chadwick   Yeah.

Bennett   Did you just actually agree with me?

Tanya   Shut up, Bennett.

Cissy   Some people can wear a coat like that. Some people look like retards.

William *enters. He is frantic. He is drinking a red drink out of a mineral water bottle.*

William   Somebody's stolen my money.

They look at him for a beat. He swigs.

Tanya   What money?

William   I had about a hundred pounds.

Tanya   What did you have a hundred pounds for?

William   It's not that much.

Lilly   Where have you been?

William   What?

Lilly   You've not been in for days.

William   What are you talking about?

Tanya   What did you bring a hundred pounds to school for?

William   It was in my bag.

Lilly   When did you last see it?

William   What do you mean, when did I last see it? What kind of a fucking cunt of a question is that? 'When did you last see it?' This morning. This morning is when I last saw it. I saw it this morning when I put it in there. Somebody's stolen it. People are always doing that to me.

Tanya   Are you sure?

William   Don't I look like I'm sure?

Tanya   I make that kind of mistake all the time.

William   Do I look like a liar?

Tanya   No.

She moves towards him.

He backs away from her suddenly.

William   Were you trying to kiss me?

Tanya   What?

William   Just then?

Tanya   No.

William   Were you?

Tanya   No, I wasn't.

William   'No, I wasn't.' Is that why you moved closer to me?

Tanya   I didn't realise I did.

William   People do that kind of thing though, don't they?

Bennett   William. What are you drinking?

He looks down at his drink.

William   Campari and grapefruit juice.

Do you want to try some?

Bennett   Are you really?

William   Why would I lie about something like that? It's my favourite drink, for goodness' sake. Here.

Bennett *takes it.*

Bennett   Ta.

He drinks.

Wow.

He drinks some more.

Chadwick, have you got any money on you?

Chadwick   I'm sorry?

Bennett   Have you, Chadwick?

Chadwick   What do you mean?

Bennett   I mean have you got any money in your wallet or in your pocket or in your bag or up your arse that you could spare for William? William's lost a hundred pounds and I think you should try and get it back to him, don't you?

Chadwick   It's nothing to do with me.

Bennett   I'm sorry?

Chadwick   I said it's nothing to do with me.

Bennett   Ha!

Chadwick   William, I'm terribly sorry that you've lost some money but I don't really think it was my fault.

Bennett   Chadwick. Get your wallet out.

Tanya   Bennett. Stop it. Now.

Bennett   What? What, Tanya? Are you actually trying to stop me here?

Chadwick, get your wallet out fucking now you fucking cunt-faced twat or I will beat the fucking bricks out of your arse with my bare fists while everybody else watches and sings little fucking songs, so help me God I will.

Chadwick   Here.

Bennett   How much is in there?

Chadwick   Nothing.

Bennett   How much, you lying fuck?

Chadwick   Twenty pounds.

Bennett   Take it out.

Chadwick   What?

Bennett   Take it out of the wallet.

Chadwick   No.

Bennett   Now. Hole-head.

Thank you.

And give it to William. He's a bit short.

Chadwick *gives the money to* **William**.

Bennett *watches. Has another drink.*

Silence.

Some time.

They all try not to move, apart from **Bennett***, who moves with some comfort.*

Bennett   It's warmer today. I think. Don't you, Chadwick? Haven't you noticed it's warmer today? They would put the heating on just as the sun comes out. How typical is that?

An Indian summer.

We're going to the dentist this afternoon. I've got the afternoon off. I'm looking forward to that. Hang out in the sunshine.

My mum's already here to collect me. I saw her. She's waiting in the reception. I decided to just walk straight past her.

Everybody's being very quiet.

How's the revision going, Lilly? Have you started yet?

Lilly   Yes.

Bennett   Sorry? You're muttering. I didn't hear you.

Lilly   I said yes. Of course I've started. The exams are next week.

Bennett *nods his head.*

He goes to **Chadwick***.*

He stares at him. He touches his cheek.

Bennett   Lovely.

What did you have this morning, Chadders?

What subject did you have?

Chadwick   Maths.

Bennett   Maths. Very good. Very good.

I had Politics.

He burps in **Chadwick**'s *face.*

Lucy Francis *enters. She's eleven. She is nervous in the room. The others notice her.*

Lucy   Mum says you've got to hurry up.

Bennett *turns to her.*

Bennett   Right. Thank you, Lucy. Tell her I'm coming.

He collects his bag and jacket. He gives **William** *his drink back. He stops right in front of* **Tanya**.

Bennett   What's the matter with you?

Tanya   Nothing.

Bennett   You look all sad. Are you really sad?

Tanya   No.

Bennett   You are though, aren't you? Do you know why? Do you want to know why you're so sad? Should I tell you?

You're sad because you're fat.

You're fat because you eat too much.

You eat too much because you're depressed. You're depressed because of the fucking world.

Right. My dentist awaits these elegant gnashers.

He gnashes his teeth at **Chadwick**. *Leaves.*

Tanya   Are you OK?

Chadwick   What?

Tanya   Are you OK, I asked.

Chadwick   Of course. Yes. I'm fine. Of course I'm OK.

Tanya   I'm really sorry. I tried to stop him.

Chadwick   Yes. I know. You don't need to –

The bell goes.

They all wait for a beat. **Lilly***'s looking at* **Cissy**.

Cissy   What?

He was messing about.

Fucking hell. It was a joke.

He's just nervous. He's terrified of the dentist.

Are you coming to English?

Tanya *looks at her. Says nothing.*

Cissy   I'll walk with you.

Tanya *nods. Exits.* **Cissy** *follows.*

Lilly   What are you going to do?

About your money?

William   Did you take it?

Lilly   What?

William   I just wondered if you'd taken it. You might have done. You never know. You might have gone into my bag and found it.

Lilly   What are you talking about?

William   Ha!

Lilly   What?

William   Tricked you!

Lilly   You what?

William   I'm just winding you up, Lilly. Just having a little joke. Do *you* want some of this?

He drinks some more Campari and offers her the bottle.

Lilly   No, thank you. I'll see you later.

William   Yeah. I look forward to that.

She leaves. Some time.

Chadwick   How was your mock?

William   It was good. It was Lloyd. He was very sharp. He's by some distance my favourite teacher. He gave me a cigarette at the end which was probably a bit unprofessional of him. But quite sweet as well.

When's yours?

Chadwick   I'm not doing a mock. I'm just going to go down and do the interview.

William   Right.

He reaches into his own wallet and gives **Chadwick** *the twenty pounds.*

Chadwick   Thank you.

William   That's all right.

Chadwick   He's –

William   Yeah.

Chadwick   I don't think I deserve some of the things that happen to me, you know?

Do you?

I don't think I'm so bad. I'm not as bad they make out. I'm not as stupid as people think.

William   I don't think anybody thinks for a second that you're stupid in any way.

Chadwick *gets his phone out. He opens it. He finds a text. He reads it and shows it to* **William.**

William   When did you get this?

Chadwick   This one came this morning.

William   This isn't from Bennett, is it?

Chadwick   No. It's probably from somebody downstairs. That's why I come up here all the time.

William   Have you had this kind of thing before?

You should tell somebody about it. This is serious, Chadwick.

Chadwick   Yeah.

Sometimes . . .

William   What?

Chadwick   Nothing.

William   Go on. Chadwick, what were you going to say?

Chadwick   There's far, far less antimatter in the universe than there is matter. Did you know that?

William   I'm not entirely sure that I did, Chadwick, no. Was that really what you were going to say?

Chadwick   Yes. That's one of the things that the experiments at CERN are investigating.

William   CERN?

Chadwick   The LHC?

The Large Hadron Collider?

William   That broken telescope?

Chadwick   It's not a telescope. It's an atomic particle accelerator.

William   That they couldn't even get working.

Chadwick   But they will.

His conviction stops **William** *for a beat.*

Chadwick   One of the things that this collider may be able to test is where all the antimatter has gone to. Some people think that it must be somewhere. That it can't just disappear. Given its absence from the known universe they speculate that this proves that there are alternative universes. And that the antimatter resides in these alternative universes.

I think the experiments that this telescope is able to develop will prove them right. Eventually.

It makes me feel rather small. We're so little. We take up a tiny amount of space, as individuals, don't we? And a negligible amount of time.

If it was possible to harness antimatter and to bring a single antimatter positron into contact with a single electron of matter it would create an explosion of untold force and energy. They could build an antimatter bomb. It would be forty thousand times bigger than a nuclear bomb.

I think that'd be better.

Don't you think it'd be better sometimes? Just to end it.

I do. I think about that far more than I ought to. I sometimes think that when you die it's like you cross this threshold. You cross this door. You get out of here.

Some time.

William   There are other ways. Of getting out, you know.

Chadwick *nods.*

William   When I'm twenty-one I'm going to inherit over half a million pounds. Did you know that? Did I ever tell you that?

Chadwick   No.

William   My dad made over twelve million pounds in the oil markets in Russia in the early nineties. He left half a million pounds of it to me in trust in his will. I inherit it when I'm twenty-one. I can do whatever I want with it.

I'm moving to New York. I'm going to go and live with Lilly.

Chadwick *looks at him.*

William   We've planned it. Ask her if you don't believe me. We're going to get a warehouse loft conversion in the Lower East Side of Manhattan. I'm going to get a Lamborghini Esprit. Lilly'll probably get a haircut like Jennifer Aniston or something like that. We'll drive around. That'll be better than being dead, I think.

Chadwick   Won't Nicholas mind?

William   What?

Chadwick   Won't Nicholas mind you living with Lilly?

William   What has it got to do with him?

Chadwick   She's going out with him.

William   Who is?

Chadwick   Lilly. She's been fucking him is what I heard.

William   She's not.

Chadwick   She has.

William   Since when?

Chadwick   Since about the first week she got here.

Pause.

William   Oh.

Chadwick   Didn't you know?

William   No. I didn't.

Chadwick   Has it come as something of a blow?

William   Well. I admit I am a little disappointed.

Silence. Some time.

Can I stay at yours tonight?

Chadwick   What?

William   Can I stay at your house tonight?

Chadwick   I don't know.

William   What would your parents say if I just came round?

Chadwick   I'm not sure they'd like it. With the exams next week and everything.

William   They wouldn't do anything though, would they?

Chadwick   I don't know.

William   I could sleep on your floor. We could top and tail.
We could get up in the middle of the night and make cheese
on toast and eat it.

Chadwick   No.

William   What are you like at home?

Chadwick   I don't know.

William   Are you different?

Chadwick   I don't think so.

William   Do you behave differently than you do here? I bet
you do. Do people like you there a bit more? I bet they do,
don't they?

Why won't you let me stay then?

Chadwick   It's not about letting you do anything. It's just
not really my house.

William   I could come round after the exams then. Couldn't I?

You know what it is that's wrong with your bone structure?
I just figured it out. It's your nose. It's a little bit too high up
your face, I think. Isn't it? A bit too high up there?

I'm going to be fucking really fucking late now. I've got lessons
all afternoon.

I have to say I feel like you've really let me down.

Scene Four

'The Woman Inside' by Cows.

It's Monday 10 November, 8.27 a.m.

Bennett, **Tanya**, **Nicholas**, **Cissy**, **William** *and* **Lilly** *are in
the common room.*

Bennett   What?

Tanya   A wasp!

Cissy   Where?

Tanya   There.

Cissy   Fuck.

Nicholas   That's not a wasp.

Cissy   Of course it's a wasp. Fuck.

Tanya   Get rid of it.

Nicholas   It's the middle of November. It's a fly.

Tanya   It's a wasp, you fucking idiot. Open a window.

William   I can't see it.

Nicholas   'Fucking idiot', that's a bit strong.

Cissy   There. My God, it's by your head.

Tanya   It's gonna sting me.

Cissy   Get it. Kill it. Fuck!

William   Don't kill it.

Cissy   What?

William   Don't kill it.

Tanya   Has it gone yet?

William   You mustn't kill it. It's a living creature.

Cissy   Are you being serious?

Bennett   It's a fucking wasp.

Nicholas   Just open the window.

Bennett   Wait.

Tanya   William, please will you open the window?

Bennett   Hold on. Watch.

Cissy   Bennett.

Bennett   Trust me. Watch.

Tanya   William, open the window.

Bennett   No. Don't. William. Don't. Watch this.

He moves to grab the wasp in his hand.

He moves suddenly and with some elegance.

He squeezes his fist closed.

Opens it.

He has caught and killed the dead wasp.

The others look at him and at the wasp. He plucks it from his fist and holds it between two fingers.

Cissy   Oh my God.

Nicholas   How did you do that?

Bennett   Magic. My dad taught me. You just have to watch the way they move.

Tanya   That's freaky.

He looks at her.

Bennett   You want to hold it?

Tanya   No, thank you. It's really odd.

William   I don't think it's odd. I think it's cruel.

Bennett *looks at the dead wasp. He gives it to* **William**. **William** *takes it. Looks at it.*

Puts it in his pocket.

Cissy   Cruel? How's it cruel? Wasps are vicious, pointless things.

Nicholas   It's pretty fucking impressive is what it is.

Cissy   Didn't it sting you?

Chadwick *enters.*

Bennett   Chadwick.

Stand there.

Now wait there.

Thanks.

No. They never do. Not if you're quick enough.

Chadwick   Lloyd's had a heart attack.

Everybody turns to look at him.

Eliot just told me. He's in Stepping Hill. He nearly died. He didn't. They don't know how long he'll be in there.

Bennett   Wow.

William   What did you say?

Chadwick   Late last night. Lloyd. He had a heart attack.

William   A heart attack?

Chadwick   It was quite severe. I think there were complications. Eliot said that somebody told him that he'd lost complete consciousness for a few seconds.

Tanya   Jesus.

William   Lloyd?

Chadwick   That's what I said.

William   Is he dead?

Chadwick   No. He's in hospital.

William   But he died? For a bit?

Chadwick   No. He lost consciousness, that's different from dying.

Bennett   You can't die for a bit.

William   I saw him yesterday.

Chadwick   Yes.

William   I don't believe you.

Chadwick   I'm not lying, honestly.

Pause.

Cissy   Fucking hell, eh?

Tanya   At his age. With that level of smoking. That's serious. And it's the History exam this afternoon as well.

Pause.

Bennett   Do you know what I liked about him?

William   He's not dead.

Bennett   I always liked the way he moved his hands. He had these little jerky movements. They were charming. Oooh! They'd take you by surprise.

William   Don't talk about him like he's dead. He's not dead.

Cissy   I'm not surprised teachers have heart attacks. They wander round like trauma victims. You look into their eyes. They're terrified. They all end up with stomach ulcers. They all suffer uncontrollable sweating. They haven't got a clue who half of the school is. It's ridiculous. They're the ones who are meant to be looking after us.

William   I'm going to go and see him. Does anybody want to come with me?

Does anybody want to come with me to see him?

Tanya   It's half eight, William.

William   What?

Tanya   Maybe after school. We could go. We don't know what time visiting is.

William   What?

Tanya   I'm not entirely sure he'll be able to take visitors for a couple of days. My grandad was like that. They kept him sleeping, mainly.

Bennett   Did I tell you you could fucking move.

Did I?

Chadwick   No.

Bennett   Then what the fuck are you moving for?

Chadwick   I wanted to put my stuff in my locker.

Bennett   Well you can't. Today, Chadwick, as a little tribute to a dying Lloyd, you are my doll. Do you understand me?

Tanya   Bennett.

Bennett   What? What, Tanya?

Tanya   Leave him alone. It's boring.

Bennett   Boring? I'm not bored. Are you bored, Chadwick? Are you bored, Nicky?

Tanya   You're such a –

Bennett   What?

What am I such a, Tanya? Come and tell me.

Ah. Fuck it. I'm playing. I'm playing. I'm being a prick.

Chadwick. Come in. Come in, lovely boy. Put your stuff away I'm being an arsehole.

How are you today, Chadders?

Chadwick   I'm fine, thank you.

Bennett   Ready for your General Studies exam?

Chadwick   Yes.

Bennett   Me too, lovely, me too. It's my last one. I'm tempted to do it with my eyes closed.

That's awful fucking horrible news about Lloyd, isn't it? I wonder what he looked like. I wonder if he stopped breathing. I wonder what colour he went. Have you ever seen anybody die, Chadders?

Chadwick   No.

Bennett   I heard you get an erection. Is he too old to get an erection, do you think?

Cissy   Bennett.

Bennett   I bet he's got a fucking huge cock. A really fucking big schlong, don't you think, Chadders?

Tanya   You're sick.

Bennett   Have you ever had an erection, Chadwick?

Tanya   Don't.

Bennett   What? I'm only asking. I'm only asking my mate Chadders.

Have you, Chadwick? Have you ever had an erection, Chadwick?

Have you ever come?

Chadwick   Yes.

Bennett   How do you know?

Chadwick   It's obvious, isn't it? Don't you know that?

Bennett   I can't imagine you coming. Do you wank all the time at home, Chadwick? What do you think about when you're having a wank? Do you think about girls or boys?

Chadwick   I think about girls. Don't you?

Bennett   Your mum doesn't count, Chadwick, can I just say that?

Or do you think about fat little Tanya mainly? You're in there, mate, by the way. You should definitely ask her out. You'd make a lovely couple.

Have you ever had a girlfriend, Chadwick? Chadwick, answer my fucking question, you uptight prick cunt.

Chadwick   What?

Bennett   Chadwick, have you ever had a girlfriend in your whole fucking life?

Chadwick   No. I haven't. Not yet.

Cissy   Ah!

Bennett   They will drop off eventually, you know? They'll dry up and drop off. Like dead fruit.

Cissy   That's not true. Don't listen to him.

Bennett   What do you think, Nicky? Poor lamb's never been kissed.

Nicholas *doesn't answer.*

Cissy   God. Can you imagine? Doing it with Chadwick. Sorry, Chadwick. No offence or anything.

Chadwick   No. None taken.

Bennett   You should give him some tips, Nicky. You get fucked all the time is what I heard.

Nicholas   Who told you that?

Bennett   Everybody knows about that, don't they, Lilly?

(*To* **Tanya**.) I can't believe you're being such a cock tease with him. It's fucking cruel if you ask me. (*To* **Nicholas**.) Haven't you got any mates who are interested in charity work?

Nicholas   No, Bennett. I haven't.

Bennett   Couldn't you ask Copley for him?

Cissy   Have you seen her face?

Bennett   Have you seen her cunt?

Her cunt is so fat.

Tanya   This is just –

Bennett   Do you know what that means, Chadwick? A fat cunt like that?

You don't, do you?

Mind you, you wouldn't know what to do with it, Chadwick, would you, son? If she came up to you and bent over your desk in the middle of Physics to mark your work you wouldn't have a clue where to start.

Chadwick   And you would?

Bennett   What did you say?

Chadwick   I said, 'And you would?' Know where to start, Bennett.

Bennett   I don't believe you said that out loud.

Chadwick   If she leant over your desk in the middle of Physics what are you saying you'd do?

Bennett   I'd fuck her until she fucking screamed.

Chadwick   Does that mean you're bisexual?

A pause.

Bennett   Tanya, have you got some lipstick.

Tanya   What?

Bennett   Have you? Have you got any lipstick, Tanya?

Cissy   Bennett, the bell's about to go. Everybody'll come out.

Bennett   Can I ask you something, Tanya old girl? Do you think I feel bad about myself because you keep on sticking up for him? Is that what you think?

He goes to **Chadwick**. *He grabs a fistful of his hair, really tightly.*

Bennett   Tanya. Take your lipstick out or I'll properly hurt him.

There.

Now Chadwick, come over to Tanya. And she'll put some lipstick on for you.

Tanya   What?

Bennett   Come on Tanya.

Cissy   Oh my God.

Bennett   Chadwick, come to Tanya. Purse your lips.

Tanya.

He spits in her face.

Do it.

Now.

Thank you.

Chadwick   It's nice.

Cissy   What?

Chadwick   I like it. It smells nice.

Bennett   You look so fucking gay, Chadwick, you make me want to do a piss.

Kiss him.

Cissy   What?

Bennett   Kiss him. For me.

She looks at **Bennett**. *She goes to* **Chadwick**. *She kisses him with a real sexuality.*

Bennett   What are you doing William?

William   Just having a bit of a dance.

Bennett *watches* **Cissy** *kiss* **Chadwick**.

Bennett   Hey, Chadwick. That's my girlfriend.

Chadwick *and* **Cissy** *stop kissing.*

Bennett   What the fuck are you doing, kissing my fucking girlfriend?

Chadwick   You told me to.

Cissy   He tasted like crisps.

Bennett   Right in front of me.

Chadwick   You told me to, Bennett. I didn't want to.

Bennett   You didn't want to? What are you saying? What are you saying about Cissy, Chadwick? Are you calling her? First you snog her right in front of me and then you go and call her like that. I should cut your face off for that. I should cut your ears off. I should cut your needle dick off. You fucking pervert fuckhead cunt.

William   Stop it, Bennett.

Bennett   What?

William   Stop it.

Just leave him alone.

Bennett   Are you actually talking to *me* now?

William   You're a complete fucking prick. Leave him alone.

Bennett   Listen to him.

William   I mean it, Bennett. Leave him alone. Now.

Bennett   Listen to the brother fucker over here.

William   What did you say?

Bennett   Oh, I think you heard me, William, didn't you?

William   Come here. Come here and say that.

Bennett   I said, 'Listen to the brother fucker over here.' I was talking about you. I was referring to your brother.

William   I'll kill you for that.

Lilly   William, calm down. He was winding you up.

William   Yeah, well, I'll wind him up. I'll wind him up like a knot.

The bell goes.

They go to move.

Where are you all fucking going? Stay there. Stay there,
Bennett. I'm not scared of you. I'm not scared of anybody.
You want to know how hard I am?

Lilly   William. It's registration.

William   Come on, Bennett. You cunt. You fuckhead. Come
on then. Any time. You and me. Outside. Now.

Bennett   Have you heard him?

Cissy   He's talking like a comic book.

Bennett   You're talking like a character from a film.

William   I could beat you in a fight really easily.

Bennett   I'm sure you could.

William   I tell you. One day, soon, you are going to get the
surprise of your life. (*To* **Chadwick**.) Don't listen to him. He's
worth nothing. He's just a big empty vacuous awful space.

Chadwick   I don't mind.

Bennett   Don't you?

Chadwick   I don't worry about you lot any more.

Bennett   Well. That's big of you.

Chadwick   Human beings are pathetic. Everything human
beings do finishes up bad in the end. Everything good human
beings ever make is built on something monstrous. Nothing
lasts. We certainly won't. We could have made something
really extraordinary and we won't. We've been around one
hundred thousand years. We'll have died out before the next
two hundred. You know what we've got to look forward
to? You know what will define the next two hundred years?
Religions will become brutalised; crime rates will become
hysterical; everybody will become addicted to internet sex;
suicide will become fashionable; there'll be famine; there'll
be floods; there'll be fires in the major cities of the Western

world. Our education systems will become battered. Our health services unsustainable; our police forces unmanageable; our governments corrupt. There'll be open brutality in the streets; there'll be nuclear war; massive depletion of resources on every level; insanely increasing third-world population. It's happening already. It's happening now. Thousands die every summer from floods in the Indian monsoon season. Africans from Senegal wash up on the beaches of the Mediterranean and get looked after by guilty liberal holidaymakers. Somalians wait in hostels in Malta or prison islands north of Australia. Hundreds die of heat or fire every year in Paris. Or California. Or Athens. The oceans will rise. The cities will flood. The power stations will flood. Airports will flood. Species will vanish for ever. Including ours. So if you think I'm worried by you calling me names, Bennett, you little, little boy, you are fucking kidding yourself.

Bennett   Blimey.

That's a bit bleak, Chadwick.

Chadwick   Just because something's bleak doesn't mean it's not true.

Cissy   I don't believe that.

Chadwick   You should do.

Cissy   We can educate each other.

Chadwick   We don't.

Cissy   We can change things.

Chadwick   We can't.

Cissy   We can. There's science. There's technology.

Chadwick   It won't help now.

Cissy   People have always said the world's going to end.

Chadwick   They were wrong. I'm really fucking not.

I was right about your lipstick, too, Tanya. It does taste nice.

He licks his own lips. Leaves.

Bennett   Ah! First period! Once more into the breach. What time's the exam?

Ten o'clock, isn't it? Lovely. That was fun that, William. I rather enjoyed myself. Same time tomorrow, old bean?

Until the exam hall, lovelies. Don't be late.

He leaves.

Cissy   We've got English.

No response.

We'll be late.

No response.

At least he'll notice you.

Tanya *leaves.*

Cissy *stands for a while. She has no idea where to go or what to say or what to do.*

She leaves.

Nicholas   Are you all right?

William   Am I what?

Nicholas   I was asking if you were OK.

William   Do I not look it?

Lilly   It's good that you stood up to him.

William   Are you both free now?

Lilly   Until the exam.

William   Well. You'll like that.

Nicholas   I can't believe they make us do a lesson. For one period . . .

William   Have they turned the heating off in here?

Nicholas   No. I'm really warm.

Lilly   I'm boiling.

William *looks at her.*

William   I feel a little bit let down.

Lilly   What by? What by, William?

William   It's hard because there are some things that have happened that are entirely my fault.

Lilly   What like?

William   You know what like.

Lilly   I don't.

William   All of you talk about it all the time.

I'm not that naive. I know I might look it. I know I might look like 'oh William'. William Billiam. William Tell. William the thick. William the Great. Do you think I'm William Shakespeare?

They look at him.

Because I might be. It's entirely possible. Look at the news!

Nicholas   What?

William   A hundred and ninety people were killed yesterday in a plane crash in Brazil. Why do you think that happened?

Lilly   It skidded. On the runway. The runway was wet.

William   Oh right. Yeah.

Nicholas   That's true.

William   That's what they tell you is true.

Nicholas   Are you saying you caused the plane crash, William?

William   Wouldn't you like to know?

I bet you really –

How long have you been going out, you two?

Nicholas   William.

William   Why the fuck won't anybody come with me to Lloyd's funeral, for fucksake!

Lilly   He's not dead. He didn't die. Chadwick said –

William   They should close the whole school is what they fucking well should do.

How many times have you fucked her, Nicholas?

Nicholas   William, shut up.

William   Or what? Is his cock really huge?

Lilly   Be quiet. You're making a fool of yourself.

William   What?

What?

Have I said something really embarrassing?

I'm sorry.

God.

I'm really sorry. I didn't even hear myself speak.

Come here. Come here, Lilly. My best friend.

Lilly   William, get off.

He kisses the side of her head.

William   I could eat you. I'd better go now.

Lilly   William, where are you going?

William   I'm going to go and see Lloyd. Get a bit of conversation. Bit of stimulation. You know what I mean?

Lilly   You've got your exams.

William   I've got what?

Lilly   You've got the General Studies exam. You've got History this afternoon.

William *looks at her briefly, slightly confused by what she's talking about. Then he leaves.*

They watch him go.

They look at each other.

Nicholas   Are you OK?

Lilly   I think so. Are you?

He nods. They hold each other's gaze for a while.

Scene Five

'Fell in Love With a Girl' by The White Stripes.

It's Monday 10 November, 4.38 p.m.

Lilly   What?

What?

Aren't you going to talk to me?

Are you just going to look at me, William, because it's creeping me out a bit?

Why are all the windows open? Did you open them?

What did you want? Where have you been all day?

Look. I got your text. You asked me to come here so I came.

It's getting dark. I'm going to go home unless you speak to me. I mean it.

William   Lloyd died. This morning. When we were in here.

I went up to the hospital after I left you and Nicholas. I was too late. I tried to get you all to come earlier. You all stopped me.

It was a horrible place.

He's the second person I ever met who's died now. How many people do you know who've died?

I was meant to have exams, wasn't I? I got lost coming home. I was wandering around.

Have I missed them? My exams? Did I miss History?

Lilly *nods.*

William   While I was wandering about I realised something about you. I realised what you are. In real life. It came to me. Like an epiphany.

Lilly   What are you talking about?

William   You're a robot, aren't you?

Lilly   What?

William   Where did they make you? What laboratory did they make you in?

When I asked you out, were you already going out with Nicholas?

You were, weren't you? Why didn't you tell me? Why didn't you say anything about it?

Can you hear that?

Lilly   What?

William   That banging?

Lilly   No.

William   Are you lying?

Lilly   I didn't know what to say. I really liked you. I really like you. I didn't want to let you down.

William   Good answer. I brought you a present when I was out and about. It's a very early Christmas present.

Lilly   Fucking hell.

William   'Fucking hell.' If my mum could hear you swearing.

Lilly   You can't give me this.

William   'You can't give me this.' Yes I can. I just did. I got one too. I got some CDs. Look I burnt them on for you.

Lilly   William, there's three hundred songs on here.

William   'William there's a hundred songs on there.' Ha!

Lilly   Did you buy all these?

William   'Did you buy all these?'

Lilly   I thought you said your mum was dead.

William   My stepmum.

Don't.

Lilly   What?

William   Look at me like that. You look exactly like her. I really hate it.

Will you do me a favour? In return for my present?

Lilly   It depends what it is.

William   Will you stop burning yourself? Because I don't think it's very good for you. I think you'd be better off stopping.

Will you, Lilly? Do you promise?

A long pause.

Lilly   I'll try.

William   Try really hard.

Lilly   William, are you all right?

William   I'm just a bit.

Lilly   What?

William   I can't think of the word.

Lilly   For what?

William   When you haven't slept enough?

Lilly   Tired?

William   Yes. I'm a bit tired.

Lilly   You couldn't remember the word 'tired'.

William   Do you know what I figured out?

Lilly   What?

William   That it's not me. It's not my fault. It's not a problem of genetics, it's a problem of geography. It's Manchester. It's Stockport.

Lilly   What is?

William   You go downtown. Yes? You go down to the Arndale. Yes? All the kids in there look like they could slice your stomach open and reach their hands inside your stomach and pull your insides out. Yes?

Lilly   They don't.

William   You walk into a room. Yes? Everybody knows you've walked into that room. Everybody's waiting for you. All these people are waiting for you. Aren't they? With their legs and their arms and their hair hanging down in front of their faces when they cry.

Some of the things you told me weren't true.

Lilly   What things?

William   You know what things. There's a lot about you which is a lie. The way you tie your tie is a lie. You're lying with the way you tie your fucking tie.

Lilly   This is exhausting me.

William   Yeah.

Lilly   I'm going home.

William   Don't.

Lilly   Why shouldn't I?

William   I'm scared of what I might do if you leave.

She looks at him.

Lilly   Yeah.

We all get scared, William.

Sometimes the world is a bit unnerving. Some people do awful things but, and you need to listen to this William, seriously, most of the time the world is all right. You need to get that into your head and stop moping about.

William   Moping? Is that what you think I'm doing?

Lilly   Most people are all right.

William   They're not.

Lilly   They're funny. They chat a bit. They tell jokes. They're kind. They're all right.

William   You so should have gone to the College, shouldn't you?

Lilly   You know, ninety-nine per cent of the people in the school are perfectly good people. Ninety-nine per cent of the young people in this country, William, and nobody ever says this, ninety-nine per cent of the young people in this country do a really good job at the actual work of being alive. They'll survive. Happily. They'll grow up. They'll end up doing jobs. Being married. Living lives which are perfectly good and reasonable and all right and happy ones. That's not a bad thing William. You know? What makes you think you're any different? What makes you think you're so special? When I was ten –

William   When you were what?

Lilly   Listen to me. I'm trying to tell you something. When I was ten I used to get headaches.

William   What are you talking about?

Lilly   They were properly fierce. It used to feel as though the front of my head was being carved in two. They could really bring tears to my eyes. I didn't tell my mum about them for weeks –

William   Why are you telling me this?

Lilly   But after about two weeks I did.

William   I think you've gone a bit mad.

Lilly   I told her. She took me to the doctor and the doctor gave me some aspirin and told me to drink more water and get some more fresh air and to eat less sugar and so I did and the headaches went away.

William   I'm not talking about headaches. This is more than a headache.

Lilly   Maybe you should tell somebody.

William   Are you trying to inspire me? With your little tiny story? You want to inspire me? Take your top off. That'll inspire me. Let me see your tits. That'd be a massive inspiration I think. That'd really cheer me up, Lilly. Honestly.

Lilly   I'm sorry I didn't want to go out with you. I wanted to go out with Nicholas instead.

I really love him.

But I always thought you'd be my mate. And I would still really like to be in spite of everything. Because actually I think you're not that well and I'm worried about you and I want to get you some help.

William   Ha!

Lilly   What?

William   Can I ask you this: when you have sex with him, with Nicholas, does it hurt?

Does it?

Please tell me.

Lilly   No.

William   Doesn't it?

Lilly   No.

William   What's it like?

Lilly   It's lovely.

William   Right. That's good. That's good for you. I don't like him. Personally. I think he's a fraud. I think he's a liar. I think he's made of lies and shit. But that's just my opinion.

Lilly   He isn't.

William   I am completely entitled to my own opinion. Don't you dare try to tell me that I'm not because I fucking am.

Some time.

Lilly   Nicholas told me that you were lying about your parents.

Why did you lie about your parents, William?

William   I didn't. I wasn't. I didn't lie.

Lilly   He told me your parents are still alive but that you had a brother and it was your brother who died when he was a baby.

William   Lies, damn lies and statistics.

Lilly   Why did you lie about it, William?

Why did you lie about your parents being dead?

Is it true about your brother?

Did you have a brother who died? Why did your brother die?

William   Can you hear it?

Lilly   What?

William   I can hear it again. That banging.

Lilly   I can't hear it at all.

William   There was a boy killed himself here once. When it was a boys' school. He climbed onto the roof of the quad. Jumped off. This was back in the seventies. Maybe it's him.

Were there a lot of gypsies in Cambridge?

Lilly   What?

William   We should sort them out, us two, I reckon. Go on a march.

Lilly   Sort who out?

William   I know we could. When two people love each other as much as we do then I think they can do anything.

Lilly   I don't love you.

William   You must do.

Lilly   I don't, William.

A long pause. Longer than you think you can get away with.

William *turns the lights off. He stands still for a long time.*

Lilly   Can you turn the light back on please, William?

William   I'm sorry. Did you say something?

Lilly   You're starting to –

William   I don't blame you. By the way. I'm rubbish, me. I'm a waste of time. I'm not even worth the space I take up. I'm not even worth the paper I'm written on. I've got no friends. I've got no imagination. I've got no ideas.

Lilly   Stop it.

William   I hate my shoes. I hate my house. I hate this school. I hate my hair. Can I have a haircut?

Lilly   What?

William   Will you give me a haircut, please? A better one. One that makes me look less of a fucking spastic –

Lilly   Don't say that.

William   – than this haircut makes me look.

Lilly   I hate that word.

William   Cut my hair.

Lilly   With what?

William   I don't care. Your hands. Your ruler. Pull it out.

I'm just. I want it to stop.

You know when I'm with you?

Lilly   I've only known you a month.

William   I feel like I'm earthed. Here.

He touches the side of her head with the palm of his hand. Nothing apparently happens or changes.

And watch what happens if I let go.

He lets go.

See?

Nothing apparently happens or changes. He smiles for a while. He stops smiling quite suddenly.

Who are you?

Lilly   What?

William   I don't know who you are.

Lilly   –

William   Can I tell you something?

Lilly   What?

William   Do you want a word of advice? A word to the wise?

Lilly   –

William   Tomorrow.

Lilly   What?

William   Don't come into school.

Scene Six

'Touch Me I'm Sick' by Mudhoney.

It's Tuesday 11 November, 8.57 a.m.

The stage remains empty for a while. **Bennett** *enters. Then*
Nicholas.

Bennett   They've marked the exams.

Nicholas *looks at him for a while.*

Nicholas   What?

Bennett   I just saw Gilchrist. She said she'll give us our
results later.

Nicholas   Fuck.

Bennett   Yeah. She had a remarkable look on her face.
It was like a combination of glee and fury.

I absolutely know that I have really properly fucked them
all up.

My parents will go fucking mental.

Nicholas   Yeah.

Bennett   They'll drag out the same old speeches. About
the fees. Do you know what we have to do to get the money
to send you to that place? Do you have the slightest idea how
much it costs every year?

I don't actually. Do you?

Nicholas   Have you seen Lilly?

Bennett   I've not seen anybody all morning. Maybe they're
all hiding. Maybe they all know something we don't.

Aren't you worried at all about your results?

Nicholas   Too late to change anything now.

Bennett   Well that's very fucking mature I have to say.

He lights a cigarette.

He looks at **Nicholas**.

Bennett   How are things going with her? With Lilly?

Nicholas   They're all right, thank you.

Bennett   She's lovely.

Nicholas   Yes. She is.

Bennett   She's surprisingly smart. I like her cos she's rock hard. She's very lucky.

Did you hear that Tanya's dad came up to the school?

Nicholas   Lilly mentioned that she'd seen him.

Bennett   Yesterday lunchtime he came and spoke to Edwards. She must have rung him during the day. The fat bitch. He kept me here till half past six last night. Bastard. He was probably marking our exams while I was sat there doing fucking lines.

Nicholas   You shouldn't have spat at her.

Bennett *looks at* **Nicholas** *for a beat.*

Bennett   No. I shouldn't have done.

It was stupid. I just really wanted to. I wanted to try it out. I wanted to know what it would feel like.

Do you ever get things like that?

Nicholas   I'm not sure.

Bennett   Have you ever wanted to set fire to things?

Nicholas   Nothing serious. Maybe the occasional dustbin.

Bennett   Have you ever wanted to blow something up?

Nicholas   Fuck, yeah. Who hasn't?

Bennett   Have you ever wanted to kiss a boy?

Nicholas   No.

Bennett   Never?

Nicholas   No.

Bennett   Liar.

Nicholas   I'm not lying.

Bennett   I wanted to kiss Thom Yorke once.

Nicholas   Yeah?

Bennett   And David Bowie.

Nicholas *looks at him for a beat. Smiles at him.*

Pause.

Nicholas   I was so hungover this morning I couldn't believe it.

Bennett   Where were you last night?

Nicholas   I went out with my brother. He's come home for Christmas.

Bennett   Already? Fucking students. How is he?

Nicholas   He's really well. Mum and Dad are happy to see him.

Bennett   How's Durham?

Nicholas   He loves it, I think.

Bennett   That's good. Are you all going away for Christmas or something?

Nicholas   I don't think so.

Bennett   We're going to fucking Reykjavik of all places.

Nicholas *looks at him. Smiles.*

Nicholas   I shouldn't have been drinking. I'm on painkillers for my ankle. I feel fucking shit now.

Bennett   What happened to your ankle?

Nicholas   I twisted it. Playing rugby.

Bennett   When was this?

Nicholas   Last week.

Bennett   You never told me this.

Nicholas *looks at him.*

Bennett   Can I see it?

Nicholas *shows him his ankle.*

Bennett   It looks red, Nicholas.

Nicholas   Yeah. You should have seen it last week.

Bennett *touches it. He winces as he touches it as though feeling* **Nicholas***'s pain.*

Nicholas   It's all right. It doesn't really hurt any more.

Cissy *enters.*

Cissy   Don't tell my mum. Don't tell my mum. Don't tell my mum. Don't tell my mum.

Nicholas   Don't tell your mum what?

Cissy   I just saw Anderson. I got a 'B' for English.

Bennett   Fucking hell.

Cissy   I know.

Nicholas   A 'B''s not bad.

Cissy   Are you being serious?

Nicholas   A 'B''s good I think.

Cissy   If she finds out she'll kill me.

Nicholas   Cissy, I think you're exaggerating.

Bennett   You don't know her mother.

Cissy   How can I stop her from finding out?

Nicholas   Don't tell her.

Cissy   She'll get the report.

Bennett   Hide it. Burn it.

Cissy Don't be fucking stupid, Bennett. She knows there'll be a report. It's the end of the term. There's always a report.

Bennett Tipp-Ex over it.

Cissy Oh you're *so* not helping.

Tanya *enters.*

Tanya What is the matter with you?

Cissy I got my English results.

Tanya Already?

Bennett She got a 'B'.

Tanya Ouch! Have you ever got a 'B' in anything before?

Nicholas She's worried her mother's going to kill her.

Tanya Yeah. She will.

Cissy If I fuck up –

Bennett You already have, sweetheart.

Cissy No, properly. If I properly fuck up. If I don't get the grades I need for my place in the summer, not in the mocks, in the real exams, then I'll go –

I don't know what I'll do.

Tanya You won't. Fuck up. You're being really stupid. These are just mocks.

Cissy I'll never get out of Stockport. I'll never leave. I'll be stuck here for ever. There's a whole world out there and I'll never see it once, not ever. All these things I want to do, I won't be able to do them.

Tanya You keep going on about that.

Cissy *looks at her.*

Tanya It's not about Stockport, Cissy. It's about you. You were made here. You keep trying to pretend that you weren't. It's ridiculous.

The two girls look at each other.

Cissy   I don't know what to say.

And I don't know what you're laughing at.

Bennett   What?

Cissy   You're meant to be my boyfriend.

Bennett   Oh, come on!

Cissy   You're meant to stick up for me.

Bennett   It was funny. She was being funny.

Cissy   All you ever do is laugh at me.

Bennett   Well. Can you blame me?

Cissy   What?

Bennett   You *are* ridiculous. For somebody so clever you're unbelievably fucking stupid. How could I fail to laugh at you?

Isn't she? Isn't she Nicky?

Chadwick *enters.*

Bennett   Chadwick, isn't Cissy fucking ridiculous?

Chadwick   I don't think so. She's always seemed rather intelligent to me.

Bennett   I'm not denying that. I'm not talking about her intelligence for fuck sake.

William *enters.*

Bennett   William. Answer me this. Why is it that every single person in this school judges everybody else by the level of their intelligence? Not by their wit. Not by their appearance. Not by their dress sense. Not by their taste in music. By how many 'A*'s they got at GCSE.

William *pulls a gun out of the inside pocket of his blazer.*

William   I've no idea.

He shoots his gun at the lights in the common room. He smashes the bulbs.

The room darkens.

It works then.

I did warn you, Bennett. Don't say I didn't warn you because I really fucking did.

He points his gun at **Bennett**.

Bennett   What? What the fuck? No. No. God. Please. Don't.

Bennett *cowers away from him. Wherever he goes to,* **William** *follows him with his gun.*

Nicholas   William.

William *turns to look at him. Points the gun at him when he does.*

William   Yeah. What?

Nicholas   Don't.

William   Don't what?

Tanya *has started crying.* **Cissy** *moves to the door.*

William   Don't. Cissy. Fucking just don't.

Nicholas   William. People will come.

William   What?

Nicholas   People will have heard the gunshot. They'll be here any second.

William   Do you think so?

I can't hear anybody coming. Can you hear anybody?

They listen.

Nicholas   Put the gun down before anybody gets hurt.

William   Don't be fucking stupid.

It feels funny. It's a lot lighter than I thought it would be. It's a lot easier to aim.

Hey, Bennett. Hey, Bennett. Get up. Bennett. Stop fucking crying and fucking listen to me.

You know when you spat at Tanya, what was it like?

What did it feel like?

What was it like for you, Tanya?

Tanya   William, stop it.

William   I heard you got a detention. Shit.

Did your parents find out?

Bennett. Did your parents find out?

Did your parents find out about your detention, Bennett?

Bennett   No.

William   Didn't they?

How come? What did you tell them? What did you tell them, Bennett?

Bennett   I told them I was at football practice.

William   Ha! Did you? How did you think of that? That's fucking brilliant. That's fucking genius is what that is.

Can I tell you something, Bennett?

No other animal in the world polices its behaviour via a third person. Did you know that?

Bennett   Did I know what?

William   If a monkey steals another monkey's nuts he doesn't go and get a third monkey to sort him out. If a cat shits on another cat's tree that cat doesn't go and tell a big huge third cat and get him to sort the first cat out. Does he? No. Of course he doesn't. Only human beings do that. I hate it. You spat at Tanya. Tanya should have stabbed you or something. She didn't. She rang home and told her dad. It's pathetic. As far as I'm concerned that means you're free to do whatever you want with her. Batter her. Shoot her. Rape her. She's the only one who should be able to stop you.

Don't you think?

Don't you think, Bennett?

Everybody's being really fucking quiet today.

Don't you think, Nicholas, shouldn't Bennett be allowed to rape Tanya now?

Nicholas   No.

William   What?

Nicholas   I said no. He shouldn't. That's horrible. That's a crazy idea.

William   What did you say?

He looks at him for a long time.

Nicholas   I said that's a crazy idea.

William   Don't say that.

Nicholas   We can't operate like –

Bennett   Don't, Nicholas.

Nicholas   We can't control a community –

Bennett   Nicholas, be quiet for God's sake.

William   Ah! That's quite sweet. She's protecting you, look.

I don't want to talk about this any more.

*He shoots **Bennett** twice. He dies. **Cissy** screams. She tries to stop herself.*

There is some quietness. Some stillness for a while.

William   Can you smell burning?

Something's burning. Can you smell?

Nicholas   No.

William   Here. Nicholas.

Nicholas   What?

William   Watch this.

He shoots **Cissy**. *She dies.*

Nicholas   William!

Tanya *is crying.* **Chadwick** *is crying.*

William   Did you say something?

Chadwick   Me?

William   Yeah.

Chadwick   No.

William   I thought you said something.

Chadwick   I didn't.

William   I thought somebody said something. Just now. About – did you say something about a fire?

Chadwick   No.

William   You did. I heard you.

Chadwick   I didn't, William.

William   It's probably just me. Is it just me? Am I the only one who heard him talking about the fire?

This happens to me all the time.

He points his gun at **Nicholas**.

William   You know when you're thinking?

Nicholas   Thinking? Yes. I know when I'm thinking –

William   When you're thinking, yeah, and in order to like make a decision, yes? Sometimes you have to weigh one side up against the other and you need to have a jolly good debate in your head about what is the right thing to do and what is the wrong thing to do, yes? And sometimes when you're doing this each side kind of has a voice in your head. You know that?

Nicholas   I think so, William.

William   Sometimes when I do that – the voices sound like they're coming from over there. Or over there. Or over there. Sometimes. Not often. That sounded as though it was coming from Chadwick. How very embarrassing. I am sorry.

Nicholas   Don't be.

William   I am. I will be. Because I am. You can't exactly choose these things can you?

Can you hear anybody coming?

They listen.

Told you.

William *turns away from* **Chadwick**. *Without* **William** *noticing* **Chadwick** *takes the opportunity to turn and run through the classroom door.*

William *notices him too late. He points his gun. He puts it down again. He laughs a little.*

He got away!

He turns and shoots **Nicholas**. **Nicholas** *dies.*

He looks around at what he's done.

There's some time. He looks at **Tanya**. *She's crying her heart out.*

William   Did you hear about Lilly?

Tanya   What about her.

William   She's dead.

Tanya   Dead?

William   Not literally. She's just in a bit of trouble.

Tanya   Why?

William   She did something.

Tanya   What?

William   Something really bad.

Tanya   What did she do?

William   What's wrong?

Tanya   Nothing.

William   You're crying.

Tanya   Yeah.

William   You're so lovely. Don't cry. Here.

He smiles. Goes to hug her. She is terrified. He hugs her. Lets go. Sits down on a table.

A long pause.

Dear God. Please – Dear God . . . Are you there? Dear God, please look after little baby Alistair and Mum and Dad and –

He breaks into uncontrollable giggles.

I always find it hard to keep a straight face.

He goes to shoot himself. He holds his gun in his mouth. After a short while he retracts it.

I'm sorry. I really need a piss. Should I do it on the floor? Should I do it in my trousers, Tanya? If I do it in my trousers will you tell?

Tanya   No.

William   Do you think it'd be all right?

She nods.

He pisses in his trousers, down his trouser leg, onto the floor of the common room.

My God. The relief.

He breaks into an enormous smile.

Scene Seven

'Desperate Man Blues' by Daniel Johnston.

It's Wednesday 24 December, 11.59 a.m.

William Carlisle *and* **Dr Richard Harvey** *are in a clinical examination room of Suttons Manor medium-security hospital.*

The walls of the room are white. It is very brightly lit.

Dr Harvey *wears an immaculately smart brown suit.* **William** *wears joggers and sweat shirt.*

William *is completing a questionnaire.*

He has to tick boxes in answers to questions.

The questionnaire is twenty-five pages long.

There is some time before **Dr Harvey** *speaks.*

Dr Harvey   Would you like to rest?

William   No.

Dr Harvey   You can do.

William   I don't want to.

He answers another question.

I like this kind of test.

It's quite funny.

Have you done it?

Did you make these questions up?

Dr Harvey   With a colleague.

William   How many are there in total?

Dr Harvey   One thousand eight hundred.

William *looks at him. Smiles.*

William   Great.

It's like doing a comprehension test. A bit.

Doing a comprehension test on your brain.

'Do you feel confident in clothes shops?'

'Do you feel confident in music shops?'

'Do you feel confident in cafés?'

'Do you feel confident in libraries?'

'Do you feel confident in supermarkets?'

'Do you feel confident at football matches?'

'Do you feel confident in school classrooms?'

'Do you feel confident in furniture shops?'

'Do you feel confident in licensed adult shops?' Is that sex shops?

Dr Harvey   That's right.

William   'Do you feel confident in greengrocers?'

'Do you feel confident in newsagents?'

'Do you feel confident in playgrounds?'

'Do you feel confident in estate agents?'

He fills in more of the forms.

Dr Harvey *watches him. He writes a little as he's talking.*

After a while **William** *puts his pen down.*

William   I'm not allowed a cigarette, am I?

Dr Harvey   I'm afraid not.

William   I could just have a cheeky one.

Dr Harvey *smiles.*

William   You laugh but I'm being serious.

I'm getting a bit tired now. You shouldn't have put the idea in my head.

It's the Droperidal. The Holoperidal.

He answers a question. He looks up again.

Is it Christmas yet?

Dr Harvey   Tomorrow.

William   It's Christmas Eve?

Dr Harvey   That's right.

William *thinks.*

William   Do you know who I am?

Dr Harvey   Sorry?

William   I never know with you lot if they tell you who I am before I meet you or if they try and keep it neutral.

Dr Harvey   I'm not sure if I know what you mean.

William   Did they tell you what I did?

That means they did, didn't they?

What's your name?

Dr Harvey   Harvey. Dr Harvey.

William   What's your first name? That's not Harvey too is it? Harvey Harvey? Dr Harvey Harvey?

Dr Harvey   No. My first name's Richard.

William   Happy Christmas, Richard.

Dr Harvey   Happy Christmas.

They smile at each other.

William   Can I ask you something: when you found out that you were coming to meet me, did you get a bit excited?

Dr Harvey   Excited?

William   It's always exciting meeting celebrities, isn't it?

You must have wondered what I'd be like, did you?

Dr Harvey   I've been doing this job long enough to know that you can never really predict what a patient is going to be like, or how they're going to behave. Regardless of how much of their record you've had access to.

William   Or what you've read about them in newspapers.

Dr Harvey   I honestly don't read newspapers.

William   But you know who I am, don't you? You know what I did? Do you know what I did? Richard, do you know what I did?

Dr Harvey   Yeah. Yes I do.

William   I bet there are a million things you want to ask me, are there?

Actually there are one thousand eight hundred things, eh?

But I bet you want to know more than whether or not I feel confident in estate agents, don't you?

Does it freak you out a bit being in here with me?

Dr Harvey   No.

William   Have you got a panic button?

Dr Harvey   Yes I do.

William   Is it underneath your desk?

Have you got any children? Have you, Richard?

Dr Harvey   I've a daughter.

William   How old is she?

Dr Harvey   She's seventeen.

William   My age.

Does it make you sick what I did?

Does it make you sick what I did?

Dr Harvey   No.

William   You're lying. I can tell by the way you look to the left. When people look to the right they're thinking. When they look to the left they're lying.

Can I have a glass of water, please?

Dr Harvey   Certainly.

He stands to leave.

William   I'll just wait here.

Dr Harvey *enjoys the joke.*

He exits.

Some time.

Nicholas *enters.*

He sits opposite **William.**

William *almost laughs. He stares at him.*

William   Nicholas? Nicky?

He goes to touch his face.

Are you OK? Are you dead?

Does it hurt?

Did I hurt you?

I'm –

William *starts to cry a little bit. He stops himself and rubs his eyes dry furiously.*

Nicholas *stands suddenly.*

He exits as though he'd forgotten something and has to rush to get it.

William *is left on his own.*

He tries to gather himself.

William   Oh fuck.

Dr Harvey *returns with a glass of water and three cigarettes and a box of three matches.*

Dr Harvey   Sorry, the cooler was empty. I had to go up to the second floor.

William   Thank you.

He drinks.

Dr Harvey   I got you these. Here.

He gives **William** *the cigarettes.* **William** *smiles broadly.*

William   Fucking hell. Thank you.

He takes a cigarette and opens the matches.

Notices there are only three. Laughs once.

Takes one. Strikes it. Lights his cigarette. Smiles broadly.

That tastes lovely.

He smokes.

See, the main question people have been asking me is why I did it?

Why do people keep asking me that?

Dr Harvey   I think people are concerned about you.

William   'Why did you do it, William? What did you do it for? Why did you do that? Why did you do this?'

He answers some more questions. As he answers the questions he talks. His ticking becomes more frantic. By the end of his speech he is almost cutting into the paper with his pen.

Dr Harvey *takes a few notes.*

William   I don't know. I don't care. It's a pointless question. It's a stupid question. It's a boring question. Next question please. Next question please. Next question please. Was it because of my mum? No. Was it because of my dad? No. Was it because of my brother? No. Was it because of my school?

No. Was it because of the teachers? No. Was it because of Lilly? No. Was it the music I was listening to? No. Was it the films I saw? No. Was it the books that I read? No. Was it the things I saw on the internet? No.

He scribbles onto the paper. Puts his pen down.

I did it because I could. I did it because it felt fucking great.

He smokes.

There was a bullet left in the gun. I was going to shoot myself. I actually put the gun to my mouth. Did you hear about that? Tanya was there, she could tell you this.

Is she all right? Tanya?

Dr Harvey   She's recovering. She and Chadwick Meade both hope to go back to school at the start of next term.

William *thinks about this.*

William   I needed a piss.

So, I just like, I just did a piss there. In the classroom. On the floor.

It felt fucking amazing. I thought if I died I'd never feel that, that, that relief.

Dr Harvey   That's caused by the release of endorphins in our bloodstreams. There are hormones called endorphins which are released when we urinate. They allow us to feel that sense of euphoria.

William *looks at him for a beat.*

William   When you went to get the water, were you watching me? You don't need to answer that, by the way.

Dr Harvey *smiles.*

William   Will you be coming back after today?

Dr Harvey   We don't know yet. I need to complete my report by the end of next week.

William *nods.*

William   What are you going to say about me in your report?

Dr Harvey   I don't quite know yet.

William   Is that a lie? I bet that's a lie. Are you not allowed to tell me when you do know?

Dr Harvey   I'm sure eventually you'll be able to see it.

William   And after you they'll probably send somebody else.

Dr Harvey   That hasn't been decided.

William   They probably will. They send new people all the time.

He answers another question then looks up again.

It needn't be like this, you know?

Dr Harvey   What?

William   Not everybody feels like I feel.

Some people. They're funny. I like them. They tolerate other people. There are people who tolerate other people. They take the piss out of themselves. They work hard to try to make things better.

You can see some of them. You can see them in Year Seven and they look all right. They're wily. You know?

My dad's lived in Stockport all his life. You can walk from house to house to all the houses he's lived in. It takes about an hour. I've done it. He's going to come and visit me, he said. I'm not entirely sure if he'll know how to get here.

He answers another question.

When I was eight I stole some money from my mum's purse. It was about two pounds. I never even spent it. I just wanted to know what it felt like. I watch porno when nobody's in my house. Loads and loads of it. You can get them on the internet for free really easily. My favourite is when it's lesbians.

Sometimes I didn't do my homework. Sometimes I copied it from – there are websites you can go to. I copied it.

I smoke. I have smoked a lot of things actually. I've drunk alcohol. I inhale Tipp-Ex sometimes.

He answers some more questions. Then stops.

I should go and get a job. Do something proper. Do something worthwhile, I think. Don't you think?

Dr Harvey   In time.

William   No. Not in time. Now.

Look. I'm not an – I'm not. I'm not an idiot. I know that something's going on. I know something's a bit wrong.

I want to be an architect. Build buildings way up as high as I can get them to go. Get some children. Just be normal. Go to hospital one day and get my head sorted out. Buy a small house. Not spend too much money.

He answers some more questions. Then stops.

He looks up. He looks at **Dr Harvey**.

Light falls suddenly.